IR

D0118362

JUL 11

GRAPHIC USA

AN ALTERNATIVE GUIDE TO 25 US CITIES

Published by Cicada Books Limited

Edited by Ziggy Hanaor
Designed by April, www.studio-april.com
Cover illustration by Gwenda Kaczor
Text and images by the contributors as specified
Set in LL Gravur Condensed, www.lineto.com

British Library Cataloguing-in-Publication Data.

A CIP record for this book is available
from the British Library.
ISBN: 978-0-9562053-2-2

Cicada Books Limited
76 Lissenden Mansions
Lissenden Gardens
London, NW5 1PR

T: +44 207 267 5208
E: ziggy@cicadabooks.co.uk
W: www.cicadabooks.co.uk

CONTENTS

Hi! I'm Ziggy, the editor of *Graphic USA*. On behalf of myself and Studio April, who designed the overall layout, thanks for buying this book.

Graphic USA follows on from our previous collaboration, *Graphic Europe*. The concept behind it is that people who work in the graphic arts, and who have an offbeat aesthetic to their work will often seek out the unexpected and inspirational elements in their environments that one wouldn't find in most travel guides. The recommendations in this book are the personal favorites of the individual contributors. They were not compiled by a team of trained researchers, and for the most part they do not include the bucket list recommendations that most tourists feel they have to tick off. They tend to reflect the alternative, independent culture that is bubbling underneath the city, feeding into its public persona, but not immediately apparent to the visiting outsider. Not all the suggestions may be your cup of tea, but hopefully for those who are part of an alternative scene themselves, they will tap into a common urban approach and will open up a different view of the city that you can dip in and out of as you desire. It's kind of like a friend writing down their hot tips for each place.

The working process for this book was similar to that of *Graphic Europe*: We drew up a list of cities spread across the country, including some smaller places as well as the usual suspects, and then started to look for people whose work really turned us on. The results were surprising. Some cities (and not necessarily the ones you'd expect) had a surfeit of amazing designers producing beautiful, quirky and independent material, whilst for others we had to look long and hard to find the free spirit who was producing something unique and relevant. Google Image Search became our best friend very quickly.

I am so pleased with our final lineup of contributors. I think their work is without exception fantastic. Their response to the brief was varied and insightful, with an often-humorous honesty in their writing and a wealth of styles and approaches to the illustrations. In Europe, every other person you meet seems to be a freelance graphic designer, in the States, however, most illustrators and designers are employed by a company and working on their own projects in their spare time. I'm therefore even more grateful to them for the enormous effort they put in, and their willingness to communicate and discuss their work.

I hope you enjoy this book and use it however you see fit – as a gallery of beautiful images, a directory of talented illustrators and designers, or as a travel guide for a weird and wonderful alternative road trip across the USA.

Ziggy Hanaor

Illustration by Elizabeth Graeber

laura ferago's
Anchorage

ANCHORAGE, ALASKA BY LAURA FERACO

Alaska was a very late addition to the United States, and still maintains a degree of isolation from the lower 48. It is a wild and extreme place, and its main city, Anchorage, is no exception. Built on a strip of coastal lowland and surrounded by six mountain ranges, Anchorage is the largest city north of Helsinki, St Petersburg, Oslo, and Stockholm. Although the proximity to the sea helps moderate the climate, temperatures in winter can often hit 5°F, and occasionally are as low as -30°F.

Just like the subarctic weather, the design world in Anchorage can be harsh and unforgiving, and only the resilient can survive. It's easy to get lost in the kitsch tourist-trap bars and T-shirt shops and the relentless resource development, but there is plenty of inspiration to be found if you look beyond all this. Firstly, the light in Anchorage is truly unique. In winter everything is tinged with a ghostly blue, and in summer the midnight alpenglow has a way of illuminating things in unexpected ways. Secondly – and more importantly – the natural surroundings of the city are nothing short of spectacular, and this in itself has a way of clearing one's mind – opening a path for fresh ideas and new approaches. At any given moment, you can see the mountain ranges of Chugach, Kenai, Talkeetna, Tordrillo, Aleutian, and Alaska from almost anywhere in Anchorage. I've never been anywhere else that offers such inspiring and humbling views. It takes only a ten-minute drive outside of the city to find wilderness so extreme that you can get lost and not be found until next summer.

As a result of these qualities, Anchorage has become something of an outdoor enthusiast's playground – the frontier spirit that attracted many to these remote climes in bygone days is very much alive, and an emerging creative subculture has started to bubble underneath the mainstream. The Native American presence, though much diminished (Native Americans account for a mere five per cent of the population these days), still lingers, keeping a watchful eye over the city. Anchorage is ultimately a haphazard collection of unique discoveries and pockets of brilliance, surrounded by a wilderness that demands respect and metes severe punishment to those who lack it. I have come to worship my puffy goose-down coat. For people in the lower 48 it's a fashion statement – for me it's a survival tool.

STAY

CAPTAIN COOK HOTEL A luxury hotel with old-world feel. The cozy, dark halls are decorated with wood carvings and murals telling tales of Captain Cook's adventures at sea. 939 West 5th Ave, Anchorage, AK 99501, www.captaincook.com

COPPER WHALE INN BED & BREAKFAST This quaint little B&B is perched just above the Tony Knowles Coastal Trail and offers jaw-dropping views across Cook Inlet to the Alaska Range and Mount McKinley. Take your breakfast in the common area and see if you can spot a bald eagle or a beluga whale. 440 L St, Anchorage, AK 99501, www.copperwhale.com

INLET TOWER HOTEL AND SUITES Contemporary decor surrounded by natural scenery. This boutique hotel is in an old building near Westchester Lagoon, in the oldest neighborhood in Anchorage. 1200 L St, Anchorage, AK 99501, www.inlettower.com

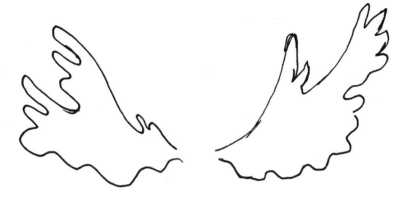

EAT

SNOW CITY CAFE A local favorite on the western edge of Downtown with a bright, modern feel and just the right kind of coziness. Breakfast and lunch are made with fresh ingredients and served with a complementary side of cheerful. Study the local art decorating the walls or gaze at the sun through the floor-to-ceiling windows. Serves beer and wine as well. 1034 West 4th Ave, Anchorage, AK 99501, www.snowcitycafe.com

URBAN GREENS A trendy sandwich shop serving up consistently delicious salads and sandwiches. My favorite is the 'tuna salad salad' – yum! High wood tables and bar-style window seating are available for the urbanites, and there's a cozy couch in the back for the more chilled out. 304 G St, Anchorage, AK 99501, www.urbangreensak.com

NAMASTE SHANGRIA A hidden gem offering an amazingly delicious selection of dishes from Burma, Nepal, India, and Tibet. It's owner run and operated and has a very friendly, casual atmosphere. 2446 Tudor Rd, Anchorage, AK 99507

SPENARD ROADHOUSE Comfort food with a modern twist is served up at this casual diner-meets-log-cabin-chic roadhouse. Highlights include s'mores to die for, bacon of the month, live local bands every second Saturday, eight local beers on tap, a full bar, and a knowledge of bourbon that would make anyone from the lower 48 jealous. 1049 West Northern Lights Blvd, Anchorage, AK 99503, www.spenardroadhouse.com

FIRE ISLAND RUSTIC BAKESHOP A small, family-run, artisan bakery offering organic breads, muffins, pastries, and sandwiches. Focus is on fresh and local ingredients and fair trade coffee and teas are available. Stop by for a hot scone in the morning or grab a sandwich to enjoy at nearby Westchester Lagoon for lunch. 1343 G St, Anchorage, AK 99501, www.fireislandbread.com

MIDDLE WAY CAFE A bright, open cafe with a lofting ceiling, displays by local artists and healthy food and drink. Creative sandwiches, salads, breakfast, and smoothies are enjoyed by an animated, alternative crowd of veg heads, vegans and carnivores. 1200 West Northern Lights Blvd, Anchorage, AK 99503

SACK'S CAFE Definitely one of the best high-end restaurants in town. An inviting dining room serves up eclectic seafood dishes with Asian influences, using locally sourced ingredients. If you're visiting in summer, grab a table outside and enjoy your meal under the Alaskan sky. 328 G St, Anchorage, AK 99501, www.sackscafe.com

CRUSH WINE BISTRO AND CELLAR Experience wine in a relaxed, friendly atmosphere. Order a glass or a bottle and discover wine at an entirely new latitude. Good food too. 343 West 6th Ave, Anchorage, AK 99501, www.crushak.com

TAP ROOT CAFE A quaint, socially conscious cafe, nestled in South Anchorage with nightly music, open mic nights, and poetry readings. Grab a seat at the bar and take your pick from the list of rotating beers. 1330 Huffman Rd, Anchorage, AK 99503

KINLEY'S RESTAURANT AND BAR This place has a popular after-work scene thanks to its full bar, extensive beer and wine lists, true 16oz pints, and happy hour menu. The stone wall behind the bar lends a modern vibe to the warm and friendly atmosphere. Don't miss the display of concert posters in the entryway. 3230 Seward Hwy, Anchorage, AK 99503, www.kinleysrestaurant.com

SIMON AND SEAFORT'S SALOON AND GRILL Saunter up to a stool by the windows in the saloon and enjoy panoramic views across Cook Inlet with your daily happy hour special. Old-school Alaskan feel complete with oil paintings, which have eyes that follow you around the room. 420 L St, Anchorage, AK 99501, www.simonandseaforts.com

BEAR TOOTH THEATRE PUB AND GRILL Local micro-brew and a movie. Life is now complete. All beers are brewed in-house and range from light ales to dark stouts. Grab whatever you fancy, sit at the bar, and meet the locals, who will be all too happy to share an adventure story or two. You can also enjoy a tasty dinner there – or eat it while watching a movie in the attached theater. 1230 West 27th Ave, Anchorage, AK 99503, www.beartooththeatre.net

MIDNIGHT SUN BREWERY Located in South Anchorage, this micro-brewery has an industrial style tasting room offering current brews on tap. All creations taste as unique as their names. "Go Green. Go Growler" is their motto. Growlers and kegs are available as to-go options. 8111 Dimond Hook Dr, Anchorage, AK 99507, www.midnightsunbrewing.com

DRINK

SHOP

TIDAL WAVE BOOKS The largest bookstore in Alaska. It's locally owned and sells a great selection of new and used books, with an emphasis on Alaska-themed books. Discover surprises on the shelf that may not exist anywhere else in the world. Midtown (open year round): 1360 West Northern Lights Blvd Anchorage, AK 99503, Downtown (open in summer): 415 West 5th Ave, Anchorage, AK 99501, www.wavebooks.com

ANCHORAGE FARMERS' MARKETS Matanuska Valley farmers display an abundance of gigantic veggies and fruit; lettuces as big as your torso and radishes that taste as sweet as apples. Local bakeries, flowers and plants also feature. There are two locations, both open on Saturdays from May to October. Anchorage Farmers' Market: 15th Ave at Cordova St, www.anchoragefarmersmarket. org, South Anchorage Farmers' Market: Subway/Cellular One Sports Centre at the corner of Old Seward and O'Malley. www. southanchoragefarmersmarket.com

CIRCULAR Eco-friendly, recycled, and smartly designed products fill this shop. Home goods, jewelry, and clothing for adults and children. Great place to find gifts. 320 West 5th Ave, Suite 132 (across from Nordstrom on 6th Ave), Anchorage, AK 99501, www.circularstore.com

OCTOPUS INK GALLERY Distinctive and beautiful handcrafted goodies for yourself or a friend, with a focus on sustainability. Jewelry, pottery, and marine-inspired hand screen-printed clothing and bags by local artists. 410 G St, Anchorage, AK 99501, www.octopusinkclothing.com

MODERN DWELLERS CHOCOLATE LOUNGE This place is like an installation in itself. It's worth visiting just to see the crazy furniture that the owners built themselves out of scrap. They stock unique jewelry, bags, homewares, and as an added bonus, drinking chocolate and handmade truffles. My favorite combo: a spicy hot chocolate with an Indian bop truffle. Grab a cup, sit yourself down, and enjoy the surroundings. Two locations. 751 East 36th Ave #105, Anchorage, AK 99510, and 423 G St, Anchorage, AK 99501, www.moderndwellers.com

ALASKA NATIVE MEDICAL CENTER CRAFT SHOP Yes, it's at the hospital, but it has the best selection and prices for native art in Anchorage. Each piece of art has a story to tell and more proceeds go directly back to the artist than most galleries. As you make your way to the craft shop keep an eye out for priceless works of art on display. 4315 Diplomacy Dr, Anchorage, AK 99508, www.anmc.org

ALASKA NATIVE HERITAGE CENTER An insight into Alaska as it was before it was settled by Russians and Americans. Reconstructed native villages show what life was like then and now for the indigenous peoples. 8800 Heritage Center Dr, Anchorage, AK 99504, www.alaskanative.net

DOS MANOS Self-described as "a funktional art gallery", this is form equals function Alaskan style. Features a constantly changing spiral staircase display of Alaskan inspired art. 1317 West Northern Lights Blvd, Suite 3, Anchorage, AK 99503, www.dosmanosgallery.com

AFTER HOURS BY DESIGN Local designers gather on the second Wednesday of every month to discuss design, trends, art, or just hang out. All are welcome and they meet up at a different bar or restaurant each time. Check the website for details. www.graphicdesignalaska.com

ANCHORAGE MARKET AND FESTIVAL Carnival-esque atmosphere with booths selling Alaskan specialities from mesmerizing aurora photography to hand carved sculptures as well as great food. It's hard to decide between the reindeer sausage or the smoked salmon. Open weekends during the summer. Cnr 3rd and E St, Anchorage, AK 99501, www.anchoragemarkets.com

FUR RONDY FESTIVAL AND THE IDITAROD From the end of February to the beginning of March the Fur Rondy festival celebrates local history and culture with dogsled races, outhouse races, running of the reindeer and more. In the first weekend of March, the more well-known dogsled race, the Iditarod, has its ceremonial start in Anchorage. www.furrondy.net, www.iditarod.com

MTS GALLERY Like the gallery, located in Mountain View, just a bit east of Downtown, the art is off the beaten path, with unique monthly exhibits of local and global artists. Third Fridays of the month are openings. 3142 Mountain View Dr, Anchorage, AK 99514, www.mtsgallery.wordpress.com

FIRST FRIDAYS ART WALK First Fridays of the month art galleries stay open late in Downtown Anchorage. Pick up a map in the *Anchorage Press*. Some galleries have catering by local restaurants, so you can eat and drink while viewing local artists' work.

ANCHORAGE MUSEUM A new wing added in 2009 complements the old concrete architecture, the towering glass standing out against the mountain backdrop. Meander through the birch forest of the public common as you approach. Inside you'll find an extensive collection of art of the north, and travelling exhibits from around the globe. 625 C St, Anchorage, AK 99501, www.anchoragemuseum.org

BEAR TOOTH THEATER AND GRILL The place to catch international films with the locals. Monday nights they screen independent, international, artsy movies. 1230 West 27th Ave, Anchorage, AK 99503, www.beartooththeatre.net

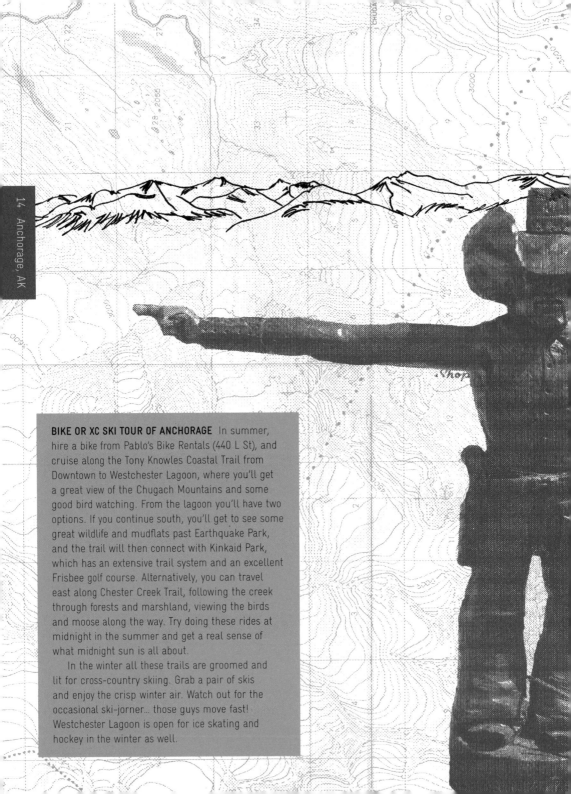

BIKE OR XC SKI TOUR OF ANCHORAGE In summer, hire a bike from Pablo's Bike Rentals (440 L St), and cruise along the Tony Knowles Coastal Trail from Downtown to Westchester Lagoon, where you'll get a great view of the Chugach Mountains and some good bird watching. From the lagoon you'll have two options. If you continue south, you'll get to see some great wildlife and mudflats past Earthquake Park, and the trail will then connect with Kinkaid Park, which has an extensive trail system and an excellent Frisbee golf course. Alternatively, you can travel east along Chester Creek Trail, following the creek through forests and marshland, viewing the birds and moose along the way. Try doing these rides at midnight in the summer and get a real sense of what midnight sun is all about.

In the winter all these trails are groomed and lit for cross-country skiing. Grab a pair of skis and enjoy the crisp winter air. Watch out for the occasional ski-jorner... those guys move fast! Westchester Lagoon is open for ice skating and hockey in the winter as well.

HIKES

If I need to clear my head, there are two great hikes in **CHUGACH STATE PARK** that help me reconnect with mother nature, and reset my brain. Common sightings on both: ptarmigan, porcupine, moose, dall sheep. Necessities: boots, water, camera, map, hat, extra layer, hiking poles, and bear spray. Winter addition: snowshoes.

NEAR POINT TRAIL Easy to moderate: first three miles wide and flat, last mile steep and narrow to the top with rewarding views of the Alaska Range, Sleeping Lady, Chugach Mountains, Anchorage, and Cook Inlet. Access at Prospect Heights trail head off of Hillside Drive. Elevation Gain: 1900 ft. Easy cross-country skiing and snowshoeing in the winter for the first three miles.

LITTLE O'MALLEY TRAIL AND THE BALLPARK Easy to moderate: five miles round trip to the back of the ballpark. Access from Glen Alps trailhead off of Upper Huffman Road. Elevation gain 1800 ft. In summer, view rock formations left by glaciers, colorful summer flowers and dall sheep. At the end of the ballpark discover bottomless mountain lakes and connect up with Williwaw Lakes Trail. Snowshoe and backcountry ski in the winter.

DRIVES

SEWARD HIGHWAY Take a drive south on the Seward Highway, along Turnagain Arm for views of the Cook Inlet, Kenai Peninsula, rocky cliffs, and untouched shoreline. Visit Beluga Point and Bird Point. If you're lucky, you may spot a Beluga whale, the vanishing white giant that follows fish up the inlet as the tide comes in. There are a number of trail heads along the Seward Highway that take you up the cliffs to beautiful viewpoints.

KENAI FJORDS NATIONAL PARK If you're up for a longer drive, continue south along Route 1 onto the Kenai Peninsula and into the Kenai Fjords National Park. The landscape as you drive south is positively mesmerizing. Eventually you'll reach the end of the road at Seward (three-hour drive from Anchorage) on the east side of the peninsula, or Homer (four-hour drive from Anchorage) on the west side. Both towns are full of culture, history and natural beauty.

LAURIE FOREHAND'S
atlanta

ATLANTA, GEORGIA BY LAURIE FOREHAND

Atlanta is situated in the heart of the American South, but unlike the rest of the area, which is known for its laid-back charm and sleepy pace, Atlanta is a proper urban hub, with a diverse music scene, high-end restaurants, designer shopping, buzzing neighborhoods, and highways. It's not a pedestrian city as such; most areas require the train (MARTA), a car, or at least a bike. However, within the individual neighborhoods, most of the restaurants, cafes, and boutiques are accessible on foot.

The key areas to know about are: Midtown Atlanta, Buckhead and Downtown Atlanta. Midtown attracts urban dwellers, who like to be close to the action. Tree-lined streets are filled with beautiful condos and charming homes, and there's an assortment of good places to eat. The highlight of the area is Piedmont Park, a great place to take a stroll, lie in the grass, play Frisbee or just indulge in some people watching. The neighborhood of Virginia Highlands is particularly worth a visit, and is home to some great bars, shops and restaurants.

Just north of Midtown is Buckhead, where I live. It's known (for better or for worse) as the 'shopping Mecca of the southeast', and is a high-end neighborhood, home to beautiful mansions, posh restaurants and designer boutiques. People either love it or hate it, but I fell in love with it as soon as I moved here ten years ago.

Finally, a short way southwest of Midtown, Downtown Atlanta is worth a visit. It's home to CNN, Turner Broadcasting, Philips Arena, Olympic Village, Georgia State University, and Georgia Tech. Its skyscrapers define the city's distinctive skyline, and it attracts urban dwellers and artists, who live in the funky old industrial buildings that have now been converted to lofts and apartments. It's also home to some amazing restaurants and hotels, as well as galleries that host some great parties on the monthly arts walk through the Castleberry Hill Arts District of Downtown Atlanta – an event not to miss if you're in town!

W DOWNTOWN This hotel was built from the ground up as a W-branded hotel, and the architecture alone says it all. A great place to stay, or just to drop in for a drink or two. In the summer months, the rooftop deck features a DJ pool party and a great view. Drinkshop is the inside bar, which serves vintage-inspired drinks in a posh setting. 45 Ivan Allen Jr Blvd, Atlanta, GA 30308, www.starwoodhotels.com

HOTEL PALOMAR One of the newest boutique hotels in Midtown, it's artfully styled with contemporary decor, and a beautiful rooftop lounge serving great cocktails. 866 West Peachtree St NW, Atlanta, GA 30308, www.hotelpalomar-atlantamidtown.com

ELLIS HOTEL A cute boutique hotel right in the heart of Downtown. The historic building has a newly updated, modern aesthetic that fits right in with the pace of the city. 176 Peachtree St NW, Atlanta, GA 30303, www.ellishotel.com

ST. REGIS A new 5-star hotel with amazing attention to detail and a 40,000 ft^2 pool piazza on the sixth level. It could make for a great city break hotel. 88 West Paces Ferry Rd, Atlanta, GA 30305, www.starwoodhotels.com

14TH @ PEACHTREE STREET

Peachtree St

OCTANE Octane is a coffee bar and lounge with a couple of locations around the city. My favorite branch is on the West Side. Free Wi-fi draws a mixed crowd of art kids, designers, and web-folk. They host pecha kucha events and barista competitions throughout the year, and their espresso martini will keep you up till the wee hours. Open late. A must visit. 1009-B Marietta St NW, Atlanta, GA 30318, www.octanecoffee.com

APRES DIEM A restaurant, cafe, bistro, bar, and lounge all in one. Continental cuisine, a good drinks menu and great coffees, plus nightly DJs and live music acts. Settle in for the evening. 931 Monroe Dr, Atlanta, GA 30308, www.apresdiem.com

WHISKEY BLUE If you're out to impress, this is the place. It's on the roof of the W Hotel in Buckhead, and offers great views and nightly DJs. Very chic! 3377 Peachtree Rd NE, Atlanta, GA 30326

HALO One of my favorite lounges in Midtown at the bottom of the historic Biltmore building. They've been around for about a decade now, but always host good DJs, and provide a great atmosphere for a night out. 817 West Peachtree St NW, Atlanta, GA 30308, www.halolounge.com

AURUM Aurum is a hot new lounge designed by Atlanta interior designer, Michael Habachy. It's got a gold, glowing theme, with an onyx bar and a well-dressed crowd. It's only open Wednesday to Saturday. 108 8th St, Atlanta, GA 30309, www.aurumlounge.com

DRINK

MARTA

LUPE Lupe is one of my favorite new taquerias, located right in Midtown on Juniper. It offers authentic Mexican dishes in a cool, contemporary environment. Specialities include goat tacos and chicken in red mole, and fantastic cocktails, such as the chipotle martini. 905 Juniper St, Atlanta, GA 30309, www.sottosottorestaurant.com

REPAST Asian influenced new American cuisine with a contemporary flair. They have one of the best wine lists in the city, and are also one of the few restaurants around with macrobiotic and gluten-free options. Try their chocolate terrain cake with olive oil and sea salt for dessert – to die for! 620 Glen Iris Dr NE, Atlanta, GA 30308, www.repastrestaurant.com

BELEZA Right next door to Lupe, you'll find this Brazilian bar/restaurant. They serve tapas-style sharing dishes, but you can just have drinks if you prefer. The decor is futuristic but homely at once. Live music or a DJ is always there to liven things up. 905 Juniper St, Atlanta, GA 30309, www.sottosottorestaurant.com

HOLY TACO Holy Taco is your friendly neighborhood taqueria in East Atlanta. The perfect place for a night out with friends. Great Margaritas. 1314 Glenwood Ave SE, Atlanta, GA 30316, www.holy-taco.com

LEON'S FULL SERVICE Leon's is a quirky spot in the Decatur neighborhood. Originally a garage, the space has been charmingly converted into a friendly neighborhood walk-up restaurant and bar. Delicious menu items and even better drinks make this place a staple. 131 East Ponce de Leon Ave, Atlanta, GA 30030, www.leonsfullservice.com

CAKES & ALE Also in Decatur, Cakes & Ale is friendly and full of personality. They use locally sourced, seasonal produce to create good southern home cooking with a soulful edge. 254 West Ponce de Leon Ave, Atlanta, GA 30030, www.cakesandalerestaurant.com

EAT

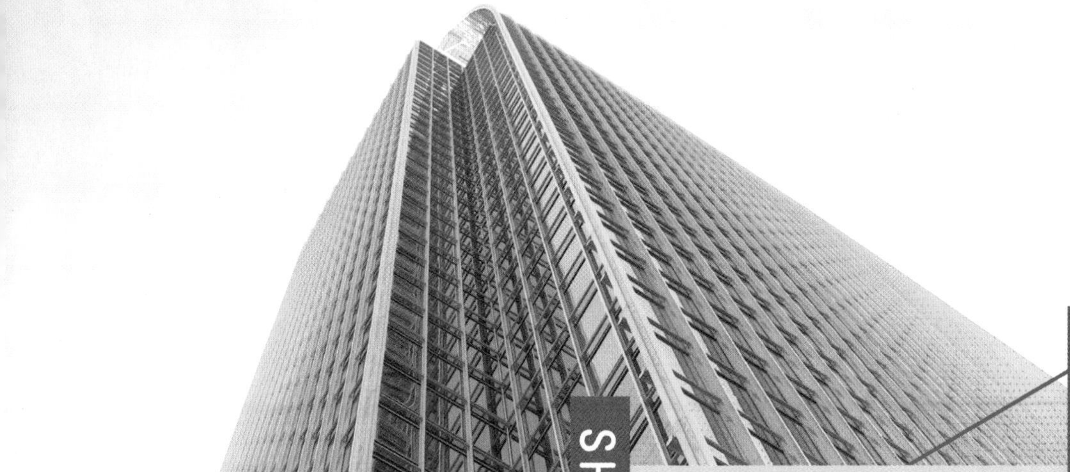

SHOP

MIDTOWN ATLANTA

BEEHIVE CO-OP A small boutique in Buckhead offering stylish, crafty, one-off gift items, homewares, stationery, and clothing by local artisans and emerging designers. 1831 Peachtree Rd NE, Atlanta, GA 30309, www.beehiveco-op.com

YOUNG BLOOD GALLERY & BOUTIQUE An independent gallery and shop for emerging designers and do-it-yourself crafters to show and sell their wares. A great place for unique gift items and cutting edge art. 636 North Highland Ave, Atlanta, GA 30306, www.youngbloodgallery.com

FAB'RIK BOUTIQUE A spot for fashionistas, Fab'rik boutique in Midtown Atlanta has hard-to-find labels and popular brands. Fashion-forward, yet not too expensive. 1114 West Peachtree St NW, Atlanta, GA 30309, www.fabrikstyle.com

K'LA A must for any shopper, this place has a great selection of really unusual fashion labels. I always get loads of compliments on the stuff I buy here. Located in Atlantic Station. 1380 Atlantic Dr, Atlanta, GA 30363

JEFFREY One of my favorite places to splurge, Jeffrey is a little slice of New York City in Atlanta, stocking the best selection of designer shoes you could dream of. The service is impeccable, and if you are looking for something specific, they will hunt it down for you. 3500 Peachtree Rd NE, Atlanta, GA 30326, www.jeffreynewyork.com

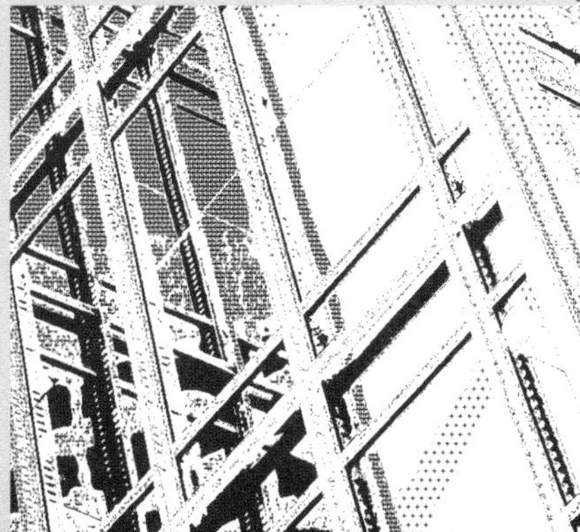

HIGH MUSEUM OF ATLANTA

CULTURE

HIGH MUSEUM OF ART The High Museum of Art is a must-see. The spectacular white Modern building was originally designed by Richard Meier, with a later addition by architect Renzo Piano. They hold a superb collection of classic and contemporary art. 1280 Peachtree St NE, Atlanta, GA 30309, www.high.org

MUSEUM OF DESIGN ATLANTA (MODA) MODA is the only museum in the southeast devoted exclusively to all things design. Inspiring exhibitions on architecture, product design, interiors, furniture, graphics, fashion, and more. 285 Peachtree Center Ave, Atlanta, GA 30303, www.museumofdesign.org

MUSEUM OF CONTEMPORARY ART OF GEORGIA (MOCA-GA) MOCA-GA is a small museum/gallery with a very specific collection showcasing local and national artists. It's definitely worth checking out to get a feel of the local art scene. 75 Bennett St NW, Atlanta, GA 30309, www.mocaga.org

WHITESPACE GALLERY Careful curatorship keeps this gallery at the cutting edge of the art scene. The space is gorgeous and refined. Every opening I have attended has been phenomenal. Located in the Inman Park neighborhood. 814 Edgewood Ave, Atlanta, GA 30307, www.whitespace814.com

EYEDRUM A non-profit art and music gallery featuring contemporary installations, new media and music performances. A hip space with an individual vibe. A guaranteed good time. 290 Martin Luther King Jr Dr, Atlanta, GA 30312, www.eyedrum.org

CASTLEBERRY HILL ART STROLL On the second Friday of the month, the Castleberry Hill Arts District hosts this fantastic event. All galleries in this cool area open their doors for late night art, music, wine and people-watching. www.castleberryhill.org/artstroll

FOX THEATRE A stunning 1920s building originally built as a mosque, the Fox Theatre brings touring off-Broadway acts, movie screenings, plays, and concert events to Atlanta. A wonderful atmosphere and great architecture – I've seen some amazing stuff here. 660 Peachtree St NE, Atlanta, GA 30308, www.foxtheatre.org

PIEDMONT PARK

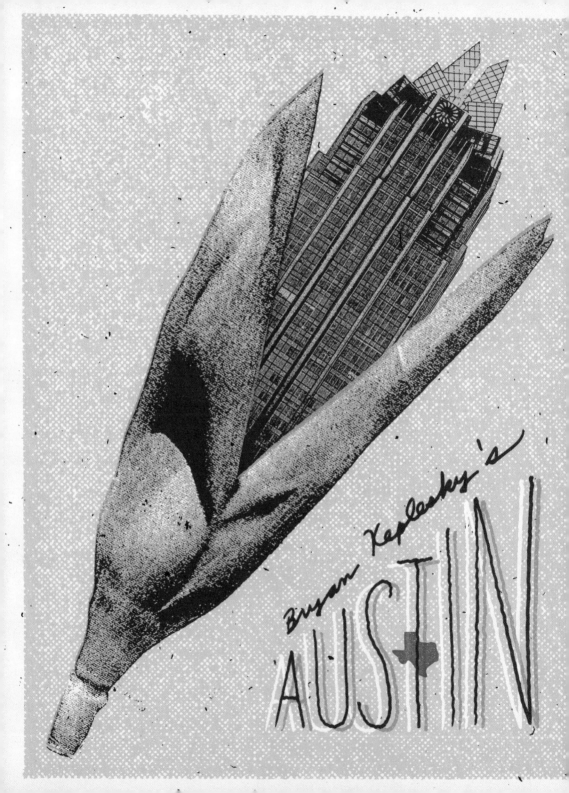

Bryan Keplesky's
AUSTIN

AUSTIN, TEXAS BY BRYAN KEPLESKY

I'm fortunate enough to call Austin my home. It's where I've worked, played, gotten into trouble, and grown creatively, personally, and professionally over the last six years. If you're visiting the city, the first thing you need to do is forget whatever notions you might have about Texas or Texans. Despite being the capital of the state, Austin has always relished its role as the loud, snotty, strange, and very drunken member at the Texas family reunion. A generation ago, Austin was a home for hippies and weirdos and as it's grown and expanded, it's evolved into a highly progressive, creative and laid back city.

I'm always wary of city branding, but our official slogan is "The Live Music Capital of the World", and in this case it's actually true. One visit to www.showlistaustin.com reveals how popular this city is with musicians of all description. This has fueled an influx of like-minded folks – people who want to screenprint posters, make art and publish zines – but will serve coffee, write software, or whatever other day job it takes to be part of this place. And this, in turn, means that bars have popped up left right and center to cater to the hedonistic requirements of all these creative folk.

Geographically, Austin can be divided into several areas, each with a unique vibe. Downtown Austin is the epicenter of live music (Red River District) and bars (6th Street). To the west is the University of Texas at Austin, the largest university in the state that continually brings an influx of culture and young people. South Austin (best represented on South Congress Avenue) perfectly captures the humble, relaxed vibe the city started out as. East Austin is the up-and-comer, home to a large Hispanic and African-American population. It was once considered pretty rough but is now in the midst of an energetic revitalization, with lots of new bars and galleries. All of this is accessible by foot, on pedal, or a quick cab ride.

One final note: Austin has a reputation as a drinking town, which I think is a bit unfair. Austin is an exceptional drinking town.

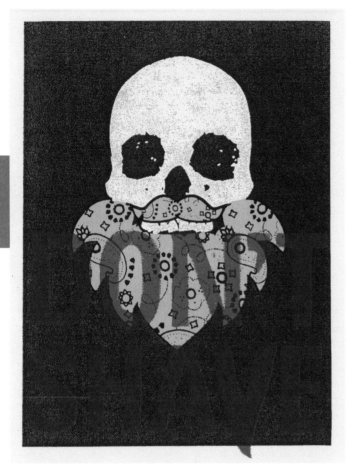

AUSTIN MOTEL An authentic 50s throwback to days when the capital city was nothing but a relaxed, folksy town populated by oddballs and dreamers, who just wanted to hang out and drink and not think about being stuck in the middle of Texas. The place is inescapably kitsch – each room has a unique and tacky wallpaper mural – but it feels like home. The motel is also internationally known for its giant, phallic neon sign. 1220 South Congress Ave, Austin, TX 78704, www.austinmotel.com

HOTEL ST CECILIA Probably the most exclusive hotel in the city. This is the where Pearl Jam or the Rolling Stones hole up for an entire week when coming into town. It's a small compound of a dozen or so elevated bungalows set back from the main South Congress drag. 112 Academy Dr, Austin, TX 78704, www.hotelsaintcecilia.com

SHERATON Even though it's a chain, this specific Sheraton is perfectly placed just outside the Red River District and only a few blocks from all the burgeoning East Side bars. When the Mohawk (see Music) books out-of-town bands, they put them up here, so if you grab a drink at the bar at around 8pm, you might just catch a glimpse of four or five dudes who look really, really out of place among all the other guests. 701 East 11th St, Austin, TX 78701, www.sheraton.com

STAY

HOTEL SAN JOSE This Modernist, one-storey hotel is completely dialed. Everything from the large (and expensive-looking) succulents that line its outer walls to the mid-century appropriations in each of the rooms reveals a keen eye for design. Complete with a pool and an outdoor patio (that doubles as an excellent public bar every night), the San Jose is my favorite hotel. Be sure to check if the Bob Dylan room is available. 1316 South Congress Ave, Austin, TX 78704, www.sanjosehotel.com

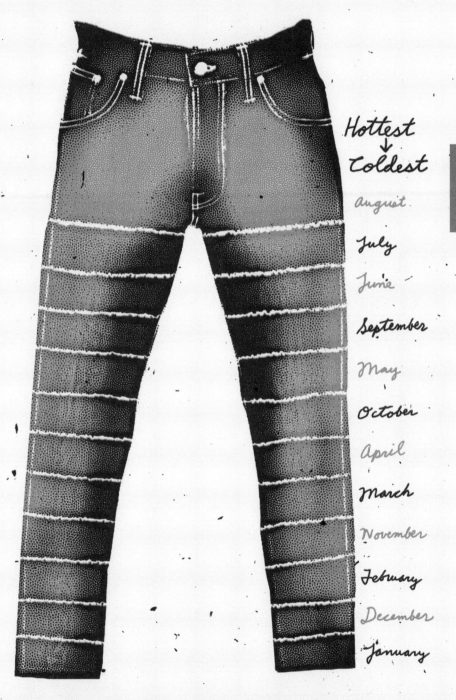

Hottest
↓
Coldest

August
July
June
September
May
October
April
March
November
February
December
January

Austin Cut-Offs Calendar

HOT DOG KING "When you eat here you dine with the King" is this amazing hot dog stand's slogan. At least I think it's something like that – I'm a bit hazy on the specifics, because its location, right in the middle of Red River Street, means that I mostly frequent it when I've been out drinking all night and not had a chance to eat. The guy who sells the Chicago-style dogs (and excellent vegetarian option) goes by the epithet of King, and I'm not one to argue. 8th St and Red River, Austin, TX 78701

SOUTH CONGRESS CAFE Weekend brunch is an Austin staple, and South Congress Cafe has always been my favorite place to go at the crack of noon on a Sunday. Bloody Marys and coffee abound and the food is always top notch. The wait can be shockingly long, but South Congress has some of the best shops in town to explore, and you'll observe some real characters when you finally get to your booth. 1600 South Congress Ave, Austin, TX 78704, southcongresscafe.com

EAST SIDE PIES This story perfectly summarizes East Side Pies: one night while hanging out with friends we all had a huge craving for pizza. After attempting to call East Side Pies no less than five times, we finally climbed into a car and drove there. When I asked if something was wrong with their phone, the guys at East Side Pies simply responded that they "didn't feel like answering it". Dealing with Austin stoners can be frustrating, but the pizza is always worth the trouble. 1401 Rosewood Ave, Austin, TX 78702, www.eastsidepies.com

CISCO'S RESTAURANT BAKERY One of the first things I learned when I moved to Austin is that people here are serious about breakfast tacos. There's no better cure for a hangover, and no better place to indulge than Cisco's. Try the Miga (scrambled eggs, onions, jalapenos and shredded tortilla chips, topped with salsa). It's rumored that Lyndon B Johnson, 36th US President and breakfast taco aficionado, used to hang out here in the 50s and 60s. 1511 East 6th St, Austin, TX 78702

MOTHER'S CAFE AND GARDEN Austin is very vegetarian/vegan friendly, and Mother's is one of the best all-vegetarian restaurants. The staff, surprisingly, appear to be lovable moms. Good cooking, a date-friendly atmosphere and fresh veggies. Be sure to pop next door for some gelato at Dolce Vita. 4215 Duval St, Austin, TX 78751, www.motherscafeaustin.com

CASINO EL CAMINO Casino el Camino is one of the last punk rock dive bars on East 6th Street. They also happen to make the best burgers in town, no question. The wait can be excruciatingly long – sometimes over an hour on busy nights. But the cooks know what they're doing, they're angry as hell, and if they tell you your burger will be ready in an hour, it will be ready in an hour and not a moment sooner. Don't despair, it's the perfect excuse to down a couple tall cans on the back patio. 517 East 6th St, Austin, TX 78701, www.casinoelcamino.net

Six Years of Hard Austin Living

- SEVERE SHORT TERM MEMORY LOSS
- NANOBOTS
- BIKE CONCUSSION
- COLLEGE EDUCATION REPLACED BY COMPENDIOUS KNOWLEDGE OF GIANT SQUID
- MD 20/20 VISION
- PERMANENT DEAFNESS
- CHAFING FROM NECKERCHIEF
- DUELING SCAR
- ELYSIUM POLTERGEIST
- GLASS SHARDS FROM RITZ BAR FIGHT
- A LOVE OF NOTHING
- SBESTOS FROM OLD EMO'S CEILING
- OVERWORKED SWEAT GLANDS
- TOM WAITS TATTOO
- ENDLESS ROPE MUSCLE
- RED RIVER LIVER
- BREAKFAST TACO FOIL
- UNDIGESTED DEATH METAL PIZZA
- INTEGRITY FAILURE
- 80 LONESTARS/MONTH x 12 MONTHS x 6 YEARS
- DISRUPTED BOWELS FROM BOWEL- DISRUPTING DOOMCORE
- ADDICTION TO LEOPARD ADRENALINE
- WRIST CANCER FROM EMO'S STAMPS
- QUA SHARK BITE
- COCKFIGHTING SCARS
- SCREENPRINTING ARTHRITIS
- CARPAL TUNNEL FROM BLOGGING
- EMBEDDED BEE STING
- STUPID SKINNY JEANS
- PERMANENT JORTS TAN LINE
- MY THIGHS SEEM OKAY
- BUSTED KNEECAPS
- TITANIUM PINS FROM KICKBALL INJURY
- BULGING CALVES
- SHIN SPLINTS FROM SKIDS
- LAST CALL ANKLE SPRAINS
- FLAT FEET

THE SIDE BAR No bar is closer to my heart than Side Bar – I've had so many great times here over the years. It's completely unassuming and utterly devoid of pretension, but what it lacks in decor, seating, and functioning bathrooms, it makes up for in atmosphere. The bartenders are glad you're there, and they show it by way of very friendly pours. Its convenient location on Red River makes it the best place to sneak into between sets at one of the nearby music venues. 602 East 7th St, Austin, TX 78701, www.thesidebaraustin.com

LONGBRANCH INN Historically, East Side nightlife was all about jazz and juke joints. That era has sadly passed, but the Longbranch keeps the flame alive. It's home to the oldest physical bar in Austin, which was relocated some time ago from the Driskell Hotel. The decor (and taxidermy) evoke that sense of history, and their jukebox is unparalleled in its mix of old and modern tunes. 1133 East 11th St, Austin, TX 78702

DONN'S DEPOT Donn's is more of a destination, rather than a usual drinking spot, mainly because the clientele skews way older. Retrofitted into an old rail car, Donn's has plush carpet, a piano and, best of all, free popcorn. Walk in on a random night and you'll see cute old couples two-stepping while the patriarch and namesake, Donn, tinkles on the ivory keys. 1600 West 5th St, Austin, TX 78703, www.donnar.home.texas.net

THE GOOD KNIGHT The last few years in Austin have seen a surge in mixology bars, serving the kinds of drinks your Grandpa made after a long day at the office. The Good Knight was at the forefront, whipping up Old Fashioneds and Pimm's Cup No. 1s, while most places were content with tossing you a Longneck. When I say this is also the darkest bar in the city, I mean it literally. It's quiet and moody, but its class is undeniable. The drink menu changes seasonally and they also serve great food off a very limited menu. 1300 East 6th St, Austin, TX 78702, www.thegoodknight.net

CHEERS SHOT BAR 6th Street is home to more college bars than I care to count and, when taken as a whole, they can be a fun time. Are any of these bars actually good? Of course not. That's really not the point. They are there to serve wild frat boys, bachelorette parties and any other 21-35 year-old. Only one 6th Street bar has managed to wrangle any genuine affection from me, and that's Cheers Shot Bar. They have about 200 different shots, all with ambiguously naughty names – the Dirty Girl Scout is my favorite. It's easy to dismiss 6th Street in favor of other areas (Red River, East 6th, etc), but despite the different subcultures, deep down everyone in Austin just wants to party and have a good time. 416 East 6th Street, Austin, TX 78701

SHANGRI-LA Austin's East Side, particularly East 6th, is currently the hottest drinking district. Most of the owners of this new crop of bars cut their teeth at some of the heavy hitters on Red River, and Shangri-La (or the Shang as it is usually referred to), is the embodiment of what makes them great. It has cheap drinks, friendly staff, and a beautiful outdoor patio that's both expansive and intimate. Oftentimes Shangri-La is someone's first foray into East Side drinking, so the crowd can be thick and random, but that's usually part of the fun. 1016 East 6th St, Austin, TX 78702, www.shangrilaaustin.com

THE LIBERTY The Liberty is Shang's rowdier little brother and has a lot of the same great offerings. The inexpensive drinks, bartenders you'd back up in a fight, and nice patio space are all here. It's rougher around the edges and the crowd is a lot more consistent in terms of its tattoos, piercings, and penchant for roughhousing. But really, that's what makes this place so great. They also have *Terminator 2* and *Star Trek: The Next Generation* pinball machines, which I have to admit are pretty awesome. 1618 1/2 East 6th St, Austin, TX 78702

CHEAPO DISCS AND FRIENDS OF SOUND

There are so many great record shops in Austin that it pains me to highlight just one, but I'll have to go with Cheapo, open 365 days a year. They have a great selection of used CDs and DVDs, but best of all is all the vinyl in the back half of the store. Obscure 45s, vintage international, and every significant musical movement of the 20th Century are at your fingertips. The inventory probably caters more to the crate digger than the curatorial, but there's nothing better than flipping through a few hundred LPs waiting to see what comes next. If you're more inclined to high-grade New Wave, electronica, and novelty, check out Friends of Sound. **CHEAPO:** 914 North Lamar, Austin, TX 78703, www.cheapotexas.com, **FRIENDS OF SOUND:** 1704 South Congress Ave, Austin, TX 78704, www.friendsofsound.com

UNCOMMON OBJECTS

Whenever I have friends visiting from out of town, I always take them here. It's hard to describe what Uncommon Objects is, and if you single out its parts you find it doesn't really describe what it is as a whole. It sells antiques, vintage furniture, signage, jewelry, clothing, old maps and woodpress type, anatomical posters, melamine flatware, and cabinets full of old postcards and photographs. All this stuff is cool, but what makes this place so special is the presentation. The entire inventory is divided into thematic nooks by color (like red, brown, or white), or subject matter (the ocean, the body, the occult). When I am looking for inspiration or want to be surprised by juxtaposition, this is where I go. 1512 South Congress Ave, Austin, TX 78704, www.uncommonobjects.com

DOMY BOOKS If you're looking to blow a paycheck on art and design books, look no further. Domy not only has a stupendous collection of zines, design manifestos and print ephemera, they also have one of the better small art galleries in town. Their packed but impeccably organized space is always worth a stop. 913 East Cesar Chavez, Austin, TX 78702, www.domystore.com

FIESTA MART This is Austin's largest Hispanic market. It's a giant, culturally authentic grocery store and a flea market combined. It's the kind of place where you can buy really good peppers and a Scarface rug in one trip. 3909 N I-35 Service Rd, Austin, TX 78722, www.fiestamart.com

SERVICE MENSWEAR AND BY GEORGE

Austin fashion boutiques are mainly of the vintage variety (there are many up and down South Congress), but Service Menswear for men, and By George for women, offer great contemporary clothes. By George is definitely high-end ladies' fashion, and exists in a world that I don't particularly understand, though many female friends attest to its pedigree. Service can also be categorized as higher-end, but not unreasonable. They have a great selection of black dress shirts, military-style jackets, and other well-appointed accoutrements. 1400 South Congress Ave, Austin, TX 78704, www.servicemenswear.com, www.bygeorgeaustin.com

OK MOUNTAIN The art scene in Austin has always been overshadowed by the live music scene. Art and artists have always thrived here, but it can sometimes be hard to notice when stacks of speakers are blaring every night of the week. East Side gallery OK Mountain is one of the few places that is changing that situation, simply by exhibiting the best up-and-coming artists (from Austin or wherever) and throwing the best opening parties. 1312 East Cesar Chavez, Ste B, Austin, TX 78703, www.okaymountain.com

ARTHOUSE Free and open to the public, Arthouse is the premier gallery for contemporary art. The exhibitions (which change about once a month) have featured international, national and Texas-based art. The openings are high-profile and great for mingling. 700 Congress Ave, Austin, TX 78701, www.arthousetexas.org

AUSTIN MUSEUM OF ART The big Texas cities (with the big Texas money) have colossal art museums, but the Austin Museum of Art is no runt. There isn't a permanent collection, but I've seen some worthwhile international touring exhibitions here. It has a great gift shop that's free to enter (the museum itself isn't free). 823 Congress Ave, Austin, TX 78701, www.amoa.org

ALAMO DRAFTHOUSE CINEMA The Alamo is an Austin institution and after seeing one movie there I never wanted to go to a multiplex ever again. They screen all the new releases, and also host an array of B-movie theme nights (Terror Tuesdays, Weird Wednesdays, for example), sing alongs, and special events. There's also food – really good food, in fact, and booze too. Various locations, www.drafthouse.com

PARAMOUNT THEATRE The Paramount is a gorgeous, classic theatre complete with plush seating, balconies, and swooping architecture. It offers movie screenings and performances including music, plays, book readings, and comedy acts. 713 Congress Ave, Austin, TX 78701, www.austintheatre.org

SOUTH BY SOUTHWEST If you want to live a year's worth in Austin in about a week, then South By Southwest (SXSW) is the way to do it. One of the premier music, film, and interactive festivals in the world, it transforms the city into a great, swarming mess of people, parties, movies, alcohol, and bands. Despite all the anxiety, crowds, traffic, and general anarchy SXSW inspires, it really is one of the things that makes this city the greatest. And the secret is you don't even have to spend money to have the best time of your life. There are more free parties, events, and happenings than one can possibly comprehend. Mid-March, www.sxsw.com

CULTURE

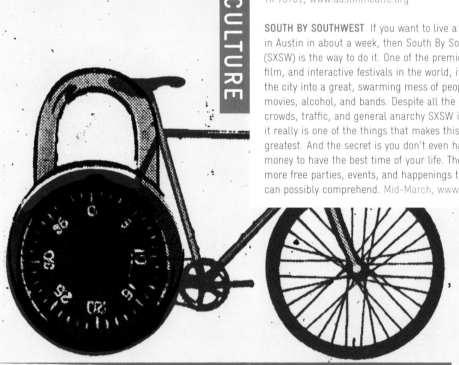

EMO'S Anchored right on 6th Street and Red River, Emo's has been the cornerstone of the live music scene for almost 20 years. It's also a total dump. There's a massive outside stage and an intimate inside stage, usually showcasing totally different kinds of music. There's nothing better than standing in the interconnecting courtyard, watching the spiked shoulder pad crowd and the vintage cardigan crowd jostling for a bit of breathing room at the same time. 603 Red River St, Austin, TX 78701, www.emosaustin.com

BEERLAND It's called 'Beerland', so what's not to like? I'm happy to say it lives up to its name, and despite it's diminutive size, it showcases the best blistering rockabilly/metal/loud bands on Red River. The doorguy has sworn to me on multiple occasions that Beerland is haunted. 711 1/2 Red River St, Austin, TX 78701, www.beerlandtexas.com

THE MOHAWK The Mohawk is one of the only venues that pulls off the trinity of good bands, good sound and good drink prices. It is without a doubt one of Austin's key clubs, and also happens to be the youngest. Run by people who genuinely care about the city, it has quickly built its reputation by booking quality shows and by being band and fan friendly. 912 Red River St, Austin, TX 78701, www.mohawkaustin.com

BARTON SPRINGS For the most part, Austin's weather is pleasant all year. From March through October it's sunny, warm (or really, really hot), and beautiful outside. When it's a nice day and you want to hop on a bike and take a dip, Barton Springs is a great option. Located within Zilker Park (the perfect place to roam around, throw a frisbee, or take your dog), Barton Springs is a series of natural water springs that are excellently maintained and impossible to not enjoy. The perfect summer day in Austin usually involves a bike, a breakfast taco and a jump in the springs. 2201 Barton Springs Rd, Austin, TX 78746

CLUB 1808 Because of the zoning restrictions of the city, East Side bars have flourished but East Side music venues are few and far between. Club 1808 is just far enough away from the spotlight (and just close enough to one of the sketchiest intersections in Austin) to have gone largely unnoticed. This is a good thing, because that's left this place free to showcase a variety of fringe bands who just want to play as loud as possible. 1808 East 12th St, Austin, TX 78702, www.myspace.com/club1808atx

RED 7 Sadly good bars and venues come and go, one of those legendary places being the Ritz (RIP). But the spirit of the Ritz lives on at Red 7, and this place is the home for all the smelly punk rockers and BMX riders that otherwise would have nowhere to go. There's skee-ball and pool tables, cheap Texas beer, and loud punk bands. Basically all the makings of a really good night. 611 East 7th St, Austin, TX 78701, www.red7austin.com

ELIZABETH GRAEBER's guide to: BALTIMORE

BALTIMORE, MARYLAND BY ELIZABETH GRAEBER

I am a Baltimore native, and although I am currently living in Washington DC, I'll always consider Baltimore my home. One of its many nicknames is Charm City, and despite its mixed reputation, the wacky charm of Baltimore, complete with a big beehive hairdo and a cigarette hanging out if its fluorescent pink lips, is still very much alive.

A few facts: Geographically, it's right on the north/south state divide, and its culture reflects that, with a warm, friendly population, great crabcakes, and a strong working class tradition. Crime is an issue (most famously depicted in the TV series *The Wire*), particularly on the West Side of the city, and nightlife can range from quirkily divey to rough as hell, depending on where you end up. On the other hand, the city is going through quite a bit of yuppification, with artists drawn to the cheap rents and warehouse spaces in previously poor neighborhoods like Hampden and Highlandtown. A lot of the rowhouses that make up Baltimore's distinctive streetscape are being done up in those areas, and left derelict and boarded up in others.

Public transport is not as good as it should be, but most of the interesting neighborhoods are easily walkable. The ones to visit are: Federal Hill, a historic neighborhood with a mixed population of blue collar old-timers and young professionals. It overlooks Inner Harbor and has the lovely Cross Street Market and lots of restaurants. On the other side of the harbor, you'll find Fells Point and Canton, with cute cobblestone streets, interesting shops, the old recreation pier and bars selling the infamous local brew, Natty Boh. Leading north from the harbor is Charles Street – the main drag of the city. Take a stroll up it, and you'll get a sense of Baltimore's diverse architecture, as well as finding plenty of galleries, restaurants and shops. At the top you'll find Johns Hopkins University, and the funky student neighborhoods (including Charles Village and the aforementioned Hampden), that surround it.

There's lots to love and hate about Baltimore. It's down and dirty, a little bit scummy, totally American, and lots of fun. One thing for sure, it's got a lot of character.

HOTEL MONACO The old B&O Railway headquarters in Downtown has now been sleekly converted into this upmarket hotel. Big rooms and a friendly touch (dog-friendly policy an added bonus for some). 2 North Charles St, Baltimore, MD 21201, www.monaco-baltimore.com

THE ADMIRAL FELL INN This is a really nice hotel right on the water in the historic neighborhood of Fells Point. It's on the higher end of the pricing spectrum, but it's really pleasant, comes complete with its own ghost story, and provides easy access to the restaurants and shopping in the cobbled streets around. 888 South Broadway, Baltimore, MD 21231, www.sterlinghotels.com

ABACROMBIE FINE FOOD AND ACCOMMODATIONS A conveniently located, mid-range B&B in the culture-rich neighborhood of Mount Vernon – across from the Symphony and down the street from the Walters Art Gallery. It has a pretty good restaurant attached. 58 West Biddle St, Baltimore, MD 21201, www.abacrombie.net

BALTIMORE HOSTEL A good budget option with lots of common space and a decent Downtown location. 17 West Mulberry St, Baltimore, MD 21201, www.baltimorehostel.org

EAT

GOLDEN WEST CAFE This funky cafe has a colourful, eccentric vibe and fits right into the small-town atmosphere of Hampden. It can sometimes feel too cool (and too popular) for its own good, but their food more than makes up for it. I recommend the Mental Oriental salad or the pumpkin pancakes. 1105 West 36th St, Baltimore, MD 21211, www.goldenwestcafe.com

IGGIE'S PIZZA Top dollar, wood-fired, thin crust pizza with fresh toppings, loads of vegetarian options, and a BYO policy. Plus it's dog-friendly. 818 North Calvert St, Baltimore, MD 21264, www.iggiespizza.com

THE EVERGREEN A charming, independently run coffee shop with mismatched seats, plants, and the work of local artists creating a homely vibe. Great coffee, sandwiches, and frozen yogurt. 501 West Coldspring Lane, Baltimore, MD 21210

THE AMBASSADOR DINING ROOM This upmarket Indian restaurant is basically tucked inside an apartment block. The ambience is always lovely – it opens up onto a large garden in summer, and has a cozy fireplace in winter. The food is not cheap, but it's good, and you can go for the lunch buffet if you're on a budget. 3811 Canterbury Rd, Baltimore, MD 21218, www.ambassadordining.com

MISS SHIRLEY'S Brunch is my favorite meal of the day, and this is one of my favorite places to indulge. Their Roland Park Omelet with asparagus, red peppers, artichoke, and goats cheese is a sight to behold. The Pratt Street branch is across the road from Inner Harbor, so a nice place to walk afterwards. 513 West Cold Spring Lane, Baltimore, MD 21210 and 750 East Pratt St, Baltimore, MD 21202, www.missshirleys.com

SOTTO SOPRA A romantic place serving creative Italian dishes. Dim lighting and well thought out decor make it a nice atmosphere – even if it does get crowded at times. It's pretty pricey, but makes a nice treat. Be sure to finish off the meal with an incredible coffee. 402 North Charles St, Baltimore, MD 21201, www.sottosoprainc.com

PAPERMOON DINER This 24-hour diner is a total one-off. Every inch of the space, including the ceiling, is covered in toys, nicknacks, pez dispensers, and weird sculptures. The food is solid, traditional diner fare, but the atmosphere is totally in its own league. 227 West 29th St, Baltimore, MD 21211, www.papermoondiner24.com

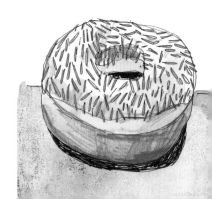

DRINK

BREWER'S ART This classy joint was recently voted the best bar in America in *Esquire* magazine. High praise that it actually manages to live up to. It has a dimly lit downstairs bar area, serving a vast selection of hand-crafted brews and bar snacks, and a brighter upstairs dining room serving proper food. The Resurrection Ale is the one to try. 1106 North Charles St, Baltimore, MD 21201, www.belgianbeer.com

MT ROYAL TAVERN The diviest of dive bars – cheap drinks, disgusting toilets, and a recreation of the Sistine Chapel on the ceiling. It attracts a strange mix of art students and middle aged drunks. Fun. 1204 West Mount Royal Ave, Baltimore, MD 21217

DOUGHERTY'S PUB A nice, chilled out, standard pub, where you can have a conversation without shouting, relax with a mixed crowd, and drink cheap beer served in pitchers by friendly staff. If it looks familiar, that's because it featured in *The Wire*. 223 West Chase St, Baltimore, MD 21201

THE DEPOT A grungy, unpretentious club that attracts a young, friendly crowd. It's pretty quiet on a weeknight, but it's still a place to go for dancing, rather than just for drinking. Fridays are 80s music nights and it gets packed. 1728 North Charles St, Baltimore, MD 21201

DIONYSUS Around the corner from Brewer's Art, the exterior of this place looks unpromising, but inside it's great. It has a cosy lounge-style downstairs bar and serves Greek food and good pizza. 8 East Preston St, Baltimore, MD 21202

Natty Boh ↓

book thing

SHOP

THE BOOK THING This is an amazing institution that has to be seen to be believed. A warehouse-sized warren of dusty rooms lined with second-hand books. The incredible thing is that all of them are FREE! I know! I've found some real gems here. In return you should really donate any old books you have lying about. Open on weekends. 3001 Vineyard Lane, Baltimore, MD 21218, www.bookthing.org

THE ZONE A total must for the vintage clothing enthusiast. Friendly staff and brilliantly selected stock in the front room of a brownstone in a very hip area. 813 North Charles St, Baltimore, MD 21201

MILAGRO A Hampden boutique selling jewelry, clothes, art, and gifts from around the world. Really nice selection of objects. 1005 West 36th St, Baltimore, MD 21211

ATOMIC BOOKS A quirky, independent bookstore selling zines, comics, and designer art toys. Conveniently located across the road from Golden West (see Eat). 3620 Falls Rd, Baltimore, MD 21211, www.atomicbooks.com

DOUBLE DUTCH BOUTIQUE Women's clothing, jewelry, handbags, and shoes by interesting contemporary indie labels, and some great one-off designs. The first Friday of the month you can sometimes get 10-20 per cent off your purchases. 3616 Falls Rd, Baltimore, MD 21211, www.doubledutchboutique.com

DAEDALUS BOOKS A well organised, no-frills warehouse bookstore selling discounted remainder books. And not just random stuff you're not interested in. Most of the stock is under $5. 5911 York Rd, Baltimore, MD 21212, www.daedalusbooks.com

VALUE VILLAGE THRIFT STORE A neighborhood thrift store stocked with good finds at rock bottom prices. 5013 York Rd, Baltimore, MD 21212

VOGUE REVISITED A neighborhood consignment shop selling discounted designer clothing and accessories. It can get crowded at weekends. 4002 Roland Ave, Baltimore, MD 21211

CROSS STREET MARKET An indoor food market with an old fashioned vibe. Sit at the bar and try the crabcakes at Nick's. 1065 South Charles St, Baltimore, MD 21230

AMERICAN VISIONARY ART MUSEUM
You can't really miss this crazy elliptical building with its 55ft wind sculpture dominating the exterior. It's a museum dedicated to 'art by everyday people' – a kind of folk art by self-taught artists – often with a political/social context; a quilt by a holocaust survivor, or a sculpture by a Baghdad surgeon for example. It's a quirky collection that can be very inspiring. 800 Key Hwy, Baltimore, MD 21230, www.avam.org

THE BALTIMORE MUSEUM OF ART
A free city museum with both contemporary and historical works. For a regional museum it's very good with some big name works and a nice sculpture garden. 10 Art Museum Dr, Baltimore, MD 21218, www.artbma.org

THE CHARLES THEATER
One of the few art-house cinemas left in Baltimore, with by far the most interesting program of indie and foreign movies. It has five screens in a very cool historic building. 1711 North Charles St, Baltimore, MD 21201, www.thecharles.com

BALTIMORE SYMPHONY ORCHESTRA
The BSO has experienced a resurgence since it was taken over by the talented female conductor, Marin Alsop. Concerts are really cheap, and they do some interesting experimental stuff as well as your standard classical fare. 1212 Cathedral St, Baltimore, MD 21201, www.bsomusic.org

THE THEATRE PROJECT
An experimental performing arts center that's been going since the 70s, bringing Baltimore world class shows and performance artists from around the globe. 45 West Preston St, Baltimore, MD 21201, www.theatreproject.org

THE WALTERS ART MUSEUM
A historic art museum located in Mount Vernon showing paintings, sculpture, artifacts, and objects. 600 North Charles St, Baltimore, MD 21201, www.thewalters.org

NUDASHANK GALLERY
A new, independent, artist-run space, showcasing emerging talent. It's on the third floor of a building which also houses several other galleries, including Gallery Four, which is another I really like. Worth dropping by. H&H Arts Building, 405 West Franklin St, Baltimore, MD 21201, www.nudashank.blogspot.com

CULTURE

EVENTS

HONFEST Honfest ('hon' being a term of endearment in Baltimorese – short for honey), is a celebration of Baltimore's kitsch, allegedly in honor of the working women of Baltimore. It takes place in the streets of Hampden in early June, and its highlight is the 'Baltimore's Best Hon' competition, in which the award goes to the best hon outfit (usually incorporating a beehive hairdo and leopard print spandex). An institution. www.honfest.net

ARTSCAPE The largest free arts festival in America happens around the MICA campus area on Mt Royal Avenue towards the end of July. It features work by artists, outdoor sculptors, fashion designers and craftspeople, performing arts events, experimental music, and family friendly activities. Check the website for the program. www.artscape.org

KINETIC SCULPTURE RACE An event in early May organized by the Visionary Art Museum (see Culture). Truck sized sculptures of animals and creatures race each other around the city for eight hours. Crazy. www.kineticbaltimore.com

GO

THE DOMINO SUGAR FACTORY The historic neon sign of the Domino Sugar Factory is a landmark of the city, so be sure to take a picture. You can get the best view from Fells Point.

FORT MCHENRY PARK A national park built around a 19th Century fort – and the birthplace of the national anthem. It's got a nice view over the water. Located just off 95, near the harbor.

NATIONAL AQUARIUM I have a soft spot for aquariums. What can I say? I love dolphin shows! This is a big aquarium located at the end of a pier in the harbor. It's well laid out, but gets busy, so book in advance or arrive when it opens! 501 East Pratt St, Baltimore, MD 21202, www.aqua.org

Yellow-Billed Cuckoo

ESTHER UHL'S
BOSTON

BOSTON, MASSACHUSETTS BY ESTHER UHL

If you believe the author Oliver W Holmes, Boston is "the center of the solar system". Personally, I think that's a minor exaggeration, but there is no doubt that, starting with the Boston Tea Party and the ride of Paul Revere, Boston has always played a central role in America's history. Today, thanks to the world-class reputations of Harvard and MIT, Boston is an important centre of education, medicine, and economy. This has helped it rise above the status of Grand Dame of America, to something much more interesting, which attracts creative, ambitious folk with open minds and innovative approaches to life. People here tend to have a certain resolve and a *joie de vivre* that one doesn't always see elsewhere in the US, and this gives the city a lively energy.

Boston is a medium-sized city built on a harbor, with the Charles River separating it from neighboring Cambridge, Watertown, and Charlestown. Over the years it has been populated by immigrants who have left their imprint on the culture, foods, and philosophies of the city. As you walk through the streets you'll be struck by the visible layers of history and the juxtaposition of the old and the new. Ancient red-brick sidewalks twist past handsome federalist mansions en route to soaring glass towers housing state-of-the-art technology. It's an attractive effect.

The city is divided into dozens of little neighborhoods that reach from North End through peaceful Bay Village and up-market Back Bay to South End with its independent galleries and shops. Each area has its own distinct character making Boston a great city to walk around and explore. The MBTA underground system is easy to use as well, and cycling is always an alternative option. While you're at it, check out the green spaces of Boston Common or take a long walk along the Charles River. One of my favorite activities in the summer is to take a trip to the beach in South Boston (Southie), and watch the sun setting over the city from Castle Island.

STAY

NINE ZERO Plush hotel with elegant furnishings, a soothing colour scheme and immaculately designed lighting. It's big and quite expensive but very relaxing, I'm sure. 90 Tremont St, Boston, MA 02108, www.ninezero.com

ONYX HOTEL This Downtown boutique hotel is run by the same guys as Nine Zero. It's got a fantastic location, is nicely designed, and not too pricey for what it is. 155 Portland St, Boston, MA 02114, www.onyxhotel.com

NEWBURY GUEST HOUSE A 32-room guest house in a Victorian red brick building in trendy Back Bay, right on bustling Newbury Street (filled with shops and cafes). The rooms are clean and contemporary and it's a reasonable option price-wise. 261 Newbury St, Boston, MA 02116, www.newburyguesthouse.com

HI-BOSTON A fairly large hostel run by Hostelling-International in the Back Bay area. It's been recently renovated and is slightly lacking in personality, but clean and fine for the money. You can get private and semi-private rooms, and it's probably the best budget option. 12 Hemenway St, Boston, MA 02115, www.bostonhostel.org

THE LIBERTY A grand 19th Century jail that was converted into a really lovely hotel – a pretty impressive architectural feat. Worth a visit even if you don't stay there. 215 Charles St, Boston, MA 02114, www.libertyhotel.com

PHO PASTEUR A family-owned Asian restaurant in the heart of Chinatown. It serves big portions at good prices, and they make the best soups I have ever eaten. 682 Washington St, Boston, MA 02111, www.phopasteurboston.net

TABERNA DE HARO Boston's most authentic Spanish tapas bar. It's got a friendly, informal atmosphere with a nice street-side patio area in the summer. They serve simple, traditional food, their regional specialities are great, and they have an impressive range of Spanish wines. 999 Beacon St, Brookline, MA 02446, www.tabernaboston.com

THE BEEHIVE A popular (by which I mean busy – so book in advance) bohemian eatery in the center of the arts complex in South End. Apart from their great food, it's always got a buzzing atmosphere thanks to the live entertainment, which ranges from world class musicians playing blues, R&B, electronica, and reggae to burlesque and cabaret acts. And they don't even have a cover charge! 541 Tremont St, Boston, MA 02116, www.beehiveboston.com

MIRACLE OF SCIENCE I always feel comfortable in this neighborhood joint – it's got a nerdie-chic atmosphere I can relate to, with a subtle science-lab vibe to the decor. The food is good, particularly the burgers, and it attracts a mix of artists, musicians, computer gurus, and MIT geeks. 321 Massachusetts Ave, Cambridge, MA 02139, www.miracleofscience.us

MERENGUE That's what you call soul food! Dominican cuisine in a rough (but on-the-up) neighborhood. It's got colorful, tropical-style decor, friendly staff and HUGE portions of incredible food. Definitely check it out. 156-160 Blue Hill Ave, Boston, MA 02119, www.merenguerestaurant.com

CUCHI CUCHI A fun 1920s brothel-style extravaganza. With stained glass windows, waitresses decked out in full flapper-gear, and a romantic atmosphere, this place is totally over the top – in a good way. The menu is a retro-eclectic selection of sampler plates (think beef stroganoff, chicken kievs and seafood stuffed avocado) – all surprisingly delicious and lots of veggie options. 795 Main St , Cambridge, MA 02139, www.cuchicuchi.cc

BALTIC EUROPEAN DELI A Polish grocery store in South Boston with an amazing selection of bread and deli foods freshly cooked in-house. If you're tired of burgers and fast food, this is the place to refresh your palate. 632 Dorchester Ave, Boston, MA 02127

EAT

33 RESTAURANT AND LOUNGE A swanky, New York-style martini bar with a downstairs lounge and a beautifully lit upstairs bar. A good place to go to impress. 33 Stanhope St, Boston, MA 02116, www.33restaurant.com

WHISKEY PARK The bar/club in Back Bay is where all the beautiful people go. Cover charge and expensive drinks, but you'll get to boogie with some real hotties. 64 Arlington St, Boston, MA 02116, www.gerberbars.com

WALLY'S CAFE The first time I went to this tiny, no-frills neighborhood jazz bar I felt a bit awkward – everything from the bartender to the musicians to the clientele was so authentic that I felt out of place. A few beers and some great live music soon put paid to that, and I'm now a big fan. 427 Massachusetts Ave, Boston, MA 02118, www.wallyscafe.com

DRINK

TOP OF THE HUB Located on the 52nd floor of the Prudential Center, this bar/restaurant offers a spectacular view of the Boston skyline from every table. It's kind of dressy (although that's not essential), but it's a nice treat to sip an amazing mojito while listening to live jazz and taking in the view. 800 Boylston St, Boston, MA 02116, www.topofthehub.net

GOOD LIFE A cozy, funky bar spread over two floors. Upstairs you can eat or have a cocktail at the bar. Down in the basement is where the party's at, with the best DJs on the turntables. 28 Kingston St, Boston, MA 02111, www.goodlifebar.com

AUDUBON CIRCLE An easy-to-miss minimalist restaurant/bar owned by the same guys as Miracle of Science (see Eat). They do great cocktails, excellent and creative food, and in summer you can hang out on their bamboo-lined patio with the other designers and hipsters. 838 Beacon St, Boston, MA 02215, www.auduboncircle.us

THE SOWA OPEN MARKET Boston's fantastic weekly artisan market hosts a wide variety of vendors. You'll find painters, sculptors, photographers, clothing and jewelry designers, milliners, florists, bakers, local farmers' produce, and much more every Sunday from May till October. 460 Harrison Ave, Boston, MA 02118, www.southendopenmarket.com

BODEGA A secret sneaker shop tucked inside what appears to be a normal convenience store. Behind a hidden door near the Snapple machine lies a fine selection of vintage and limited edition sneakers. 6 Clearway St, Boston, MA 02115, www.bdgastore.com

HONEYSPOT This is where I buy my beloved partner birthday presents. A great selection of gifts, cards, stationery, jewelry, and more. 48 South St, Jamaica Plain, MA 02130

MAGPIE This store is out in Somerville but is definitely worth checking out if you're in the neighborhood. Super cute and full of hand-crafted goodies and indie-designer home accessories. 416 Highland Ave, Somerville, MA 02144, www.magpie-store.com

POD A well-edited collection of products in a small space tucked away in Brookline. Beautiful textiles, French soaps, and antique Victorian postcards, all artfully laid out. 313 Washington St, Brookline Village, MA 02130, www.shop-pod.com

RUGG ROAD PAPER COMPANY An artist-run store with a friendly atmosphere selling gorgeous cards and handmade paper from around the world. 105 Charles St, Boston, MA 02114, www.ruggroadpaper.com

BLACK INK AND THE MUSEUM OF USEFUL THINGS I always lose track of time in Black Ink. They have so many one-off quirky items ranging from magnets to children's books to ceramic animals and rubber stamps. They have another shop called The Museum of Useful Things in Cambridge, selling objects for the home and office with an edgy design aesthetic. **BLACK INK:** 101 Charles St, Boston, MA 02114, **THE MUSEUM OF USEFUL THINGS:** 5 Brattle St, Cambridge, MA 02138

WINDSOR BUTTON An immense sea of buttons and a great selection of yarns. If you're into knitting you'll love this place. 35 Temple Pl, Boston, MA 02111, www.windsorbutton.com

SHOP

SOUTH END This is one of my favorite shopping areas. On every corner you'll find an interesting boutique offering a selection of design objects, jewelry, and homewares by local artists and designers. Gifted, Michelle Willey, and Turtle are three of my favorites. **GIFTED:** 53 Dartmouth St, Boston, MA 02116, www.madebymarie. com, **MICHELLE WILLEY:** 8 Union Park St, Boston, MA 02118, www.michelewilley. com **TURTLE:** 619a Tremont St, Boston, MA 02118, www. turtleboston.com

NEWBURY STREET For an upmarket Boston shopping experience, this is the place to go. Besides the usual stores, you'll find some really cool independent boutiques, and fun stuff like Johnnycupcakes or the Puma design store. Plus, loads of cafes where you can rest your weary, shopped-out feet.

ORPHEUM THEATRE A music venue that hosts some great acts. It's kind of worn and dated, but that's part of its charm. 1 Hamilton Pl, Boston, MA 02108, www.orpheum-theater.com

CANTAB LOUNGE Another music venue, which hosts an open mic poetry slam every Wednesday from 8pm. It's very variable – sometimes you feel it and sometimes you don't, but it makes a nice change of scene. 738 Massachusetts Ave, Cambridge, MA 02139, www.cantab-lounge.com

BOSTON CENTER FOR THE ARTS A non-profit center for the performing and visual arts. They have four theater spaces, and they get some great experimental stuff in. It's in a good South Boston location too, so check out what's on and make a night of it. 539 Tremont St, Boston, MA 02116, www.bcaonline.org

AXIOM A top gallery showcasing new and experimental media. They also have a program of live music, workshops, and other events. 141 Green St, Boston, MA 02130, www.axiomart.org

MASS MOCA A vast complex of buildings that used to house a textile factory, and has now been tastefully converted into a fantastic center for the arts. They host musical events, dance, film, theater, art, and everything in between. Big names are often drawn there, and I've seen some mind-blowing stuff – including a fantastic Sol LeWitt exhibition. It's out of town, but worth the trek. 87 Marshall St, North Adams, MA 01247, www.massmoca.org

THE INSTITUTE OF CONTEMPORARY ART (ICA) Contemporary art in all media, housed in a beautiful modern waterfront building. The collection is outstanding, with amazing exhibitions that are punctuated by the stunning views from the floor to ceiling windows. Plus they have a great, intimate little space where they host live music. Grab a beer from the cafe and sit on the water in the sun. 100 Northern Ave, Boston, MA 02210, www.icaboston.org

INDEPENDENT FILM FESTIVAL BOSTON This usually happens around April every year. I love getting the chance to see films from around the world – and there's always a buzzing atmosphere. www.iffboston.org

THE COOLIDGE CORNER THEATRE A friend once told me that this independent movie palace was originally built as a church and later redesigned as an Art Deco movie theatre. It's friendly, inexpensive, and fun, with bonuses like midnight movie screenings and kiddie matinees. The best place to see independent and classic films in Boston. 290 Harvard St, Brookline, MA 02215, www.coolidge.org

OPEN STUDIOS CAMBRIDGE / SOUTH END Once a year Boston's designers and artists open their studios to the public, offering a glimpse behind the scenes of the working practices of people you worship or can't abide. It's fun to stroll around checking out other people's work. www.useaboston.com, www.noca-arts.org

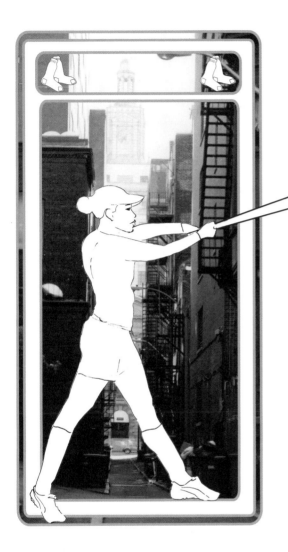

JEANETTE NEIL DANCE STATION
So I love dancing. It's the way I clear my mind, body, and soul after a stressful day. This lovely studio is my escape and my safe haven. It holds open classes, so you can come and dance without having to sign up for the rest of your life. Their teachers – especially their hip hop teachers are positively inspirational. 261 Friend St, 5th floor, Boston, MA 02114, www.jndance.com

HARBORWALK The Harborwalk is one of Boston's urban planning triumphs. 50 miles of walks, all cleverly linked up, take you around the shoreline from Charlestown, Deer Island, North End, and all the way to South Boston. It's easily accessed from Downtown (start at the ICA or the aquarium), and is great for cycling, boating, swimming, picnicking, or just going for a stroll. My favorite walk (or run – even better!) is along Pleasure Bay, a calm, enclosed lagoon with a sandy swimming beach, with a detour to Castle Island, where I circle the fort and take in the awesome ocean views.

CHILL

CHRISTIAN SCIENCE CHURCH POOL The Christian Science Church is an imposing, domed 19th Century building in the middle of the city. In the 1960s the church commissioned a big plaza to be built in front of it by the firm of the wonderful architect I M Pei. The result was the amazing 670 ft reflecting pool and fountain, which is a real Boston landmark. I love just staring at it on a sunny day. 210 Massachusetts Ave, Boston, MA 02115

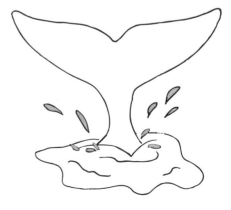

THE

OLY

CITY

CHARLESTON, SOUTH CAROLINA

BY JAY FLETCHER

To most, Charleston is a nod to gentler days gone by, known for its history, grace, and charm. To me, Charleston is a city rich in superlatives. We make a lot of "best of" lists. Flipping through the pages of most any travel rag will often reveal our relatively small city scoring top marks for best beaches, best weather, best dining, best manners…. It always amazes me how often I see my quaint little home touted amongst mega-destinations like New York, San Francisco, Chicago, and the like. Then again, it doesn't. Within a few square miles of my front door I've eaten some of the best food, seen some of the most inspirational sights, and met some of the most pleasant people you could ever hope to come across. "Quality of life" is a phrase you hear constantly echoed in local circles. Charlestonians are a proud bunch, equally protective and welcoming, who can't imagine life elsewhere. And don't want to.

Originally named Charles Towne when established by English settlers in 1670 and nicknamed "The Holy City" due to an overwhelming number of churches (in fact, there's a height restriction ordinance enforced on new construction to keep the city's signature steeple-dotted skyline intact), Charleston is one of America's oldest and most historic cities. Pirate raids, sporadic assaults from Spain and France, pivotal moments of the American Revolution, the opening battle of America's Civil War, and a devastating earthquake felt as far north as Boston and as far south as Cuba are just a few notches on Charleston's unique and storied timeline. Today, apart from the tourism, it also has a vibrant economy based on an important and active seaport and a burgeoning IT industry.

Strolling the city's gas lantern-lit cobblestone alleys is like exploring a time capsule, lush and largely untouched history on display at every turn, the past alive and mingling with the city's diverse and vibrant present. This is the true beauty of Charleston – how wonderfully the city coexists with itself as a modern antique, looking backwards and forwards at the same time.

STAY

WENTWORTH MANSION Built in 1885 as a private residence, the Wentworth Mansion now serves as one of Charleston's most unique and opulent hotels. Hand-carved marble, intricate woodwork, and Tiffany stained glass windows are just a few of the perks. The hotel restaurant, Circa 1886, is fantastic. If it's too pricey, stop by anyway and politely ask if you can admire the view from the rooftop cupola. 149 Wentworth St, Charleston, SC 29401, www.wentworthmansion.com

FRENCH QUARTER INN Adjacent to Charleston's famous market area, the French Quarter Inn manages to be upscale without being snooty. The decor is classic, French urban in style, and the staff has a reputation for top customer service. The restaurant, Tristan, is popular, and the nightly wine and cheese reception is a guest favorite. 166 Church St, Charleston, SC 29401, www.fqicharleston.com

THE INN AT MIDDLETON PLACE This is one of the city's few modern hotels. Awarded for its Lloyd Wright-inspired design, it sensitively complements the neighboring 18th Century plantation. Warm, handcrafted wooden furniture and paneling adorn each room, along with floor-to-ceiling windows offering views of the inn's natural surroundings. 4290 Ashley River Rd, Charleston, SC 29414, www.theinnatmiddletonplace.com

SEASIDE INN If you're looking for a more moderately-priced, saltier, beach-going experience, this is the place. Located 15 minutes from Downtown on the Isle of Palms, the rooms are mere steps from the ocean and the surrounding area is home to several good restaurants, bars, and shops. You came to see Charleston, but you just might not leave the island. 1004 Ocean Blvd, Isle of Palms, SC 29451, www.seasideinniop.com

TRATTORIA LUCCA Living in a city known for world-class cuisine, and picking your favorite restaurant is like asking a father of twenty to pick his favorite child. That said, Trattoria Lucca is near the top of my list. This place brings a true Italian dining experience to a city known for shrimp and grits and macaroni cheese. The restaurant is cozy, the chef mingles with his diners, and the food melts in your mouth. Be sure to sample as many of the appetizers as you can. 41-A Bogard St, Charleston, SC 29403, www.luccacharleston.com

TACO BOY The original Taco Boy at Folly Beach is a stone's throw from the Atlantic, and a newer venue has now opened up in Downtown. Great atmosphere and food. Try the tempura shrimp tacos with a Mexican coke, and finish your night off with a hunk of tres leches cake. 217 Huger St, Charleston, SC 29403 and 15 Center St, Folly Beach, SC 29439, www.tacoboy.net

CAVIAR & BANANAS One part upscale market and one part gourmet cafe, Caviar & Bananas is a slick little spot with something for everybody. There's charcuterie, cheeses, sushi, a coffee bar, and a decadent selection of pastries. Or you can swing by and pick up the fixings for a meal at home. Do yourself a favor and try the duck sandwich. 51 George St, Charleston, SC 29401, www.caviarandbananas.com

MONZA Wherever you live, you know how it goes – there are the pizza places that deliver, and then there's that one-off pizza joint that everybody goes to. Monza is the latter. The dining room is polished with a minimalist vibe, and a subtle vintage Italian racing theme. The pizzas are named after people you've probably never heard of. Start with the Sausage and Peppers and then take the Materassi for a spin. 451 King St, Charleston, SC 29403, www.monzapizza.com

CHARLESTON GRILL Without a doubt, the best meal I've had in Charleston (which is saying something) was served to me at Charleston Grill. Think dark wood, dim lighting, and a waiter who says things like "the chef would like you to try...". Not for the budget-conscious, this stuff will revolutionize what you thought you knew about food. Don't forget to say hi to Mickey – the guy who made you feel like a million bucks when you walked through the door – and tell him Jay sent you. 224 King St, Charleston, SC 29401, www.charlestongrill.com

THE WRECK A hidden local favorite in Old Village overlooking picturesque Shem Creek. You'd be forgiven for thinking that the name was derived from the building, but actually it refers to the Richard and Charlene, a trawler that was wrecked during Hurricane Hugo in 1989. Don't be put off by appearances – this place serves up freshly-caught seafood, boiled peanuts, hush puppies, red rice, banana pudding, and other Southern delicacies. 106 Haddrell St, Mount Pleasant, SC 29464, www.wreckrc.com

POE'S TAVERN Known for killer style and unpretentious yet delicious bar food, this place is just plain cool. Largely open-air, laid back, and oozing with character, Poe's Tavern is a hugely popular post-beachgoing hangout. Finding parking within a quarter mile during the summertime is all but impossible, but definitely worth the hassle. 2210 Middle St, Sullivan's Island, SC 29482, www.poestavern.com

CLOSED FOR BUSINESS This place is new on the scene, but has quickly become my watering hole of choice. The atmosphere is what you'd get if a design blog and a ski lodge had a baby – floor-to-ceiling wood, a staff clad in all plaid, huge illuminated marquee letters, loads of taxidermy, and walls plastered with interesting prints. The booze selections are just out of the ordinary enough to make you feel exotic. If you get hungry, try the Pork Slap. 453 King St, Charleston, SC 29403, www.closed4business.com

THE LIBRARY ROOFTOP Set atop the Vendue Inn, right on the edge of Charleston Harbor, there's no better place to knock back a pint, admire the view and watch the sunset. Be warned: the elevator ride to the top can be interesting. It's old, it's small, it's hot, and there's always some joker who starts talking about how well you'll get to know each other when it gets stuck. 23 Vendue Range, Charleston, SC 29401, www.vendueinn.com

CHAI'S LOUNGE AND TAPAS With an Asian-inspired, upscale-yet-comfortable vibe, this place has become a hub of Charleston's nightlife circuit for a lot of the young professional crowd. Enjoy fantastic tapas with paper lanterns dangling around you, or step outside onto the patio and sample a mojito that'll make you have two. 462 King St, Charleston, SC 29403, www.chaislounge.com

COAST Located in a former indigo warehouse, this is a bar/restaurant with ambience in spades. Booths are covered with tin roofs, surf movies play on loop, and inflated puffer fish serve as light fixtures. It attracts a good crowd, which often spills out into the adjacent alleyway. It's got a whopping wine list and a solid menu with a seafood focus. Try the buffalo shrimp or Baja fish tacos. 39-D John St, Charleston, SC 29403, www.coastbarandgrill.com

AC'S The term 'dive bar' may have been coined specifically for AC's. It's dark, it's grimy, and it's a blast. Patrons from all walks of life can be found here on any given night, from the most polished college students to the most unpolished college dropouts. 467 King St, Charleston, SC 29415, www.acsbar.com

SHINE One of the newer bars in town, Shine has quickly become the spot to find Charleston's hip and funky creative class. The space is smooth and modern with elaborate rococo wallpaper, vintage chandeliers, and handmade bamboo tables. The food alone is worth the trip, and with a DJ often spinning on the weekends, an unassuming dinner can quickly turn into a night out. 58 Line St, Charleston, SC 29403, www.shinecharleston.com

CHARLESTON WATERSPORT

Between plates of fried chicken and pints of Ben & Jerry's, I try to stay active and enjoy Charleston's natural beauty as much as possible. Flat as a pancake, hot as an oven, and surrounded by water, your best bet on being outdoorsy here is to take up a hobby that requires you to get wet. Whichever aquatic pastime you decide upon – be it surfing, paddleboarding, kayaking, waterskiing, or wakeboarding – Charleston Watersport's got the tool for the job. They offer rentals as well. 1255 Ben Sawyer Blvd, Mt Pleasant, SC 29464, www.charlestonwatersport.com

ARTIST AND CRAFTSMAN SUPPLY

This place always makes me wish I was back in art school. That crisp smell of pencils and canvas is as tantalizing to me as a whiff of warm apple pie. They sell solvents, pigments, papers, and anything else your creative pursuit might require. As odd as it sounds, make sure to visit the bathroom – every poster, flyer, or invitation designed in Charleston seems to make its way there – it can be very inspiring. 143 Calhoun St, Charleston, SC 29401, www.artistcraftsman.com

SHOP

THE CHARLESTON FARMERS' MARKET

Marion Square in the heart of Downtown hosts a farmers' market every Saturday from April through December, 8am-2pm. Locals flock to socialize with neighbors and stock up on fresh produce and flowers. They also have live entertainment, some crafty stalls, and lots of brunch and lunch options. Marion Sq, Charleston, SC 29403

OUT OF HAND

When my girl and I first got together, she unabashedly let me know: "if you ever want to buy me a present but don't know what to get, just buy something from Out of Hand." Even though the store is quite feminine, I have to admit that when I made my first visit I became less concerned with what to get her and more focused on what to pick up for myself. From daintily distressed picture frames to exotic soaps that, well, make a guy wanna buy exotic soaps, a trip to Out of Hand is like visiting the tree of some fantastical, whimsical creature who's been squirreling away trinkets and treasures you never knew existed. 113C Pitt St, Mt Pleasant, SC 29464, www.shopoutofhand.com

HALF-MOON OUTFITTERS

With three locations in the Charleston area, Half-Moon is your one-stop-shop for all things adventurous and outdoorsy. Just stepping inside makes me want to take on Everest. Well, base camp, anyway. 280 King St, Charleston, SC 29401, www.halfmoonoutfitters.com

WORTHWHILE

Worthwhile is the kind of place where you walk in the door not looking for anything, and leave with a metal insect made of watch parts, a book outlining life lessons for your unborn son, and/or the nicknack you saw on a design blog yesterday but never thought you'd actually see in person. Worthwhile's unique array of pretty things is always a treat for the senses. 268 King St, Charleston, SC 29401, www.shopworthwhile.com

PECHA KUCHA NIGHT CHARLESTON
Having launched in Tokyo in 2003, Pecha Kucha nights are now a worldwide phenomenon. For the uninitiated, the rundown is simple: a roster of presenters each show 20 images at a pace of 20 seconds per image. How presenters will use their time is anybody's guess, but the format keeps energy levels high and everyone on their toes. Charleston's PK nights are held every few months, with the location with the location revealed just a couple days prior to the event.
www.pechakuchacharleston.com

CHARLESTON INTERNATIONAL FILM FESTIVAL Each spring the Charleston International Film Festival showcases the talent of emerging filmmakers and screenwriters with four days of independent cinema, shorts, documentaries, and animated films, along with nightly after-parties, industry panels, and educational workshops. www.charlestoniff.com

CHARLESTON WINE AND FOOD FESTIVAL
Each spring, the city's many culinary wizards band together to form the Charleston Wine and Food Festival. The event also attracts celebrity chefs and Food Network stars from across the country, along with winemakers and other assorted food industry vendors.
www.charlestonwineandfood.com

DRAYTON HALL Considered one of the finest examples of Georgian-Palladian architecture in the United States, Drayton Hall is one of America's only pre-Revolutionary houses to remain in near original condition today. Drayton Hall has been meticulously preserved, rather than restored – meaning nothing has been changed, added, or refurbished. 3380 Ashley River Rd, Charleston, SC 29414, www.draytonhall.org

CULTURE

GO

THE OLD SULLIVAN'S ISLAND BRIDGE At the end of Pitt Street in Mt Pleasant's Old Village you'll find the remains of a bridge, which used to span the Intracoastal Waterway, joining Sullivan's Island to the mainland. All that's left is a few pilings, but the spot is now a unique park with a long pier walk jutting out into the salt marsh. The view is a 360-degree wonderment, with the Atlantic Ocean on one side and Downtown Charleston on the other. The end of Pitt St, Old Village

WHITE POINT GARDEN More commonly referred to as "The Battery," White Point Garden lies at the southernmost point of peninsular Downtown, and showcases Charleston's finest antebellum homes. It's a major tourist hangout, offering unprecedented views of Charleston Harbor and Fort Sumter (the site where the Civil War began). East Battery and Murray Blvd Charleston, SC 29401

MARION SQUARE Sandwiched between the intersections of Downtown's major thoroughfares, Marion Square is a six-acre grassy field, which marks the epicenter of Charleston. There are numerous events and festivals held there throughout the year, and it is used by locals as a daily picnicking, sunbathing, and general gathering spot. If the sun is shining you're sure to stumble upon a pickup sporting event of some sort. Calhoun St and King St, Charleston, SC 29403

REDUX STUDIOS Redux, a non-profit arts organization housed within a 6,000 ft² warehouse, has become the beating heart of Charleston's creative community. The facility includes gallery spaces, private artist studios, a print shop, darkroom, wood shop, classroom, and film screening area. If you're planning a visit, be sure to check Redux's website beforehand as exhibits and events are constantly changing. 136 St Philip St, Charleston, SC 29403, www.reduxstudios.org

GIBBES MUSEUM OF ART For over 100 years, the Gibbes has served as Charleston's 'traditional' art museum, with over 10,000 objects in their permanent collection showcasing the region's rich cultural history. It's also cool as a cucumber in the summer – a great place to escape the heat. 135 Meeting St, Charleston, SC 29401, www.gibbesmuseum.org

THE TERRACE A lot of locals, including myself, have a mantra when it comes to this place: "If it's playing at The Terrace, I'll go see it." Charleston's only movie theater is dedicated to showing the best independent and foreign cinema, and seems to have impeccable taste at every turn. They also sell beer and wine, along with a candy counter that'd make Willy Wonka jealous. 1956 Maybank Hwy, Charleston, SC 2941, www.terracetheater.com

Daniel Blackman's

Chicago

CHICAGO, ILLINOIS BY DANIEL BLACKMAN

I moved to Chicago a couple years ago, and it's a daunting task to try and describe its complex geography. Chicago is an expansive city with villages, neighborhoods, and districts connected by buses, bridges, and 'El' stops, and you have to choose which areas feel most comfortable to you. I tend to spend most of my time in the neighborhoods of Bucktown, Wicker Park, and Logan Square. I have to confess that these areas are all hipster hangouts that were once a little bit down-at-heel and have become increasingly trendy. However, that doesn't make them any less fun or beautiful – it just means you need to watch out for fixed gears, neon tank tops, and Ray Bans.

Chicago is a very green city literally and figuratively – it has a great recycling program, zillions of roof gardens covering more than 4.5 million ft^2 of rooftops, and it is one of the most bike-friendly cities I've ever been in. The lake front bike path, which runs around the edge of Lake Michigan, is 18 miles long with museums, parks, and zoos along the way. If renting a bike isn't really your thing, then the best way to get around is with the El. The train lines all connect at The Loop in the center of the city, and then radiate out in all directions. The areas my entries tend to focus on (Bucktown, Wicker Park and Logan Square) are all on the Blue Line.

Living in Chicago is an ongoing adventure for me. I feel like I'm always finding a new bar, park, restaurant, gallery – or even an entirely new area. It's a city of hidden treasures that are easily accessed if you're willing to seek them out. From a design point of view, I love Chicago because it isn't nearly as pretentious as some of the other major cities in the US. The architecture is fantastic, the lake is beautiful, and there are plenty of opportunities – both commercial and independent – for creative people. The artistic community is diverse and open to newcomers and emerging talent. It's a friendly place, with a lot to offer on all fronts.

THE JAMES HOTEL A high-end but friendly hotel conveniently located bang in the heart of Downtown. I hear that it's a great place to stay if you have the money, and you can get anywhere from there. 55 East Ontario, Chicago, IL 60611, www.jameshotels.com

THE WIT HOTEL This is another posh hotel which is pretty amazing. Again it's right in Downtown by The Loop, and has tons of amenities. The decor is modern in a really refreshing way, and it has a good cocktail lounge on the top floor. 201 North State St, Chicago, IL 60601, www.thewithotel.com

THE WICKER PARK INN This B&B is as close as you're going to get to my neck of the woods. Nestled in the middle of Wicker Park it offers good value for money and gets good reviews. 1329 North Wicker Park Ave, Chicago, IL 60622, www.wickerparkinn.com

THE DRAKE HOTEL If you've got the cash, this is the place to stay. It's a beautiful Art Deco building in Downtown, close to Michigan Avenue and the lake, with a grand lobby and big rooms. A real sense of the city's history. 140 East Walton St, Chicago, IL 60611, www.thedrakehotel.com

HOSTELLING INTERNATIONAL CHICAGO If you're really on a budget this is the hostel to go for. It gets great reviews – topping various 'best hostel' lists. And the location is pretty good too in the South Loop. 24 East Congress Pkwy, Chicago, IL 60605

HOT DOUGS
SINCE 1948

AM

LULA

AM

PM

BIG STAR

PM

KUMA'S CORNER
SINCE 2005

EAT

LULA CAFE In a quiet, shady corner of Logan Square you'll find this little gem, serving the best brunch in town. You might have to wait in line, but it's worth it – especially if you get to sit on the patio. Dinner is also good, but brunch is unrivalled – and reasonably priced. 2537 North Kedzie, Chicago, IL 60647, www.lulacafe.com

HOT DOUGS If you think 20 minutes is a long time to wait in line for a hot dog, you've never experienced the wares of Hot Dougs. It is an AMAZING place to get dogs – anything from the traditional Chicago-style dog to a Foie Gras and Sauternes Duck Sausage with Truffle Aioli, all with a large serving of fries. Oh yes. 3324 North California Ave, Chicago, IL 60618, www.hotdougs.com

BIG STAR This taco joint in Wicker Park is the new 'it' spot. Whiskey, Mexican coke, and tacos. You can't go wrong. They spin country and rock... mostly Cash and Jennings. 1531 North Damen Ave, Chicago, IL 60622

KUMA'S CORNER The best burgers in the city. Each burger is named after a metal band, and the atmosphere is dark, with loud metal blaring. Get there as soon as they open. It's not uncommon to wait for hours for a table. Good artsy beer selection. 2900 West Belmont Ave, Chicago, IL 60618, www.kumascorner.com

PICANTE This taqueria has saved my life on numerous occasions, serving amazing Mexican food extremely fast. It's easy to miss even though it's located right on Division and Damen. 2016 West Division St, Chicago, IL 60622, www.picantechicago.com

ENOTECA ROMA A more up-market joint for a nice sit down Italian meal. The pear ravioli is my favorite. They also have a good selection of wine, and if you don't want to break your wallet on a bottle, they have plenty of wine flights to choose from. 2146 West Division St, Chicago, IL 60622, www.enotecaroma.com

VIOLET HOUR Expensive cocktails and appetizers in a dim, romantic, loungey setting. Just across the street from Big Star, it's a good spot to go to for a drink or two… anything beyond that and it starts to get pretty heavy on your pocket. 1520 North Damen Ave, Chicago, IL 60622, www.theviolethour.com

BAR DEVILLE Amazing little bar in Ukrainian Village with super-talented bartenders specializing in prohibition era cocktails. A nice place to go with friends. Fridays and Saturdays can be a bit busy, but worth it. Anyone who drinks Jaeger Bombs is not welcome. 701 North Damen Ave, Chicago, IL 60622

THE WHISTLER Another great place for cocktails in Logan Square. If you're there at a weekend and there's a long line, head across the street to the Two Way where you'll find twenty-somethings socializing with forty-year old neighborhood drunks. Yay! 2421 North Milwaukee Ave, Chicago, IL 60647, www.whistlerchicago.com

THE BURLINGTON It's a bit off the beaten path, but this great bar has lots of atmosphere with its tin roof and church pew seating. The staff is friendly and the beer is cheap. 3425 West Fullerton Ave, Chicago, IL 60647, www.theburlingtonbar.com

MAP ROOM If you like worldly beers, this is the place to go; hands down the biggest beer menu in Chicago. Nice ambience with thousands of old National Geographics and old topographic maps plastering the walls. 1949 North Hoyne Ave, Chicago, IL 60647, www.maproom.com

RAINBO A total dive bar, just the way I like it. Insanely cheap beer, a crowd of hot, sweaty hipsters, and an old-school photobooth. I have had some great nights here. 1150 North Damen Ave, Chicago, IL 60622

DRINK

SHOP

ARCHITECTURAL ARTIFACTS
A cross between a museum and an antiques store, this beautiful building is spread over three floors, and filled with everything from marble fireplaces to old signs and 1930s foozball tables. Def worth checking out 4325 North Ravenswood Ave, Chicago, IL 60613, www.architecturalartifacts.com

QUIMBY'S BOOKSTORE Design bookstore filled with everything from fine art books to local zines and underground smut mags. Badass place to spend an afternoon. 1854 West North Ave, Chicago, IL 60622, www.quimbys.com

BELMONT ARMY Four floors of great vintage and consignment clothing in Lakeview. The basement is all army/navy gear, and the rest is well-selected and organized hipster apparel. 855 West Belmont Ave, Chicago, IL 60657, www.belmontarmy.com

PENELOPE'S A Wicker Park boutique stocking European indie labels and high-end fashion at relatively reasonable prices. 1913 West Division St, Chicago, IL 6062 www.penelopeschicago.com

SALVAGE ONE A place much like Architectural Artifacts but completely unique in its own right. Huge three-story warehouse filled with old nicknacks and treasures. 1840 West Hubbard St, Chicago, IL 60622, www.salvageone.com

SAINT ALFRED The best place in town for kicks. They carry special edition shoes, great clothes and caps. The staff is super nice and helpful. 1531 North Milwaukee Ave, Chicago, IL 60622, www.stalfred.com

POST FAMILY COLLECTIVE
A gallery and artists' space run by a collective of seven artists, with interesting events and exhibitions by young talent. Check out the prints for sale in their online shop. 1821 West Hubbard St #202, Chicago, IL 60622, www.thepostfamily.com

CO-PROSPERITY SPHERE
These guys put on amazing shows and are associated with some pretty badass artists. They are also affiliated with *Lumpen Magazine* and *Proximity Mag*, both local zines worth checking out. 3219-21 South Morgan St, Chicago, IL 60608, www.coprosperity.org

THE MUSIC BOX THEATRE
Wow. A true gem of a theatre. It's independently owned and plays a lot of art-house films. If you're in Lakeview, stop by and see a piece of old Chicago. 3733 North Southport Ave, Chicago, IL 60613, www.musicboxtheatre.com

MUSEUM OF CONTEMPORARY ART
Does what it says on the cover. It has consistent curatorship, bringing in talented contemporary artists, and putting on interesting exhibitions. 220 East Chicago Ave, Chicago, IL 60611, www.mcachicago.org

THE ART INSTITUTE OF CHICAGO
HUGE museum with tons of art from all periods and a beautiful new modern art wing. Plus it's ideally located right next to Millenium Park and the lake. The top floor has great views, a restaurant, and outdoor sculptures. 111 South Michigan Ave, Chicago, IL 60603, www.artinstituteofchicago.org

CULTURE

MUSIC

EMPTY BOTTLE
Perfect venue. Small, loud, total dive, cheap beer, and great bands. 1035 North Western Ave, Chicago, IL 60622, www.emptybottle.com

SCHUBAS
Another small venue with a restaurant and nice bar attached. Usually has pretty good shows and is relatively cheap. 3159 North Southport Ave, Chicago, IL 60657, www.schubas.com

PITCHFORK MUSIC FESTIVAL

Yep those asshole music critics are from Chicago. Check out their website if you haven't yet encountered their scathing album reviews. They add a lot to the music scene and put on a world-renowned music festival every July. Best time of year. www.pitchforkmedia.com

HIDEOUT BLOCK PARTY A great one-day festival put on by the guys over at the Hideout Bar every September. They get great bands in and at $10 a ticket it's a total bargain. Good people, local brews and fun times. 1354 West Wabansia, Chicago, IL 60622, www.hideoutblockparty.com

CHICAGO INTERNATIONAL FILM FESTIVAL Two-week film festival that usually takes place every fall. Tons of films all around the city. www.chicagofilmfestival.com

POTAWATOMI
INDIANS

P   I

CHICAGO   NATIVES

BOTTOM LOUNGE Huge three-storey bar/venue with a really nice roof deck that offers a great view of the city. 1375 West Lake St, Chicago, IL 60607, www.bottomlounge.com

METRO Really old theatre worth seeing, showcasing a lot of bigger bands. It is somewhat expensive and they don't allow re-entry – which is total crap. 3730 North Clark St, Chicago, IL 60613, www.metrochicago.com

WELCOME to

Gwenda Kaczor's

DENVER

DENVER, COLORADO BY GWENDA KACZOR

Maybe it has something to do with its history – reaching back to the
Old West and gold mining – or its geography, being surrounded by the
Great Plains and in the shadow of the beautiful Rocky Mountains, but for
whatever reason, Denver is one of the most welcoming cities I've ever
lived in or visited. There's an openness and independent spirit here that
has helped Denver evolve into a progressive, world-class city without
losing its unique character and charm.

It's a city that strikes a remarkable balance between urban and
outdoor lifestyles. There are wonderful parks (literally hundreds of them),
easily accessible nature trails in the surrounding mountains, and an
environmentally conscious ethos throughout the city. On the other hand
there are also some amazing and diverse museums, several vibrant arts
districts, cool music venues, and a nationally recognized performing arts
complex, all of which create a rich cultural scene. Another thing that I
particularly like is the countless local festivals and events that take place
throughout the year, giving a sense of all the different communities that
make up the city.

Getting around is pretty easy. The historic Downtown area is walkable,
or you can rent a bike or take the lightrail. The 16th Street Mall runs
through the center and is a one-mile pedestrian promenade reaching
from the beautiful state capital building at one end to the historic Union
Station on the other, with sports stadiums, shopping, restaurants, and
interesting nightlife along the way. Outside of Downtown, you'll discover
many unique neighborhoods that are charmingly contradictory: classic
brick buildings and pretty Victorians lie alongside urban districts with
industrial warehouses and amazing street art. You'll often find the old
and the new right next door to each other – creating a compelling blend
of the past and the modern that is uniquely Denver.

Of course, you can't come here without enjoying the mountains,
a mere 30 minutes outside the city. They are mind bogglingly beautiful in
every season, and with our average of 300 days a year of sunshine, you
really can't go wrong. Welcome to Denver!

THE OXFORD HOTEL The Oxford is a beautiful, classic Art Deco style hotel located in the heart of Lower Downtown. It's in an ideal location and they have a legendary bar where those in the know go for the best martinis in town. 1600 17th St, Denver, CO 80202, www.theoxfordhotel.com

BROWN PALACE HOTEL This hotel is a beloved landmark in Upper Downtown, steeped in history and tradition, and known for hosting presidents and celebrities. If you can't afford to stay here, I'd recommend just stopping by for a traditional high tea. 321 17th St, Denver, CO 80202, www.brownpalace.com

THE CURTIS HOTEL This is a really fun hotel if you're up for something different. Each floor has a different pop-culture theme, ranging from Star Wars to Elvis. It's mid-priced and located in Central Downtown. Their bar/restaurant is fun as well – great for people watching. 1405 Curtis St, Denver, CO 80202, www.thecurtis.com

EAT

FUEL CAFE This place feels like a hidden gem – it's a hip, industrial restaurant, located in a creative, urban live-work community that's a bit off the beaten path. They're passionate about using seasonal ingredients and their menu is always changing. A great place to come before or after a First Friday art walk. 3455 Ringsby Ct #105, Denver, CO 80216, www.fuelcafedenver.com

EL TACO DE MEXICO There are a lot of great Mexican restaurants in Denver but this unassuming and often crowded place has the reputation of being the most authentic – and it's great if you're on a budget. Place your order at the counter. I recommend the smothered chilli relleno burrito. 714 Santa Fe Dr, Denver, CO 80204

CITY O' CITY I could hang out at this bar and cafe all day – and many do. Its laid back environment attracts a wonderfully diverse crowd: artists, students, and nine to fivers. Kick back, have a drink or a coffee and some homemade vegetarian food. 206 East 13th Ave, Denver, CO 80203, www.cityocitydenver.com

MERCURY CAFE This is one of the first places I felt at home at in Denver. Much more than a cafe, it's a cultural hub. It's powered by renewable energy, serves food that is organic and local, and the ambience is eclectic with a hippy sensibility. Creative people of all kinds come here for everything from poetry slams to tango to live music. 2199 California St, Denver, CO 80205, www.mercurycafe.com

ROOT DOWN This is a funky neighborhood restaurant and bar on the edge of Downtown in a former gas station, which has maintained a lot of the original decor. It always attracts a cool crowd, serves interesting food, and, if you can find a place on the patio, offers an amazing view of Downtown Denver. 1600 West 33rd Ave, Denver, CO 80211, www.rootdowndenver.com

BEATRICE AND WOODSLEY With its magical interior complete with real Aspen trees, this place is like stepping into another world. The tapas-style food is as creative as the décor. It can be expensive but it's worth it. 38 South Broadway, Denver, CO 80209, www.beatriceandwoodsley.com

Z CUISINE AND A' CÔTÉ I really love this little French bistro and its wine/absinthe bar (right next door). It's located in the middle of a quaint neighborhood just outside of Downtown. High-end, small, and authentic, with a passionate chef and dishes created using local and organic ingredients. Try their La Vie En Rose cocktail – my favorite! 2239 and 2245 West 30th Ave, Denver, CO 80211, www.zcuisineonline.com

BASTIEN'S RESTAURANT AND STEAKHOUSE I adore going to this quintessential 1960s steakhouse on East Colfax. It's like time has stood still in the iconic octagon-shaped building with its classic neon sign and an awesome old Vegas feel. Sinatra plays in the background. Try to get a seat in the sunken dining room! 3501 East Colfax Ave, Denver, CO 80206, www.bastiensrestaurant.com

THIN MAN This popular Uptown bar is my favorite in Denver. It has a certain intellectual mystique, with bartenders who remember you and Catholic-themed decor. I love the ambience, interesting crowds and long narrow bar. It's hard not to become a regular. If you prefer coffee, just go next door to their equally popular coffee house, St Marks. 2015 East 17th Ave, Denver, CO 80206, www.thinmantavern.com

ROCK BAR This is a total hipster, retro bar in an old hotel on East Colfax. It was recently reopened, but the decor hasn't changed since the 70s. Their early evening happy hour is nicely chilled out, but I'm told the scene gets a lot crazier after midnight. 3015 East Colfax, Denver, CO 80206, www.rockbar-denver.com

SKYLARK LOUNGE I love the neighborhood vibe of this South Broadway mainstay. It's all old-school rockabilly vintage, with an amazing collection of classic photos and movie posters covering the walls. They often host great live music. 140 South Broadway, Denver, CO 80209, www.skylarklounge.com

MY BROTHER'S BAR There's no sign outside this beloved neighborhood institution – they don't need it. It's the oldest still-operating bar in Denver, which made its name as a Neal Cassady/Beat Poet hangout back in the day. They only play classical music and cater to a wonderfully diverse crowd. One of my favorite places, burgers, and patios in Denver. 2376 15th St, Denver, CO 80202

PARIS ON THE PLATTE CAFE AND WINE BAR Situated in an up-and-coming neighborhood, Paris on the Platte survived the downing of Denver's viaducts, and the old bookstore has been converted into a very cool wine bar. The coffeehouse is still next door – the oldest in Denver. It draws an eclectic, creative crowd, who come to enjoy the art and unique ambience. 1553 Platte St, Denver, CO 80202, www.parisontheplattecafeandbar.com

THE CRUISE ROOM BAR One of the most special bars I've ever been to, this quintessential martini bar is in the Oxford Hotel and the Art Deco design is breathtaking. Once you find the somewhat hidden location, try to grab one of the few booths and order a classic cocktail or their famous martini. 1600 17th St, Denver, CO 80202, www.theoxfordhotel.com

SHOP

DOUBLE DAUGHTER'S SALOTTO For something very different in the middle of Downtown, check out this Gothic lounge. The oversized doors lead into a fantasy-style interior with eerie lighting and weird red leather booths. If you're hungry, you can order pizza from next door. 1632 Market St, Denver, CO 80202, www.doubledaughters.com

LARIMER SQUARE A historic city block that's survived unscathed since the 1860s. It's a popular destination, full of amazing restaurants, bars, and shops. My favorites: Gusterman's Silversmiths if you love jewelry, The Market for tea, and Bistro Vendome for their idyllic outdoor patio. Larimer St between 14th and 15th Aves, Denver, CO 80211, www.larimersquare.com

TATTERED COVER I can spend all day in this amazing independent bookstore. In a great Downtown location, it's spread over many levels with couches, a coffee bar, and a newsstand. Lovely staff and amazing guest speakers. 1628 16th St, Denver, CO 80202, www.tatteredcover.com

TWIST AND SHOUT We're lucky enough to still have a fantastic, local, independent music store that draws in music lovers of all kinds. You can listen before you buy, check out in-store appearances, and find imports, rarities and cool memorabilia. 2508 East Colfax Ave, Denver, CO 80206, www.twistandshout.com

ANTIQUE ROW If you love antiques or anything used-but-loved, check out Antique Row on South Broadway. There are blocks of vintage stores and dealers occupying historic buildings. I never leave without a new treasure. 400 to 2000 South Broadway, Denver, CO 80210, www.antique-row.com

FANCY TIGER If you're interested in handcrafting or handmade clothing by small independent designers, go to either Fancy Tiger Crafts or Fancy Tiger Boutique, right across the street from each other. Both stores have a cool hipster vibe – get inspired to make something yourself! 1 and 14 South Broadway, Denver, CO 80209, www.fancytiger.com

BUFFALO EXCHANGE I love this consignment store because I can always find something fun within my budget, and the inventory of vintage and new clothes and accessories is always changing. It's a fun place to shop, with a cool clientele and great music. 230 East 13th Ave, Denver, CO 80203, www.buffaloexchange.com

MEININGER ART SUPPLY If I ever need anything art related – supplies, papers, books, or just inspiration, I know this independent art store will have it. It's been in the same family since 1881. 499 Broadway, Denver, CO 80203, www.meininger.com

CULTURE

SANTA FE ARTS DISTRICT Denver really comes out on First Fridays – and this area of Santa Fe Drive is always packed with people enjoying the art, live music, and surprise street performances. Santa Fe Dr, between 4th and 12th Aves, Denver, CO 80204, www.artdistrictonsantafe.com

ANDENKEN One of the most progressive art spaces in town, with a focus on street art and cutting edge work from local and national artists. They're located in a converted warehouse in an industrial neighborhood just east of Downtown and always draw an enthusiastic young crowd. 2990 Larimer St, Denver, CO 80205, www.andenken.com

IRONTON STUDIOS Ironton is an artists' community at the heart of the up-and-coming River North Art District (RiNo) – an industrial area northeast of Downtown. It houses one of my favorite contemporary galleries with a great sculpture garden. 3636 Chestnut St, Denver, CO 80260, www.irontonstudios.com

MCA DENVER MCA Denver is the city's first contemporary art museum, located in Lower Downtown. The unique building is a great new addition to the city. They exhibit an eclectic mix of photography, new media, and modern art, and have an interesting program of events. I love the views of Downtown and the mountains from the rooftop. 1485 Delgany St, Denver, CO 80202, www.mcadenver.org

DAVID B SMITH GALLERY This exciting gallery Downtown is where I come to get inspired. Supported by an online audience of international collectors, it offers a fresh perspective, showcasing emerging artists. 1543 Wazee St, Denver, CO 80205, www.davidbsmithgallery.com

KIRKLAND MUSEUM A great collection of 20th Century decorative arts, including works of Art Nouveau, De Stijl, Bauhaus, Art Deco, and Pop Art. It also houses an inspirational retrospective of Colorado's well-known painter, Vance Kirkland. 1311 Pearl St, Denver, CO 80203, www.kirklandmuseum.org

MAYAN THEATER I love this beautiful local treasure, which was saved from demolition and restored. It's one of only three remaining theaters designed in Art Deco Mayan Revival style, and has a great program of independent and foreign language films. 110 North Broadway, Denver, CO 80203

FESTIVALS One of my favorite things about Denver is its festivals. You can find at least one almost every month, and many more during Spring/Summer. They can give you a real taste of the city. My favorites are: A Taste of Colorado, Cherry Creek Arts Festival, 5 Points Jazz Festival, and Larimer Square's street-painting festival, La Piazza. www.denver.com/festivals

MUSIC

EL CHAPULTEPEC One of the coolest and seediest dive bars in Denver with the best live jazz jams anywhere. Get there early for drinks and a place to sit – it's very small and can get really crowded as the night goes on. Famous musicians have been known to drop by and join in. 1962 Market St, Denver, CO 80202

LARIMER LOUNGE For indie music, leaning towards rock and punk, this is the place to go. It's a low key, very intimate and somewhat divey venue, a little off the beaten track. I love the enclosed backyard/patio – nice if you need a quick break from the show. 2721 Larimer St, Denver, CO 80205, www.larimerlounge.com

RED ROCKS AMPITHEATRE This is a unique outdoor ampitheater, nestled in a stunning rock structure 15-minute's drive west of Denver. The location and view of Denver is just as much a part of the experience as the music. 17598 West Alameda Pkwy, Morrison, CO 80465 www.redrocksonline.com

ELLIE CAULKINS OPERA HOUSE This recently revamped concert hall in the Downtown Denver Performing Arts Complex is a gorgeous place to see live music. If opera isn't your taste, they also present other concerts as diverse as folk/roots to alternative/acoustic. 14th St and Curtis St, Denver, CO 80202, www.operacolorado.org

BLUEBIRD THEATER I've seen some incredible concerts at the Bluebird. It was once a vaudeville theater and then a cinema. Today it's a super-hip venue for contemporary rock shows. If you can't face standing all night, get there early and grab a seat in the balcony. 3317 East Colfax Ave, Denver, CO 80206, www.bluebirdtheater.net

OUT OF TOWN

One of Denver's advantages is its proximity to nature. Within moments you can be on an amazing mountain trail, hiking, biking, snow-shoeing, or cross-country skiing. There are also natural hotsprings that offer amazing mountain views. The smaller towns of Boulder, Lyons and Goldens in the foothills, are character-filled and well worth visiting.

DETROIT, MICHIGAN BY ANGELA DUNCAN

I used to say I'd never live in Detroit, but after three years in Ferndale, an arty suburb just north of the city, I've grown to love it and can't wait to brag about how truly rad it is. The city is alive with ambitious young creatives, fostered by the famous Cranbrook Art Academy and the College for Creative Studies. The music scene is seriously thriving, and because of our state's new tax incentives, we've got more Hollywood movies being made here than you can stalk in a weekend.

Detroit's rise and fall is common knowledge. At the turn of the century it was known as 'The Paris of the Midwest'. Its strategic location on the Great Lakes waterway meant that it emerged as a transportation hub, and the first half of the 20th Century saw the city establish itself as MotorCity, with money to burn on Art Deco skyscrapers and jobs for all. Its decline started in the late 70s with the import of cheaper cars from foreign makers, and it's never really recovered. In recent years there's been an effort to regenerate, especially along the waterfront – but nonetheless, one in five houses are abandoned throughout the city. Artists and urban regenerationists love that kind of blank canvas, so as you wander through, you'll notice a striking contrast between modern, creative, independent business and crumbling, boarded-up buildings and vacant lots (now home to a growing population of pheasants and foxes).

There's lots of interesting stuff to see. Bring your camera, rent a car, and start driving. Downtown you'll find galleries, shops, restaurants, and places to stay. On the east side of town, there's incredible hand lettering on almost every building, the smell of fried chicken, and the squeal of blinged-out tires on hot pavement. In contrast, you'll find big, beautiful homes along the shore of Lake Huron. Mexicantown, to the west, is alive with great little places to eat, and Midtown, home to the Center for Creative Studies, is packed with students and cafes. Birmingham and Royal Oak are suburbs about 20 minutes north of Downtown, where you'll find vintage and design shops, cafes, and restaurants.

From an artist's perspective, Detroit is a real treasure trove of awesome and weird stuff. Its history means it's always game to try something new and there's a real willingness to partner with artists that makes it a sexy place to be right now. Explore the city with some good company, fresh coffee, and open eyes. You won't be disappointed.

BOOK-CADILLAC HOTEL This was the world's tallest hotel when it opened in 1924. Its glamorous Italian Renaissance-inspired styling has attracted its fair share of presidents, gangsters, and Hollywood stars, and a recent $200 million renovation has brought it back to its former classy glory. It's Downtown near Greektown and the riverfront. 1114 Washington Blvd, Detroit, MI 48226, www.bookcadillacwestin.com

THE INN ON FERRY STREET From $80 a night, you can have a comfortable, historic Detroit experience in a Victorian home with modern amenities. Stay in a room in one of four houses, or rent an entire house with friends. Cozy and convenient. 84 East Ferry St, Detroit, MI 48202, www.innonferrystreet.com

DETROIT MARRIOTT AT THE GM RENAISSANCE CENTER This 73-story hotel (the tallest hotel in the Western Hemisphere no less) sits on the Detroit River, with an awesome view of Canada across the water. Comfortable, modern, and central. Renaissance Center, Detroit, MI 48243, www.marriott.com

THE TOWNSEND HOTEL This is where the movie stars stay when they're in town for shoots. All European elegance, it's in the posh suburb of Birmingham, with its bustling cafe culture, a few minutes away from Cranbrook Art Academy. 100 Townsend St, Birmingham, MI 48009, www.townsendhotel.com

EAT

SLOW'S BBQ Hands down my favorite restaurant in Detroit! It's fairly new, with modern design and a hip atmosphere. They serve up great BBQ and Southern-style concoctions with a big beer selection. They must put crack in their food, because the place is always packed. 2138 Michigan Ave, Detroit, MI 48216, www.slowsbarbq.com

EL BARZON This place is awesome. The menu is a delicious mix of Italian and Mexican, both executed really well and not expensive. The atmosphere is pretty fancy, and they have an excellent wine list. Situated in Mexicantown, (southwest Detroit), the area is a delight all its own, with plenty of sights and eats. Other good restaurants nearby include Xochi Milco and Nueva Leon. 3710 Junction Rd, Detroit, MI 48210, http://198.171.52.19 (Yep, that's their website)

THE FLY TRAP This 'finer diner' in the suburb of Ferndale serves up savory dishes with West Coast flair. Every soup, dressing, jam and aioli is made from scratch (including their famous hot swat sauce). They were featured on *Diners, Drive-Ins and Dives* on the Food Network. I worked in their kitchen for a summer, and let me tell you, Gavin (the chef and owner) knows exactly how to make his customers swoon. I want their gingerbread waffles right now! 22950 Woodward Ave, Ferndale, MI 48220, www.theflytrapferndale.com

No finer place, for sure.
Downtown
Everything's waiting for you!

AVALON BAKERY This place warms my heart. A well-loved, successful bakery Downtown. They love Detroit and want to help it grow. They have a huge variety of breads, scones, muffins, rolls, and otherwise awesome treats. 422 West Willis St, Detroit, MI 48201

THE DAKOTA INN This is where my friends and I go when we want to have a romping good time somewhere different. It's totally authentic German, so the food's interesting, and there's always karaoke, with a little old man leading on piano and singing to everything. It's a blast to sing along to the schnitzelbank song. 17324 John R St, Detroit, MI 48203, www.dakota-inn.com

THE MAGIC STICK This is the most popular place among my group of musician/artist young professional friends. It has a pizza parlor, bar, and bowling alley downstairs and a bar, stage, and pool upstairs. Big place. It's where local bands open for bigger touring acts, and where Drew Barrymore and Ellen Page hung out when they were filming in town. 4120–4140 Woodward Ave, Detroit, MI 48201, www.majesticdetroit.com/stick.asp

THE BRONX BAR This awesome dive bar is in the Midtown, Cass-Corridor area. It's always dark inside, and full of art kids. The decor is that of a Wes Anderson movie, with strange lighting and odd stuff on the walls. One of my favorites. 4476 2nd Ave, Detroit, MI 48201

CLIFF BELL'S Amazing vintage 1930s Detroit decor here. Intricate gold-framed oil paintings, patterned wallpaper, high ceilings, small tables and a large, bustling circle bar. Pretty classy, but reasonably priced, with great local music gearing towards jazz and folk. The Moth Podcast records live, unscripted stories here once a month – definitely worth catching if you can! 2030 Park Ave, Detroit, MI 48226, www.cliffbells.com

THE LOVING TOUCH This bar is a massage parlor turned pool hall, hence the ridiculous name, and is the newest addition to Ferndale. It's basically a big, open pool hall with vintage signs, skylights, and a great jukebox. I often end up here with big gang friends on a weekend, along with the entire 20-something population of Ferndale and Royal Oak. 22634 Woodward Ave, Ferndale, MI 48220

THE OLD MIAMI This started out as a veterans bar in the 40s, and the vets still come, although now they mingle with the crowd. It's the best place in the "D" to have a Corona barefoot on a porch swing in the backyard. It's like a mullet: serious in the front, party in the back. 3932 Cass Ave, Detroit, MI 48201

CADIEUX CAFE The obscure Belgian sport of featherbowling and 25 Belgian beers. Need I say more? It's on the east side of Detroit, but worth the short drive. 4300 Cadieux Rd, Detroit, MI 48224, www.cadieuxcafe.com

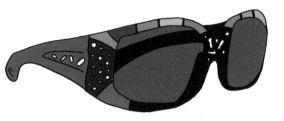

SHOP

EASTERN MARKET This gigantic, open-air produce market is open to the public every Saturday, year-round. It's always exciting. You'll find an abundance of local, fresh produce amongst other things. Be sure to check out R Hirt Company, a fine cheese and wine store in the vicinity. There's also a really great little antique shop across the street. 2934 Russell St, Detroit, MI 48207, www.detroiteasternmarket.com

NAKA This cute, modern little shop in Ferndale sells high-quality, handmade indie and DIY items. A few local artists sell here, with many vendors from around the world. 171 West 9 Mile Rd, Ferndale, MI 48220, www.nakastore.com

LEOPOLD'S BOOKS Up the street from the Detroit Institute of the Arts, this awesome little bookstore has an impressive collection of modern graphic novels, comics, indie art publications, and otherwise interesting books. Definitely worth a visit. It shares an entranceway with a great little creperie. 15 East Kirby St #114, Detroit, MI 48202, www.leopoldsbooks.com

JOHN K KING BOOKS This is an absolute must see. The building is a converted warehouse turned treasure trove of vintage books, prints, magazines, and publications. Give yourself a good chunk of the day to browse the stacks at a leisurely pace. It's practically bursting at the seams with magical finds. 901 West Lafayette Blvd, Detroit, MI 48226, www.rarebooklink.com/cgi-bin/kingbooks

STORMY RECORDS AND GREEN BRAIN COMICS Stormy Records, the coolest record shop in the Detroit area, is situated above Green Brain Comics, which in turn is a great little graphic novel/comic shop. "Hella awesome," says my friend John Krohn. It's a one-two punch for those who love music and art. 13210 Michigan Ave, Dearborn, MI 48126, www.stormyrecords.com

BAKER'S KEYBOARD LOUNGE This is the world's oldest jazz club, open since 1935. It looks exactly like you'd imagine, only more amazing. Great drinks, awesome food, and always busy on the weekends. It was rumored to be in danger of shutting down, but seems to be back on its feet. Come here to see top local, national and international acts. 20510 Livernois Ave, Detroit, MI 48221, www.bakerskeyboardlounge.com

MOTOWN HISTORICAL MUSEUM You'll probably want to check this place out. To be honest, I haven't been, but I would like to go. Maybe I'll meet you there when you're in town. 2648 West Grand Blvd, Detroit, MI 48208, www.motownmuseum.com

THE BURTON THEATER This place rules. Started by indie twentysomethings I met during a furious kickball game in Hamtramck, this little theater is located inside an old elementary school Downtown, complete with drawback curtains and a popcorn machine. But the most amazing thing about this place is the movies – they screen rare, arty/cult/indie films that you can't find anywhere else in town... or in the Midwest, in many cases. 3420 Cass Ave, Detroit, MI 48201, www.burtontheatre.com

DETROIT INSTITUTE OF ARTS (DIA) You can't visit Detroit without spending some time at the DIA. They have great exhibitions, and live music every Friday in a room painted from floor to ceiling with a huge Diego Rivera mural. I played in a French clarinet jazz ensemble at one Friday event. It was a blast, and the room was packed. Check their site for new exhibitions and events. 5200 Woodward Ave, Detroit, MI 48202, www.dia.org

MUSEUM OF CONTEMPORARY ART DETROIT (MOCAD) This place! This place is great. They have a big gallery space showing a good contemporary art collection, and they also hold great events with high-caliber, cutting-edge musicians. Definitely stop by their website to see what's going on during your stay. 4454 Woodward Ave, Detroit, MI 48201, www.mocadetroit.org

CONTEMPORARY ART INSTITUTE OF DETROIT (CAID) I've been to some incredible music shows and fantastic all-day summer music events at CAID. There's always great contemporary art on the walls and in the gallery upstairs. Super gritty, arty place. Very Detroit. 5141 Rosa Parks Blvd, Detroit, MI 48208, www.thecaid.org

THE CROFOOT This is my favorite place to see music. I've seen acts like Bon Iver, The National, Born Ruffians, and The New Pornographers here, and I'm sure they'll have something great happening during your stay. It's in Pontiac, (about 30 minutes north of Downtown Detroit), and worth the drive. Its neighbor, The Eagle Theater, is a newly renovated, awesome venue also worth checking out. 1 South Saginaw, Pontiac, MI 48342, www.thecrofoot.com

DETROIT URBAN CRAFT FAIR This yearly, one-day event is worth putting on the list. Every November, it showcases Detroit's handmade, DIY artists and makers at their finest. Their site will also fill you in on all the other events to catch throughout the year. http://detroiturbancraftfair.com

DETROIT SYMPHONY ORCHESTRA Have a relaxing evening and go see the orchestra.... Directed by Leonard Slatkin, our orchestra has earned its fine reputation. Max M Fisher Music Center, 3711 Woodward Ave, Detroit, MI 48201, www.detroitsymphony.com

Let's hear it for

DETROIT

Motor City

YEAH!

super freak

OOOH BABY

I-heard it

throug

GRAP E!

DO

SIGNED
SEALED
DELIVERED

honey

bunch

NATIONAL CONEY ISLAND Get a coney dog at National Coney Island! Historical! www.nationalconeyisland.com

WINDSOR CANADA Drive over there. Drive back. Fun!

CHECK OUT THESE LOCAL BANDS! Zoos of Berlin, The Silent Years, Javelins, Frontier Ruckus, Chris Bathgate, Daniel Zott, Suburban Sprawl Music: www.suburbansprawlmusic.com, Single Barrel Detroit: www.singlebarreldetroit.com.

SOME USEFUL BLOGS TO CHECK OUT: www.detroitlives.org Artist's tourism blog. www.sweet-juniper.com Awesome family living and blogging in Detroit.

MICHIGAN CENTRAL STATION Go and see this amazing abandoned train station. It's magnificent. Really. Check it out on Wikipedia if you don't believe me. 2198 Michigan Ave, Detroit, MI 48216

BELLE ISLE A beautiful island just off the Downtown waterfront. Drive over the bridge from Jefferson Ave to get there. It's a huge parkland, perfect for a jog, walk, photography expedition, picnic, or nap in the sun. And you get a REALLY great view of the city skyline. www.fobi.org

THE HEIDELBERG PROJECT A community art project on a large scale – an urban ghetto area has been transformed into a huge, 3D mural addressing issues of racial segregation and community action. Take a drive through – it's weird! www.heidelberg.org

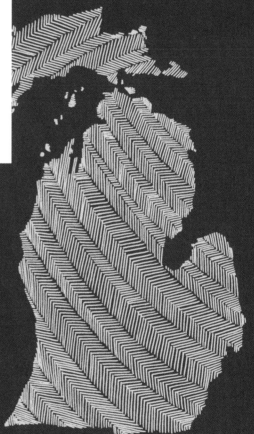

MITTENFEST IV

RAMZY MASRI & MORGAN ASHLEY ALLEN'S

KANSAS CITY

KANSAS CITY, MISSOURI

BY RAMZY MASRI AND MORGAN ASHLEY ALLEN

Kansas City is a place of stark contrasts – between historic and contemporary, rich and poor, clean and dirty. It is bohemian: full of galleries and studios converted from derelict warehouses. It is green: sprawling with parks and open spaces that echo the fertility of the land the city sits on. More than anything, it is a unique crossroads between the American East and West, a place defined by its many contrasts, and by the creative spirit of its inhabitants. Armies of artists and designers have taken a once-abandoned Downtown and transformed it into the pulsing arts Mecca of the Midwest, with open doors every first Friday of the month. Street performers, musicians, and vibrant galleries make up a grand street party, bustling in the spring and summer months when the fair weather and leisurely pace of the city lures visitors to stick around for a while.

I was one of those who stuck around for a while. I call Midtown home: a part of town south of the Downtown area, full of historic craftsman bungalows and frontier-style brick store fronts. Some locals see this part of town as dangerous or ghetto. In reality, Midtown is much like the rest of urban Kansas City, neglected years ago after a booming age of growth, and in the process of being revived. Midtown is a quirky place, famous for Westport Landing, the last stop early American pioneers made before heading out to the untamed west on the Santa Fe Trail. Today, it's a last stop for those looking for a cold beer.

Kansas City is close to my heart because it is raw. It isn't a pristine metropolitan paradise. It isn't a massive slum. It's in between; and for the most part it isn't afraid to confidently be what it is, despite the reputations and allure of larger cities like New York or San Francisco. The bottom line: Kansas City is weird. This bizarre quality is native only to Kansas City, and for a creative spirit, what could be better inspiration?

STAY

THE RAPHAEL HOTEL This is the type of hotel where you'd expect the bellhop to have a monocle. Kick back in old-world charm at this Country Club Plaza inn. 325 Ward Pkwy, Kansas City, MO 64112, www.raphaelkc.com

HOTEL PHILLIPS These luxury Art Deco digs could easily serve as a sultry backdrop for a steamy noir classic – all marble and rich mahogany. It's like something out of New Orleans' French Quarter – or somewhere that Bruce Wayne would stay. 106 West 12 St, Kansas City, MO 64105, www.hotelphillips.com

SOUTHMORELAND ON THE PLAZA For the B&B package, this 1913 colonial a few blocks from the Country Club Plaza is all quaint decor and sweet people who will tend to your every need – feeding your fireplace and baking your cookies. Take a stroll around the sculpture park or just around Southmoreland neighborhood; There's lots of unique turn-of-the-century character to see. 116 East 46th St, Kansas City, MO 64112, www.southmoreland.com

YJ'S SNACK BAR I don't think anybody knows what YJ'S stands for, but that's just one of the oddities about this cafe/eatery. Local artist David Ford has carved out a much-loved haunt that feels like two parts eccentric house, one part saloon in the heart of Kansas City's Crossroads Arts District. YJ's serves three meals a day, but the menu is restricted to 'whatever's cookin''. Stop by for a street-side cup of coffee and a peek at resident weirdos. 128 West 18th St, Kansas City, MO 64121

EL CAMINO REAL A dainty kitchen churning out hand pressed tortillas, surrounded by an intriguing mural of rural Mexico featuring a giant eagle, snake in talon, perched on a bloated cactus. Yes, this is the place for tacos. 903 North 7th St, Kansas City, KS 66101

TOWN TOPIC The thing I love most about this city is what some have coined "salt." And this is the place to find it. Don't let the lack of seating or long lines deter you; this old-fashioned burger and malt dive is where you get cozy with locals who have kept it busy since the 50s. If it's closed, head to the sister location around the block. 2021 Broadway St, Kansas City, MO 64108

POTPIE Your waiter at PotPie will most likely be wearing overalls or gingham – not as a gimmick, but because it's what a man should wear. Excellent food. Try the steamed mussels. If your mama was a 5-star chef, this is what she'd serve you on her day off. 904 Westport Rd, Kansas City, MO 64111, www.kcpotpie.com

EDEN ALLEY Eden Alley will make you forget you're at a vegetarian restaurant. Try absolutely anything on the menu. It will give you goosebumps. Hell, it may even convert you. 707 West 47th St, Kansas City, MO 64112, www.edenalley.com

BLUE BIRD BISTRO Nested (no pun intended) in the West Side, this quaint spot is all about organic, sustainable food. It's all very on trend, but the food is damn good. Try their vegan orange cake and walk off your meal with a stroll around the neighborhood. 1700 Summit St, Kansas City, MO 64108, www.bluebirdbistro.com

YOU SAY TOMATO Let there be no mystery what goes into your brunch. You Say Tomato (coffee shop, luncheonette, and grocer) sells the ingredients right next to the table you eat them on. And if that doesn't comfort you, the staff will surely put a smile on your face, singing your name when your order's up. 2801 Holmes St, Kansas City, MO 64109, www.ystkc.com

GRINDER'S An optical wonderland of exposed brick, graffiti, and bizarre decor – Grinder's is the place to eat on the first Friday of the month. Skip the deli, grab a slice of Bengal Tiger pizza, study (don't skim) the beer list, and don't let that bleach-haired food critic and TV host fool you – this place is actually good. 417 East 18th St, Kansas City, MO 64108, www.grinderspizza.com

OKLAHOMA JOE'S Lots of cities boast 'the best BBQ joint in the country', but rest assured, Okie Joes is the real deal. In fact just writing this has got me salivating and sad that I'm not there right now. If you eat in one place in KC, let it be Okie Joes. Unless you're a vegetarian. 3002 West 47th Ave, Kansas City, KS 66103, www.oklahomajoesbbq.com

R-BAR Imagine the Kansas City of the past; a wild no-man's land of saloons and bawdy, red-faced pioneers sucking down whiskey and drawing their revolvers. R-Bar is a romantic vision of this past. Bottle-lined wooden cabinets glow under the buttery dim light of the hanging lanterns, and old-timey bands play banjos and fiddles. Amazing cocktails and food. Just go. 1617 Genessee St, Kansas City, MO 64102, www.rbarkc.com

MANIFESTO Shh. Don't tell anyone. Kansas City used to be a hotspot of speakeasies during the prohibition era, and this bar is a remnant of this history. You enter through an alleyway, and can only get in with a reservation. A dark stairway and dimly-lit corridor lead you to a small and intimate bar, lit only by candle-light. Hands-down, Kansas City's best cocktails. 1924 Main St, Kansas City, MO 64108

DAVE'S STAGECOACH INN The dive you would go to in your own town. Sure, the smells are unidentifiable and the hot-plate burgers are questionable, but the drinks are cheap and the jukebox is like trail mix. 316 Westport Rd, Kansas City, MO 64111

TAQUERIA MEXICO Situated on what locals call 'The Boulevard', Taqueria Mexico is famous for its dollar margaritas and tacos. Cheap and authentic. 910 Southwest Blvd, Kansas City, MO 64108

HARRY'S BAR & TABLES Sitting at the window of Harry's you can watch the scantily clad and inebriated hoards of Westport stumble past on their pub crawl, and enjoy the show from a safe distance. Not many know of the 50 odd brands of scotch, 30 types of cigars and steak and seafood a la carte served at this joint. 501 Westport Rd, Kansas City, MO 64111

SHOP

PEGGY NOLAND Peggy Noland is a perfect example of the kind of citizen Kansas City gives birth to. This kooky fashion designer decorates her store thematically – one time it was filled completely with stuffed animals, another with shredded garbage bags. I wouldn't go there to shop – the clothes are really out there – but definitely worth a look. 124 West 18th St, Kansas City, MO 64108, www.peggynoland.com

SPIVEY'S BOOKSTORE Mr Spivey is old. Like Stonehenge. He hangs out in the back with his dogs and cats, and a visit feels like going to the cemetery with a personal tour from the crypt keeper: winding, decrepit bookshelves filled with dusty tomes, maps, and oddities. Some books are so old the pages crumble in your hands like cornflakes. 825 Westport Rd, Kansas City, MO 64111, www.spiveysbooks.com

SUPER FLEA If you have 50¢, a free weekend morning, and a solid constitution, go. A huge labyrinth of metal cages full of VHS tapes, motel furniture, weird tchotchkes and more glass bongs than an LA dispensary. A spectacle. 6200 St John Ave, Kansas City, MO 64123, www.kcsuperflea.com

RERUNS Reruns has painstakingly collected KC's most fashionable junk through the ages. Of the two locations, don't bother with the high-priced, finely curated boutique, do the dirty work yourself and head to the warehouse to dig up some real gems. They've kindly sorted the clothes for you by decade. **WAREHOUSE:** 1408 West 12th St, Kansas City, MO 64101, **BOUTIQUE:** 4041 Broadway, Kansas City, MO 64111, www.re-runs.com

DONNA'S DRESS SHOP One glimpse at Donna's vintage clothing shop will win over your sweet, ruffled, polka-dotted heart. Donna herself is the real deal: the beehive, I assure you, is not a wig, and the horn-rimmed glasses? Prescription. She's always bringing in fresh stock – both vintage and new. 1410 West 39th St, Kansas City, MO 64111, www.donnasdressshop.com

RIVER MARKET ANTIQUE MALL Four floors stocked full of anything and everything. Most places like this send me into a tizzy, but these booth renters are well organized and serious (sometimes too serious for a modest wallet). Take advantage of the cookies and coffee at the door – you'll need the energy climbing stairs and scanning halls. 115 West 5th St, Kansas City, MO 64105, www.rivermarketantiquemall.com

THE FISHTANK The Fishtank is a venue for actors, writers, performers, and local personalities to tell tales and share a belly-laugh. Depending on the troupe on call when you go, you will most likely leave with the same sensation you had after ab day at the gym. But it isn't all comedy. Sobering stories, romantic epithets, and social commentary – it's a diverse and entertaining program. 1715 Wyandotte St, Kansas City, MO 64108, www.fishtanktheater.com

GRAND ARTS One of Kansas City's finest galleries, set in a modern building, and holding consistently good exhibitions. The hors d'oeuvres served at opening receptions are worth the trip alone. 1819 Grand Blvd, Kansas City, MO 64108, www.grandarts.com

HAMMERPRESS Started by KCAI Alumnus, Brady Vest, Hammerpress specializes in reviving the fine art of letterpress, using the old type to create incredible posters, cards, notebooks, and many other one-of-a-kind curiosities. Paper ephemera aren't the only buyables here – check out the small boutique where you can purchase perfume, cologne, jewelry, etc, and even get your hair cut! 110 Southwest Blvd, Kansas City, MO 64108, www.hammerpress.net

THE BLOCH BUILDING AT THE NELSON-ATKINS MUSEUM OF ART People have a love-hate relationship with this architectural phenomenon. Designed by Steven Holl, it does a spectacular job of looking beautiful, but like the Guggenheim in New York City, strikes an interesting balance between form and function. Take time to explore this Neo-Modernist cathedral – check out the Bridget Rileys, Donald Judds and the African Collection as you bask in white geometry. 4525 Oak St, Kansas City, MO 64111, www.nelson-atkins.org

LA ESQUINA GALLERY / WHOOP DEE DOO Going to a show at La Esquina feels like going home. It's an intimate space, perfect for some up-close art viewing, and very well-suited for Whoop Dee Doo – a mock public-access children's TV show characterized by variety, energy, and the bizarre – kind of like a big talent show with lots of audience participation. 1000 West 25th St, Kansas City, MO 64108

SCREENLAND THEATER What could be better than a good movie? A good movie with matching booze – a bottle of French cognac before watching Amelie, or an ectoplasm cocktail for a Ghostbusters marathon, for example. Screenland is known for its creative bartenders, plush red LaZ Boys, and excellent programming including old classics and monthly screenings of *Rocky Horror* and *The Big Lebowski*. 1656 Washington St, Kansas City, MO 64108, www.screenland.com

GO

CLIFF DRIVE SCENIC BY-WAY You'll find the entrance to the lovely Cliff Drive in the historic Northeast area, with its beautiful old chateaux belonging to the city's rich old families. The drive twists and turns along the limestone cliffs high above the Missouri River and through the woodland of Kessler Park (George Kessler was the landscape architect who designed the whole thing). You can walk, jog, or just drive along it in search of romance. Our grandparents weathered this path in their time, and tell fond stories of the perfect make-out spot.

THE WEST BOTTOMS Heading down the 12th Street Bridge coming from Quality Hill is like looking down into the ruins of the Colosseum from an upper tier. The old industrial hub of KC is one of the most historic areas of the city, and although its regeneration has started, it's still largely derelict. Enjoy the view and then walk around the area; it's like a time warp into a scene from *On the Waterfront*. Magnificent and vibrant and one of the most characterful areas in the city.

LOOSE PARK Jacob R Loose Park is like New York's Central Park, complete with a rose garden, fountains, wide open fields, and a lake. Trails wind you through a carefully manicured landscape, reminiscent of the countryside not far away. Take a picnic, stare at the sky, and have an existential crisis. 5200 Wornall Rd, Kansas City, MO 64112

TAL ROSNER'S

LOS ANGELES, CALIFORNIA BY TAL ROSNER

I first came to LA ten years ago – an art student from Jerusalem visiting his big brother. The camera barely left my eye for a moment – the palm lined boulevards, the skyscrapers and bridges, the freeways breathing traffic like oxygen, the legendary Hollywood sign... I had seen its iconography in so many movies and paintings that it felt instantly like home, and I've been living here on and off ever since.

LA is not an easy city to get around. With the exception of a limited metro system in the Downtown area, there's virtually no public transport, and a car is essential. Even with a car it can be confusing. There is no real heart to the city, just a multitude of organs connected by traffic arteries. It's basically a series of neighborhoods that expanded until their borders merged, creating a never-ending expanse of residential and commercial terrain that nonetheless varies enormously in character as it transitions from one area to the next.

My favored parts of the city are Silver Lake and Los Feliz – residential areas with few tourists, and plenty of restaurants, bars and shops drawing the hipsters in. West Hollywood is traditionally gay, and another place I really like. It's where you'll find the more classic touristy hangouts, and slightly cleaner-cut venues. Downtown is not an area that everyone likes, but I'm actually a fan. It's quite historic, and has recently seen a big culture boost with the development of Disney Hall, REDCAT and MOCA (see Culture). I'm not a big one for Santa Monica and Venice Beach, but many of my friends that live around there never leave – it's a very self-sufficient village vibe – with the beach providing respite from what could otherwise be a claustrophobic atmosphere.

There is no escaping the centrality of the film industry to LA. It is very much the blood in its concrete veins, and perhaps as a result of the excesses of that industry, LA has earned a reputation as a big, blonde urban floozy. But it's not all silicone and fake smiles. There is a pioneering spirit that lies deep in the city's history, which means people have an open-mindedness and a positivity that allows the arts to flourish in new and exciting ways. I sometimes think that it's the confidence in the buff, tanned, physically perfect superficiality of the city that allows individuality to thrive beneath.

CHAMBERLAIN WEST HOLLYWOOD A conveniently located boutique hotel, with nicely designed, spacious rooms and a great view from the rooftop pool area. I have a particular fondness for the well-stocked toiletries in their bathrooms. 1000 Westmount Dr, Los Angeles, CA 90069, www.chamberlainwesthollywood.com

STANDARD WEST HOLLYWOOD A comparatively reasonable option on Sunset Strip. It's got a kind of *Miami Vice* retro vibe, with young clientele and an amazing balcony overlooking the city. There's an aquarium in the lobby where a scantily clad model poses every evening. Fun. 8300 Sunset Blvd, Los Angeles, CA 90069, www.standardhotels.com/hollywood

BEVERLY LAUREL MOTOR HOTEL On the cheaper side of the spectrum, this motel is unrivalled in its location. I stayed here for a week once and had lots of fun. It's got lots of old-school, original features, with the pool as a central hub – and it's attached to Swingers – a hip diner/cafe. 8018 Beverly Blvd, Los Angeles, CA 90048, www.beverly-laurel.hotel-rn.com, (323) 651-2441

METRO 417 APARTMENTS These are self-contained apartments in Downtown with a range of prices (depending on the size). It's in the converted Subway Terminal Building, which has been immaculately restored to its former Art Deco glory. 417 South Hill St, Los Angeles, CA 90013, www.metro417.com

ROOSEVELT HOTEL A piece of Hollywood history – this place hosted the first ever Academy Awards, and was home to Montgomery Clift, Marilyn Monroe, and other classic stars. It was sensitively revamped a few years ago, and is a trendy spot to be seen. The pool is beautiful, as are most of the clientele. 7000 Hollywood Blvd, Los Angeles, CA 90028, www.hollywoodroosevelt.com

HUGOS I'm a vegetarian and I love Hugo's. Serving creative organic food, it has a great selection of veggie options (although carnivores are also catered to). It's great for brunch and the staff are always friendly. It can get busy sometimes. 8401 Santa Monica Blvd, Los Angeles, CA 90069, www.hugosrestaurant.com

BUDDHA'S BELLY Reasonably priced Asian fusion in a nice, minimalist atmosphere. I come here for lunch after an arduous shopping experience. Their salads and bento boxes are great, and I'm told their Alaskan black cod is spectacular. Great $4 drinks at happy hour. 7475 Beverly Blvd, Los Angeles, CA 90036, www.bbfood.com

THE LITTLE DOOR Exquisite French food at top dollar prices. But it really is worth it. The atmosphere is lovely, romantic, and intimate, with a beautiful courtyard and a patio. The interior is done up in rustic French style. The food is southern French, and just fantastic. Next door there's a deli-cafe (the Little Next Door) serving cheaper, lighter fare, which is great for lunch. 8164 West 3rd St, Los Angeles, CA 90048, www.thelittledoor.com

DELANCEY'S If you're having East Coast cravings, this is a New York pizzeria in the heart of Hollywood. Nice interior, great thin crust pizza with lots of toppings, a big beer selection, and open till 2am. 5936 Sunset Blvd, Los Angeles, CA 90028, www.delanceyhollywood.com

CLIFF'S EDGE A Mediterranean restaurant in Silver Lake with a warm, fun atmosphere. It's all one big festive garden – with light-strung trees growing through the roof, and simple but beautifully prepared Greek and Italian food. They also have a bar that does a fine martini. 3626 Sunset Blvd, Los Angeles, CA 90026, www.cliffsedgecafe.com

FIGARO BISTROT This place is not that vegetarian-friendly, but I'm recommending it nonetheless, because the food is really good (equally so for breakfast or dinner), the decor is lovely (French bistro style), and it's in the heart of Vermont Avenue in Los Feliz, which is a great area for shopping and drinking. 1802 North Vermont Ave, Los Angeles, CA 90027, www.figarobistrot.com

VERMONT RESTAURANT AND BAR While we're in the Vermont area, this is another nice place that's a little bit more upmarket than Figaro. It's got a funky, buzzy atmosphere and serves 'New American' food – whatever that means. Not bad for celeb spotting. My most recent sighting was Robert Downey Jr looking very chilled out. 1714 N Vermont Ave, Los Angeles, CA 90027, www.vermontrestaurantonline.com

101 Los Angeles, CA

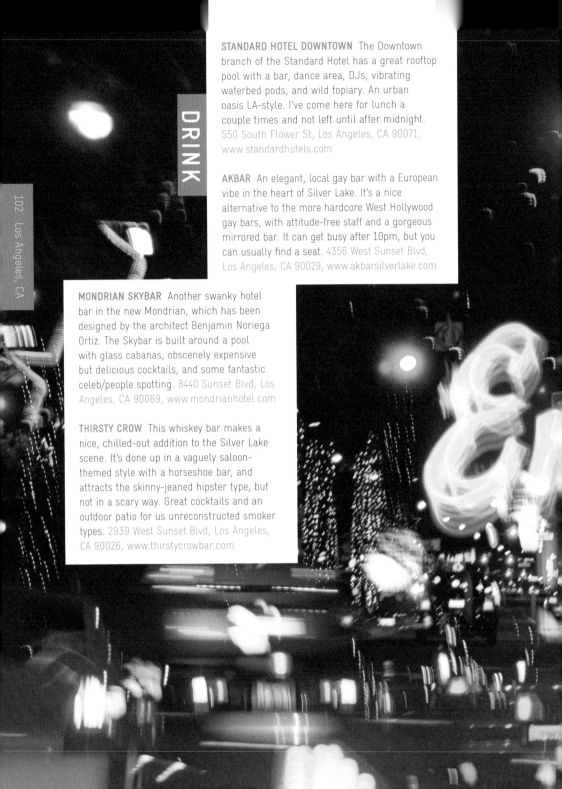

STANDARD HOTEL DOWNTOWN The Downtown branch of the Standard Hotel has a great rooftop pool with a bar, dance area, DJs, vibrating waterbed pods, and wild topiary. An urban oasis LA-style. I've come here for lunch a couple times and not left until after midnight. 550 South Flower St, Los Angeles, CA 90071, www.standardhotels.com

AKBAR An elegant, local gay bar with a European vibe in the heart of Silver Lake. It's a nice alternative to the more hardcore West Hollywood gay bars, with attitude-free staff and a gorgeous mirrored bar. It can get busy after 10pm, but you can usually find a seat. 4356 West Sunset Blvd, Los Angeles, CA 90029, www.akbarsilverlake.com

MONDRIAN SKYBAR Another swanky hotel bar in the new Mondrian, which has been designed by the architect Benjamin Noriega Ortiz. The Skybar is built around a pool with glass cabanas, obscenely expensive but delicious cocktails, and some fantastic celeb/people spotting. 8440 Sunset Blvd, Los Angeles, CA 90069, www.mondrianhotel.com

THIRSTY CROW This whiskey bar makes a nice, chilled-out addition to the Silver Lake scene. It's done up in a vaguely saloon-themed style with a horseshoe bar, and attracts the skinny-jeaned hipster type, but not in a scary way. Great cocktails and an outdoor patio for us unreconstructed smoker types. 2939 West Sunset Blvd, Los Angeles, CA 90026, www.thirstycrowbar.com

CITY SIP A hole-in-the-wall Echo Park wine bar with a very solid list and nice tapas and cheese plates to go with it. Cozy and intimate. Definitely worth going there at happy hour – they do all sorts of deals with free wine flights when you order food. 2150 Sunset Blvd, Los Angeles, CA 90026, www.citysipla.com

BARBRIX Another fun, local wine bar with a great, modern interior and a lovely patio. Nice lighting, nice staff, and really nice tapas (better food than City Sip). It's very cute. A good date destination. 2442 Hyperion Ave, Los Angeles, CA 90027, www.barbrix.com

THE EDISON This is where I take visitors to LA to impress them. It's a Downtown club/bar in an Art Deco power station with a subterranean vintage feel and well-crafted cocktails. It's pretty dressy, so don't come in jeans. 108 West 2nd St, Los Angeles, CA 90012, www.edisondowntown.com

SHOP

THE GROVE There's no two ways about it; this is a shopping mall built in a kind of Spanish piazza style, with the added bonus of a fountain that is synched to the background music (that's what you want in a shopping mall!) If it sounds tacky, that's because it kind of is, but it's also really useful, with such staples as an Apple Store, Crate and Barrel, Anthropologie, and Abercrombie and Fitch. It also has cinemas and a farmers' market. If you're in the right frame of mind it can be fun. 189 The Grove Dr, Los Angeles, CA 90036, www.thegrovela.com

SKYLIGHT BOOKS An independent bookstore in Los Feliz with two adjacent shops – one selling fiction and the other specializing in art and design. The staff are knowledgeable and helpful, and they host some interesting author events. Great for presents. 1818 North Vermont Ave, Los Angeles, CA 90027, www.skylightbooks.com

AMOEBA This is a must-see – it's just an experience really. Amoeba is the largest independent music store in the world, and it's basically everything you would expect from a quirky little indie music store – only it takes up an entire city block. Rack after rack of used CDs, DVDs and vinyl will fulfill even the most obscure musical preference. 6400 Sunset Blvd, Los Angeles, CA 90028, www.amoeba.com

THE MOCA STORE The Museum of Contemporary Art bookshop has an inspired selection of books, cards, gifts, and magazines. I bought a great T-shirt last time I was here. 250 South Grand Ave, Los Angeles, CA 90012

YOLK I can't leave this Silver Lake shop without buying something, whether it's design nicknacks, cushions, Marimekko fabrics, homewares, or baby clothes for my goddaughter. It's all attractively laid out so everything feels fresh and hip. 1626 Silver Lake Blvd, Los Angeles, CA 90026, www.shopyolk.com

FRED SEGAL An LA establishment that has featured in numerous movies over the years. It's the one stop shop for LA fashion, stocking all the high-end brands from beachwear to suits. Mauro's in the West Hollywood branch does a good Italian lunch. 8100 Melrose Ave, Los Angeles, CA 90046, www.fredsegal.com

MELROSE AVENUE BETWEEN FAIRFAX AND LA CIENAGA
This stretch of Melrose is just a fun area to walk around and window shop. From trashy biker-chic to second hand grunge to Marc Jacobs to weird Goth stuff, it's all there, and usually with beautiful interiors.

CULTURE

ARCLIGHT HOLLYWOOD Los Angeles is the capital of film, so we will start with the cinemas. I like little indie theaters as much as the next man, but sometimes it's just not what you're looking for. It's like comparing an Olivetti to the latest MacBook. ArcLight is a multiplex cinema with two branches that has streamlined the art of movie going into a stress-free and thoroughly immersive experience. With all the latest ticketing, sound and projection technologies, a million screening times to choose from, a fine line in butter and caramel popcorns, and ushers that act as comperes, introducing the films comedy-style before they start – it's the only place to see the newest releases. 6360 West Sunset Blvd, Los Angeles, CA 90028, www.arclightcinemas.com

LAEMMLE'S SUNSET 5 And this one is the Olivetti. Or as close to an Olivetti as LA will allow itself to get. A five-screen theater in a Hollywood mall showing indie, foreign and art-house movies. The people that come here tend to be young and friendly. 8000 West Sunset Blvd, Los Angeles, CA 90046, www.laemmle.com

WALT DISNEY CONCERT HALL This explosion of aluminum in Downtown LA was designed by Frank Gehry, and apart from being an architectural masterpiece, is the home of the Los Angeles Philharmonic. I've had my work screened here, so I have a particular fondness for it. The orchestra itself, led by Gustavo Dudamel since 2009, is internationally renowned. Also check out Green Umbrella, a monthly experimental/contemporary program. 111 South Grand Ave, Los Angeles, CA 90012, www.laphil.com

REDCAT Next to the Disney Hall is this lounge/performance space/gallery. The lounge area does books, drinks, food, and free Wi-Fi, with various free events such as music and readings. The performance space hosts some very interesting, experimental works from around the world, and is one of LA's avant-garde pioneers. 631 West 2nd St, Los Angeles, CA 90012, www.redcat.org

MOCA Another Downtown culture hub not far from the Disney Hall. The building was designed by Arata Isozaki in the 80s, and its previous home, the Geffen Contemporary, has been preserved as an offshoot in Little Tokyo. It's worth checking to see what's on at both locations. 152 North Central Ave, Los Angeles, CA 90013, www.moca.org

MUSEUM OF JURASSIC TECHNOLOGY Um. I'm not quite sure how to describe this museum. Open only at weekends, it's a kind of Gothic shrine to the poetic aspects of natural history and science, with vitrines showcasing curiosities of art, science and anthropology from throughout the ages. A total one-off. The Russian tearoom upstairs is a miniature recreation of Tsar Nicolas II's study in the Winter Palace, and is run by the gorgeous Nana. Tell her Tal sent you. 9341 Venice Blvd, Los Angeles, CA 90232, www.mjt.org

HAMMER MUSEUM A really good medium-scale museum linked to UCLA's departments of art and architecture. The curatorship is excellent and there's always something interesting going on, as well as a solid permanent collection, a lovely courtyard, and free film screenings. 10899 Wilshire Blvd, Los Angeles, CA 90024, www.hammer.ucla.edu

SANTA MONICA MUSEUM OF ART A small exhibition space with a nice shop located in Bergamot Station, which with its little galleries and studios, is kind of like the Chelsea of LA. It's non-profit, and they put on some interesting, edgy shows. 2525 Michigan Ave, Los Angeles, CA 90404, www.smmoa.org

LACMA A huge art museum with a collection that reaches from ancient times till today. It's housed in a series of impressive buildings designed by big name architects, with an entrance pavilion by Renzo Piano. It's the kind of place you can easily spend an entire day. The new wing of the Broad Contemporary Art Museum is particularly worth seeing. 5905 Wilshire Blvd, Los Angeles, CA 90036, www.lacma.org

GO

GRIFFITH PARK OBSERVATORY This is an LA landmark that's basically free to enjoy. You can drive up there, but it's nicer to park on Fern Dell Drive (opposite the Trails Cafe) and hike there and back. It takes about an hour and you feel like you've completely left the city – until you get to the top, when it all spreads out before you spectacularly, with a particularly good view of the Hollywood sign. The observatory itself is also really nice – a beautiful 1930s building with good IMAX-style shows. 2800 East Observatory Rd, Los Angeles, CA 90027, www.griffithobs.org

RUNYON CANYON A 130-acre park just two blocks from Hollywood Boulevard. There are entrances on Fuller Avenue, Vista Street and just off Mulholland. Once you get there, you'll find loads of trails of varying difficulty. It's a popular destination, as it's so close to the residential areas, and you'll see lots of beautiful people walking their highly groomed dogs on the easier hikes. The higher you go the better view you get of the city. 2000 North Fuller, Los Angeles, CA 90189, www.lamountains.com

POINT DUME/ZUMA BEACH In Malibu, a short drive from town, just off the Pacific Coast Highway, you'll find the lovely spot of Point Dume. It's a cliff top overlooking a peaceful beach. A great place to clear your head, drink a bottle of wine, watch the sunset, and, if you're lucky, spot some dolphins. Zuma Beach is just a short drive further on. It's a large beach that's clean, chilled out and a lot less touristy than some of the inner city ones (although it does get busy in peak season). The water can be cold, but it's a great place to catch some rays. Plus it's free – unlike some of the others around. **POINT DUME**: Westward Beach Rd, Malibu, CA 90265, **ZUMA BEACH**: 30050 Pacific Coast Hwy, Malibu, CA 90265

EL MATADOR While we're in Malibu, this beach further up from Zuma is truly wonderful. It rarely gets crowded (it's that much more of a drive and you have to trek down some serious stairs to get there), and it has a kind of island-y vibe that feels a million miles from LA. There are some crazy caves and rock formations worth exploring. A magical spot – especially midweek. 32100 Pacific Coast Hwy, Malibu, CA 90265

ANNENBERG POOL This outdoor pool is part of the Annenberg Beach House, a community hub set up by a big philanthropic trust. It's in a gorgeous spot in Santa Monica right by the sea, and it's open to all – no membership – very un-LA! You can do various yoga classes or other activities or just enjoy the beautiful pool. 415 Pacific Coast Hwy, Los Angeles, CA 90402, http://beachhouse.smgov.net

OCEAN PARK CYCLE RIDE Next to Venice Beach you'll find the neighborhood of Ocean Park, which has a slightly more humble, artsy vibe. At the end of Ocean Park Blvd (where it meets the ocean), you'll find a bike and rollerblade hire shack. Take your pick and use the dedicated cycle path to explore Venice Beach to the south (crazy/stoner/hippie vibe) or Santa Monica to the North (you'll find a tacky pier and further up there you can explore the beaches and enjoy the artistic neighborhood vibe).

CATALINA ISLAND A tiny island off the coast of LA that makes for a fun day trip. The Catalina Express (boat) leaves from Long Beach or San Pedro, and takes about an hour. Once you're there there's plenty of hiking, mountain biking, kayaking, snorkeling, fishing, and surfing. Or you can just hang out on the beach. One of the weird things about this island is that it's home to a substantial population of American bison – the offspring of a handful that were brought there in the 20s as part of a film set, and were left due to budgetary constraints.

MEMPHIS, TENNESSEE BY ALEX WARBLE

Memphis is first and foremost a Southern city. In terms of geography, weather, and culture, it makes no pretenses about its redneck origins. This means some great things and some less great things. Let's get the basics out of the way: It's situated on a bluff over the Mississippi River, with a wet, sub-tropical climate. The winters are relatively mild, but wet and grey, and the summers are great if you like saunas. Between June and September it can be hot as hell and extremely humid.

Memphis is a proud scab of the civil rights movement. There is a black majority, and there's a lot of racial tension that goes right back into the city's history. But the points at which the cultures meet can lead to some incredibly fertile artistic ground. It's because of this that the city became the birthplace of rock n' roll, and that musical heritage is very much alive today. It pushes the other arts scenes forward – it's a city ablaze with a pulsating creative fire. And yet, despite its passions, it's also very laid back, with a slow pace of life that is hard to battle in 100 degree heat. The deep, dark, sparkling Mississippi takes its time rolling by, and so do the people of Memphis.

There are some parts of Memphis which you all would do best to avoid – high crime and unemployment make for some shady areas. However, you also get some really beautiful, leafy old-school Southern neighborhoods like Annesdale, Snowden, Hein Park and Central Gardens. The Downtown area used to be an abandoned ghost town, but it's become a much more vibrant and safer place. It's where you'll find the infamous Beale Street, which was branded 'home of the blues' and as a result is full of tourist traps and second-rate clubs. If you really want to experience what the city has to offer – music-wise and generally – you'd do much better to hang out in Midtown. Overton Square in Midtown is where you'll find the old cinema and the new playhouse as well as a load of awesome restaurants, bars, and clubs.

I love Memphis. The hand painted signs, the music venues, the coffee shops – oh and did I mention the barbeques? Memphis has the best barbeques in the country and possibly in the world. If you don't like the smell of scorched, marinated pork, just go home now. I feel like Memphis is on the verge of something big and influential with the music and arts scenes at the core of it. It's got no pretensions, just raw resourcefulness and the means with which to express that.

RIVER INN, HARBOR TOWN Great boutique hotel overlooking the Mississippi and a rooftop patio from which to enjoy the view. Romantic rooms, amazing breakfast, and nice service – this one gets great online reviews pretty consistently. 50 Harbor Town Sq, Memphis, TN 38103, www.riverinnmemphis.com

TALBOT HEIRS GUESTHOUSE Family run Southern comfort in a good Downtown location. This B&B offers really good value for money, and is nicely done up, with super-friendly hosts. 99 South 2nd St, Memphis, TN 38103, www.talbotheirs.com

PILGRIM HOUSE HOSTEL This place is located in the First Congregational Church in Cooper Young – a little ways outside of Downtown. It's got a big kitchen and a library, and I've heard it's all very friendly. You can stay in a dorm or a private room for next to nothing, and the only drawback is that you have to do a chore (washing up or sweeping) to contribute. 1000 South Cooper St, Memphis, TN 38104, www.pilgrimhouse.org

THE ARCADE Awesome diner which was last redecorated some time in the 50s. It's featured in various movies, and is 100 per cent Southern. They serve cheeseburgers, sweet potato pancakes, biscuits and gravy, and fried peanut butter and banana sandwiches. Haute cuisine. 540 South Main St, Memphis, TN 38103, www.arcaderestaurant.com

FRANK'S DELI A grocery store/ restaurant. The magic happens at the deli counter at the back, serving amazing potato salad and sandwiches that are the size of your head and then some. Wash it back with a beer from the fridge. Smoked turkey breast sandwich. That's the daddy. 327 South Main St, Memphis, TN 38150

DINO'S A damn good Italian family restaurant that's a little bit off the beaten track – the kind of hole-in-the-wall, old fashioned place that feels like a secret find. They serve huge portions of homemade pastas in a simple and friendly atmosphere. 645 North McLean Blvd, Memphis, TN 38107, www.dinosgrill.com

KWIK CHECK A basic-looking dive convenience store/cafe run by a Korean and Greek man and wife, serving a mix of foods from both cultures. Put your doubts aside and try their awesome falafels. 2013 Madison Ave, Memphis, TN 38104

OTHERLANDS My favorite coffeeshop in town, where I start most of my days with their fine banana nut bread and a cup of joe on the patio. It draws in a whole mess of creative types taking advantage of the free Wi-fi and feeding off each other's caffeine rushes. At the weekend they hold live music nights and get some good acts in. 641 South Cooper St, Memphis, TN 38104, www.otherlandscoffeebar.com

BOSCO'S A nice restaurant in a quiet area of Midtown serving stone-baked pizza and American food. Wood floors, brick walls, work by local artists on the walls, and a young, buzzy atmosphere. An excellent beer selection seals the deal with many brewed in-house. 2120 Madison Ave, Memphis, TN 38104, www.boscosbeer.com

BBQ I have already mentioned that Memphis is the BBQ capital of the world. It might not sound like much of a claim to fame, but once you taste the wares you'll understand the hype. A few of the places you'll be able to experience the joys are: BBQ Shop, Cozy Corner, Leonard's, and Corky's. Ribs, pulled pork sandwiches, and everything else piggy coated in any kind of BBQ sauce your carnivorous little heart desires. **BBQ SHOP:** 1782 Madison Ave, Memphis, TN 38104, **COZY CORNER:** 745 North Parkway, Memphis, TN 38105, **LEONARD'S:** 5465 Fox Plaza Dr, Memphis, TN 38115, **CORKYS:** 5259 Poplar Ave, Memphis, TN 38119

DRINK

Hi Tone

HI TONE CAFE | 1913 POPLAR
THE BEST SOUNDING VENUE IN ALL OF MEMPHIS. TOURING INDIE BANDS GALORE- LAYED BACK AMBIANCE ~ -PING PONG! - MOST DAYS LIVE MUSIC - OTHER TIMES DANCE PARTIES & AWESOME DRINK SPECIALS. AMAZING FOOD! MAGICAL PIZZA.

thehitonememphis.com
(901) 278-8663

P&H CAFE So you might have gathered that I'm not one for flashy venues, but P&H (Poor and Hungry) really is a total cave. Dark, smoky, and dirt cheap. They only serve beer, and the menu is pretty much limited to hamburgers. It's the kind of place where everyone is welcome 1532 Madison Ave, Memphis, TN 38104

POPLAR LOUNGE A den-like lounge that's good for chilling out with friends over a beer. They get good bands in – particularly bluegrass. It calls itself 'world famous', but really it's a neighborhood bar, great if you want to get down with the locals. 2586 Poplar Ave, Memphis, TN 38112, www.poplarlounge.com

BUCCANEER The best dive bar ever and my favorite place to see local music. You know you're in the right place by an awesome sign of a mustached pirate holding a wooden sword. Enter and you'll find a small, smoke-filled ultra-bar that feels like a haunted house with red vinyl accents. It's like a pirate ship where you and your friends keeping jumping off the plank and getting back on.... 1368 Monroe Ave, Memphis, TN 38104

ALEX'S TAVERN The best place to end the night. This place serves beer and surprisingly good food till 5:30am. It's been going since the 50s and is part of Memphis history, with a great old jukebox and pictures of celebrities lining the walls. The surrounding area is a bit shady – be warned. 1445 Jackson Ave, Memphis, TN 38107

NOCTURNAL This club used to be the famous Antenna Club, punk staple of the 80s and 90s that saw many a major band cut their teeth. They still get good acts and good DJs in. Cover is cheap and so is beer. 1588 Madison Ave, Memphis, TN 38104

WILD BILL'S A hole-in-the-wall blues club in a shady old strip mall that is one of the best live music venues in town. It only serves beer in 40oz bottles, and draws in a mixed, older crowd. Forget Beale Street, this is the real deal. 1580 Vollintine Ave, Memphis, TN 38107

HI TONE The Hi-Tone is a venue that pairs local musicans with acts from around the world in the most professional way. It's the best sounding venue, with live music on most nights of the year, including some big indie acts. A great, relaxing atmosphere with a full bar, drinks specials, and a good menu... and an AWESOME mural on the outside painted by yours truly. 1913 Poplar Ave, Memphis, TN 38104, www.hitonememphis.com

SHANGRI LA RECORDS A vinyl WONDERLAND! No better spot in the world for Soul 45s! New and used records line the walls of this charming shop that embodies the true musical spirit of Memphis. 1916 Madison Ave, Memphis, TN 38104, www.shangri.com

GONER RECORDS And if you haven't had enough records, hit up Goner for more garage, punk, and soul. They have their own label and are responsible for Gonerfest – a four day music festival in venues around Midtown every September. 2152 Young Ave, Memphis, TN 38104, www.goner-records.com

BOOKSTAR I'd love to say this is an independent bookstore, but the truth is it's owned by Barnes & Noble. Nonetheless it's a pretty special place, housed in the old Plaza movie theater with all original features intact including the sign, projection booth and box office. The Starbucks inside is a later addition. 3402 Poplar Ave, Memphis, TN 38111

EASY WAY Easy Way is an awesome grocery store selling excellent fresh fruit and veg and nice deli goods with three branches around the city. The retro black and orange sign makes me feel all at home. 814 Mount Moriah Rd, Memphis, TN 38117

FLASHBACK Vintage clothing and retro nicknacks and homewares dating back to the 40s. It's not cheap, but everything is well chosen and nicely laid out. 2304 Central Ave, Memphis, TN 38104

MEMPHIS FARMERS' MARKET Located in the new open-air bus station in Downtown Memphis, this farmers' market is open on Saturday mornings from April to October selling local produce, baked goods, granola, jellies – all top fare. Huge fans keep the space cool. Front St and GE Patterson Ave, Memphis, TN 38150, www.memphisfarmersmarket.com

THE LAMPLIGHTER IS THE MOST PERFECT HOLE IN THE WALL BAR. PEOPLE FLOCK THERE FOR EXCEPTIONAL JAZZ MUSIC, TALL CANS OF PBR, A GAME OF POOL, A GAME OF CHESS, ITS KINDA LIKE THE HIPSTER VERSION OF CHEERS.

CULTURE

CONCEPT GALLERY A medium-sized space in the South Main Arts District (such as it is) showcasing some edgy local talent, including work by my good self on occasion. 314 South Main St, Memphis, TN 38103, www.theconceptgallery.com

D EDGE ART & UNIQUE TREASURES A little gallery/shop selling original framed canvasses, usually with a kind of Southern folk-art vibe as well as art objects and furniture. They have a couple really good artists on their books. 550 South Main St, Memphis, TN 38103

DAVID LUSK GALLERY This gallery represents a few of my friends and colleagues, and is the most professional gallery gallery in town. The work tends to be youthful and fun/witty – definitely worth checking out. 4540 Poplar Ave, Memphis, TN 38117

PLAYHOUSE ON THE SQUARE A new, impressive, and much deserved building for Memphis's only professional theater company. It has a great atmosphere and they put on some awesome stuff. 51 South Cooper St, Memphis, TN 38150, www.playhouseonthesquare.org

THE ORPHEUM A theater in an amazing 19th Century building that has been carefully restored, but is still apparently haunted. They put on Broadway shows and sometimes classic movies like *Rocky Horror* and *Breakfast at Tiffany's*. 203 South Main St, Memphis, TN 38103, www.orpheum-memphis.com

MALCO STUDIO ON THE SQUARE All the good movie theaters in town are owned by Malco (Malco Paradiso, Malco Ridgeway 4), but this is the best of the lot. The five screening rooms are small and cozy, but the technology is top dollar. They show a lot of arty/indie movies and serve booze and cheese plates at the bar. 2105 Court Ave, Memphis, TN 38104, www.malco.com

THE PYRAMID A massive sports arena built in the early 90s in homage to the city's namesake in Egypt. It never took off and is a total turkey. What will it become? It's the mystery of the pyramids all over again. Auction Ave, Memphis, TN 38103

COOPER YOUNG FESTIVAL Cooper Young is an up-and-coming neighborhood. Every September, they hold a nice little festival with crafty stalls and some good music. www.cooperyoungfestival.com

THE LEVITT SHELL Awesome outdoor venue in Overton Park where Elvis played his first concert. It's newly renovated (really well renovated actually), and holds a series of free concerts by local musicians every summer. 1930 Poplar Ave, Memphis, TN 38104, www.levittshell.org

STAX MUSEUM Stax Records made the careers of some amazing artists – Issac Hayes, Otis Redding, Booker T & the MGs…. This museum in the renovated studios is well worth a visit. It really shows how the city's musical history evolved. 870 East McLemore Ave, Memphis, TN 38106, www.soulsvilleusa.com

SUN STUDIO Sun Studio really is the birthplace of rock n' roll, and this is kind of a bucket list recommendation. The tour is expensive and 'interactive', which basically means you can play air guitar and sing on an original Sun Studios mic – but it's still kind of a must-see. 706 Union Ave, Memphis, TN 38103, www.sunstudio.com

GO

SHELBY FOREST STATE PARK This park is only 20-minutes drive from the city, but feels a million miles away with hiking trails, streams, Frisbee golf, natural swimming ponds, fishing, and camping. You can cycle down Jackson's Hill for some nice views of the river. 910 Riddick Road, Millington, TN 38053

THE RIVER AT SUNSET The Mississippi defines Memphis, and it's so beautiful at sunset. You can get the best views from a riverboat tour or from Mud Island River Park (take the monorail over there), or from Harbortown.

ALEX WARBLE

MIAMI, FLORIDA BY MICHELLE WEINBERG

I emigrated to Miami 12 years ago from New York with no intention of relocating permanently. I was invited by a foundation to do my work, and was generously provided with a studio, an apartment, and introductions to the small but friendly art community. It was a charmed existence, wheeling my then four-year-old son on Lincoln Road, the focal point of South Beach, where there was always a crowd, even in the heat of that first summer. A great bookstore, vintage shops, cafes, and row upon row of intimately-scaled, pastel apartment buildings, all a stones throw from the wondrous ocean... plus tropical breezes that keep it cooler than Manhattan in mid-summer. It was everything an artist from New York needs, and I've never looked back.

Miami is a fantastic place to visit. As a stopping point along the way to the Keys or the Everglades, it's good for a short trip or a longer stay, and the art scene is growing by leaps and bounds. It's a huge city, with a vast amount of diversity. There is much poverty that stays relatively out of sight if you cling to the shore and the well-to-do suburbs. But a short drive outside the tourist zones will reveal the strange, grubby, amazing cityscape that has provided me with so much inspiration for my work.

The culture is also incredibly diverse. I once read an interview with someone who said that he liked Miami because "it's so close to the United States." All too true. Miami feels more like the unofficial capital of Latin America than an American city. Cubans raised Miami to the grown-up stature it enjoys today, and a further influx of people from Central and South America means that Spanish is spoken literally everywhere. Miami is also the American Riviera, in that many Europeans, particularly from France, Italy, and Switzerland water here in the winters as well.

As a transplanted New Yorker, I am never satisfied with a homogenous culture and I restlessly seek out the places, food and music that all these cultures bring to the city. As a result, some of the places I've listed are off the beaten track and more convenient if you have more time. One last note: Miami is not a town known for excellence in customer service, so don't be surprised by a vacant stare when you inquire about something. That said, I hope I'm recommending some of the more amenable places where attention to detail – and to you – is evident.

STAY

VICEROY If you want over-the-top luxury in the classic Miami way, head to the Viceroy, with decor by the extremely trendy and gem-crazed Kelly Wearstler. Not as pricey as South Beach locations, but easily surpassing many of them in amenities, the Viceroy has a pool and bar setup high in the clouds, and a fabulous spa with immaculate, sunken white marble hot tubs in a posh solarium where you can soak and watch the cruise ships depart from Government Cut far below. A day spa pass is $30 – not bad – so you can try it a la carte. 485 Brickell Ave, Miami, FL 33131, www.viceroymiami.com

MIAMI RIVER INN Travel back in time to Victorian-era Miami in this family-owned establishment that offers a quiet alternative to the flashy high-rise *Miami Vice* experience. Located near Downtown, on the historic and fascinating Miami River, it's also affordable. 118 Southwest South River Dr, Miami, FL 33130, www.miamiriverinn.com

TOWNHOUSE HOTEL The Townhouse Hotel is one of those lovely Deco hotels perched right on the beach. Smallish rooms, hip restaurant, hip decor, hip staff. It also has a fantastic rooftop bar with seductive and from which comfy seating to enjoy the moonlight. Owned and operated by Mr Amir Ben-Zion, also the owner of Miss Yip Chinese restaurant (see Eat). The guy clearly knows what he's doing. 150 20th St, Miami Beach, FL 33139, www.townhousehotel.com

KATANA Because I live nearby, Katana is a weekly ritual for me, my son, and my boyfriend. It's a delight. Sushi on color-coded plates swooshes by on boats in a little moat. At the end of the meal, the plates are stacked up and counted. There are fancier Japanese restaurants in Miami, but none as fun. And you walk away with change in your pocket. Only open evenings after 6pm. 920 71st St, Miami Beach, FL 33141

KON CHAU You'll need a car to get here, but Kon Chau is a bit of a discovery in South Miami for cheap, authentic, and delicious dim sum. It's conveniently located next to Lucky Oriental Market, which is perhaps the most comprehensive Chinese market in Miami. 8376 Bird Rd, Miami, FL 33155

MIAMI JUICE This great all-natural juice and food place has just moved to larger quarters to accommodate the crowds demanding their daily fix of amazing smoothies and fruit salad. Other dishes have an Israeli/healthy emphasis, and staff are friendly. 16210 Collins Ave, Sunny Isles Beach, FL 33160, www.miamijuice.com

MISS YIP Miss Yip is hands down the best Chinese restaurant in Miami. Located right off Lincoln Road, it's got a super cool atmosphere, excellent Lychee martinis and Peking duck. It's where I go when I want a real treat. Can be combined with a trip to the Regal Cinema to catch the latest Hollywood blockbuster. 1661 Meridian Ave, Miami Beach, FL 33139, www.missyipchinesecafe.com

TAP TAP A South Beach institution, Tap Tap is a creative Haitian restaurant that couldn't exist anywhere else in the world – not even in New York or Haiti. Its walls are covered with traditional voodoo murals, and live music makes it a rowdy, fun place to be. The mojitos are my favorites. 819 5th St, Miami Beach, FL 33139, www.taptaprestaurant.com

CÔTE GOURMET This is a bit out of the way in quiet Miami Shores, mainland Miami. A car is required, but it's worth it for the French food prepared with love by a true mom and daughter operation. Excellent salads and a fresh pea soup with the most beautiful green color! Can be pricier for dinner. It's somewhat hidden inside a medical office building – go figure. 9999 Northeast 2nd Ave, Miami Shores, FL 33138

FOX'S SHERRON INN Fox's is a classic, dark-paneled eatery – really old school. Good for getting close to your lover in a booth and spilling a martini all over yourself, which is what I did. The food is surprisingly good, but it's the atmosphere, sooty paintings and low lighting – a bit of Old Florida, that makes it unique. 6030 South Dixie Hwy, Miami, FL 33143

JOEY'S A fantastic new addition to Miami's Wynwood Arts District, where there were formerly no options to eat anything at all – good, bad or indifferent. Here is a casual, but elegant place with a lovely outdoor patio, a great wine list, an authentic pizza oven, really yummy Italian light bites, panini, and larger plates. A little oasis of affordable luxury that attracts lots of art world aficionados. 2506 Northwest 2nd Ave, Miami, FL 33127, www.joeyswynwood.com

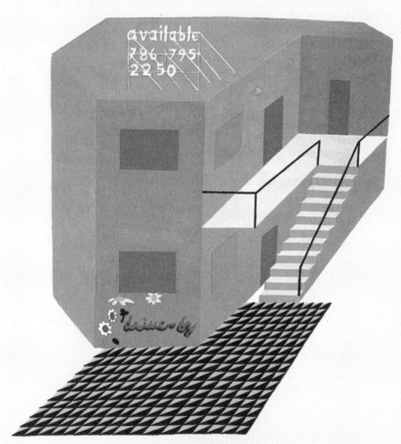

MAGNUM I'm not a great frequenter of bars, but Magnum is an original and merits a visit. One of the earliest gay bars in Miami, it retains the look and feel of a cosy speakeasy, all red velvet walls and heavy mirrors. The giant bar is very friendly, and the menu is classic and satisfying. But it's the piano bar with a rotating bunch of singers who rip through Broadway tunes (my least favorite) and old standards (really great) that is the main draw. Open late, healthy cocktails, super friendly and welcoming atmosphere. 709 Northeast 79th St, Miami, FL 33138, www.magnumlounge.com

BIN NO. 18 Bin 18 is just about my favorite place to go after art openings, near to Downtown and Wynwood and the Design District. Refreshingly theme-less, devoted to locals rather than dragnetting unsuspecting tourists (as in Lincoln Road), it's a wine bar with an excellent beer selection, and great cheese and charcuterie boards. I highly recommend the full meals there as well, but I rarely get around to them! 1800 Biscayne Blvd Ste 107, Miami, FL 33132, www.bin18miami.com

RED LIGHT Although Red Light is also a restaurant with a pretty creative menu, it is a decent full bar. Sit downstairs and outside along the murky rivulet or canal (God knows what it is!) under colorful lanterns and enjoy a cocktail while the neon glow of the latest incarnation of the strip joint plays on the surface of the water. It's the epitome of Miami, and right across from Magnum, in case you want to make a whole night of it. 7700 Biscayne Blvd, Miami, FL 33138, www.redlightmiami.com

DRINK

BUENOS AIRES BAKERY My neck of Miami Beach is known as Little Buenos Aires, as so many entrepeneurial Argentinians have opened restaurants and cafes there. This one is my favorite. Excellent coffee - strong or milky, and a huge selection of mini-sandwiches, sweets, quiches, and tortilla Española served all day. A great spot to hit before or after the beach. 7134 Collins Ave, Miami Beach, FL 33141, www.buenosairesbakeryandcafe.com

A LA FOLIE Two locations, both in South Beach. The one on Española Way is good for taking in the South Beach atmosphere and nightlife (and the Miami Beach Cinematheque), but the Sunset Harbor setting offers a water view and has better parking. Both serve authentic crepes, baguettes, sandwiches, and excellent coffees and teas. Not expensive. 516 Española Way, and 1701 Sunset Harbor Dr, Miami Beach, FL 33139, www.alafoliecafe.com

SHOP

RED, WHITE, AND BLUE THRIFT STORE

I believe you never really know a place until you invest several hours rifling through the castoffs of its residents. Miami is a remarkable destination for thrift-shopping. Northerners shed their winter clothing, and old folks with cool vintage stuff die here. Flamingo Plaza, in the distinguished enclave of Hialeah (sarcasm, sorry) boasts at least four football-field sized thrift shops, but if you're not ready for an entire day, head directly for Red, White, and Blue in the corner. You'll be amazed. Pick up a used suitcase to cart your stuff home. 12640 Northeast 6th Ave, Miami, FL 33161, www.redwhiteandbluethriftstore.com

NIBA

NiBa, the creation of Nisi Berryman, stocks the most delightful selection of things for the home. From furniture to pillows, artworks, jewelry, and all manner of decorative bibelots, NiBa is colorful, cutting edge, and just dreamy to wander into. A centerpiece of the Design District. 39 Northeast 39 St, Miami, 33137, www.nibahome.com

KARELLE LEVY

Hands down the most inventive knitwear you will ever see, Karelle Levy's studio/showroom is a place of art production as much as it is fashion. One-of-a-kinds are pricey, like buying art, but her regular stuff is affordable, and she often has sales. 180 Northwest 25th St, Miami, FL 33127, www.krelwear.com

MARIMEKKO

I grew up under the influence of Finnish design religion Marimekko in the 1960s in New York, but many Americans have never even heard of it. Thanks to Miamian Cristina Dominguez for opening a rare American Marimekko outpost in Miami, right in the Design District. 3940 North Miami Ave, FL 33127, www.marimekkomiami.com

COCONUT GROVE FARMERS' MARKET
Unlike the farmers' markets I know in New York City, in which many purveyors meet at a location, this one is the product of Glaser Organic Farms, located in the Redlands agricultural district, south of Miami proper. A vast array of raw foods, nut butters, nori wraps, and the most astonishing desserts complement a huge selection of local and national produce. Saturdays 10am-7pm. 3300 Grand Ave, Coconut Grove, FL 33133, www.glaserorganicfarms.com/market.html

EPICURE This South Beach market is the nearest thing to the fancy food emporiums I frequented in New York. I go for the cheeses alone – but only on payday, as it's somewhat pricey. Their bakery and readymade foods are excellent – perfect picnic fare. 1656 Alton Rd, Miami Beach, FL 33139, www.epicuremarket.com

BOOKS & BOOKS When describing Miami, the word literate does not immediately come to mind, however Mitchell Kaplan singlehandedly saves us with Books & Books. As is the fashion, the bookstore sports excellent cafes at its South Beach and Coral Gables locations, as well as a really respectable series of readings and concerts by locals, nationals and internationals. Check out poetry by another transplant to Miami, Campbell McGrath, and look for *Miami Contemporary Artists,* a coffee table book on the local art scene (featuring yours truly). 265 Aragon Ave, Coral Gables, Miami, FL 33134, and 927 Lincoln Rd, Miami Beach, FL 33139, www.booksandbooks.com

GALLERY DIET Miami's art scene has grown exponentially since I arrived in 1998, creating a favorable environment for young gallerists like Nina Johnson to have a go at it. Her program focuses on installation and performance. Introduce yourself when you visit – she's a delightful presence. Second Saturdays are the monthly artwalk nights. You'll have to negotiate crowds, but it's lively. 174 Northwest 23rd St, Miami, FL 33127, www.gallerydiet.com

THE WOLFSONIAN MUSEUM Comprising the mammoth collection of one Mitchell Wolfson Jr, the Wolfsonian presents artifacts from the applied arts: graphic design, architecture, and industrial design. Dynamic temporary exhibitions complement excerpts from the permanent collection. It has a fantastic bookstore/cafe where you can conduct informal research with impunity. 1001 Washington Ave, Miami Beach, FL 33139, www.wolfsonian.org

MIAMI ART MUSEUM Located in the heart of Downtown Miami, MAM hosts major retrospectives of internationally recognized artists while supporting local and national artists in regular programming. A great art bookstore included. On the same plaza is the main branch of Miami-Dade Public Library, which has an impressive exhibition program as well. 101 West Flagler St, Miami, FL 33130, www.miamiartmuseum.org

LOCUST PROJECTS One of the best-known alternative spaces in Miami, Locust Projects recently migrated from Wynwood to its new home in the Design District. Features a changing program of group and solo exhibitions by emerging artists from around the world in addition to work by local artists. 155 Northeast 38th St, Suite 100, Miami, FL 33137, www.locustprojects.org

SWAMPSPACE An eccentric, changing exhibition space masterminded by Oliver Sanchez. You never know what to expect as each month this intimate and discreet storefront space is transformed by another artist. Just around the corner from Locust Projects. 3821 Northeast 1st Ct, Miami, FL 33137, http://swampspace.blogspot.com

PRIVATE COLLECTIONS It's hard to pick just one! A bonafide South Florida phenomenon, private collectors' vast exhibition spaces rival museums. The newest, De la Cruz Collection, is a stunning example of art and architecture working in sync, staffed by Design and Architecture High School students who are studying down the block: 23 Northeast 41st St, Miami, FL 33137, www.delacruzcollection.org. Next up, the Rubell Collection is the one that started it all: 95 Northwest 29th St, Miami, FL 33127, www.rfc.museum. CIFO stands for the collection of Ella Cicernos-Fontanals and is located in a Downtown building whose façade is adorned with a mosaic bamboo forest designed by local architect Rene Gonzales: 1018 North Miami Ave, Miami, FL 33136, www.cifo.org.

ART BASEL MIAMI BEACH Each year, in the first weekend of December, Miami hosts droves of art collectors, curators, writers, dealers, and some artists too for the winter companion to Art Basel. The main fair is housed in the Miami Beach Convention Center, but satellite fairs, parties, performances, local gallery and museum extravaganzas, and more fill the weekend calendar – and often the weeks before and after. It's mind-boggling and hugely fascinating. Design Miami dovetails with the art event, and is also well worth visiting. www.artbaselmiamibeach.com and www.designmiami.com.

MIAMI BEACH CINEMATHEQUE The Cinematheque, under the direction of the indefatigable Dana Keith, is the sole outpost for foreign, independent and experimental cinema in Miami. Check their schedule online. 512 Española Way, Miami Beach, FL 33139, www.mbcinema.com

RHYTHM FOUNDATION The most adventurous, international music events you'll hear. Check the website for the schedule. All the photos of the musicians are taken by my good friend Luis Olazabal. www.rhythmfoundation.org

TIGERTAIL Try and catch a performance from one of Miami's best producers if you can. All the information is online. www.tigertail.org

MIAMI RIVERWALK Seven works of public art by local artists (including myself) are installed on a wall that curves alongside the Miami River, right where it meets the open bay. It's a great spot to walk and picnic.

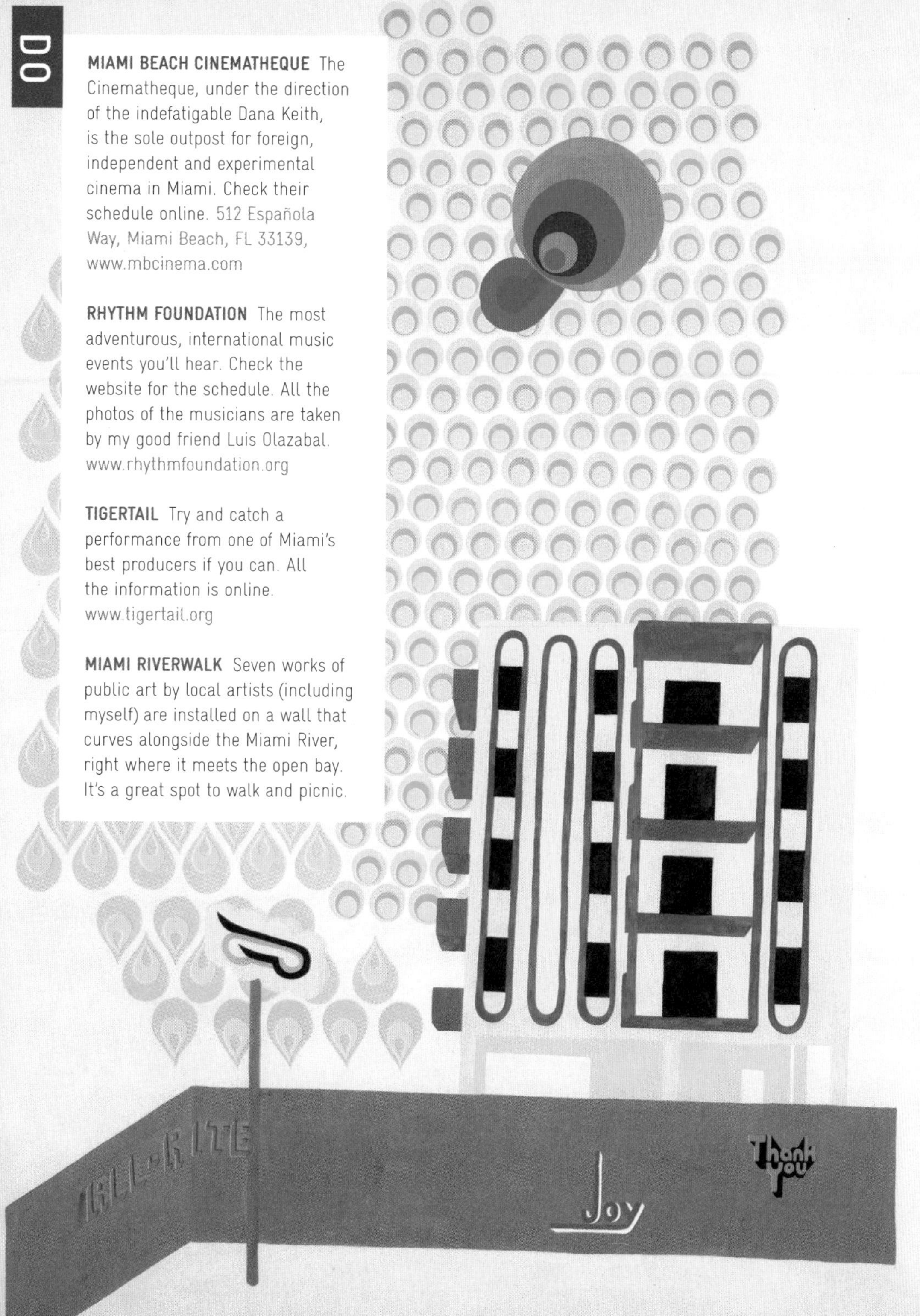

MIKE
KROL'S
Milwaukee

WITH HELP

FROM

ANDY
BRAWNER

MILWAUKEE, WISCONSIN BY MIKE KROL

Milwaukee: Beer. German food, Polish food. Beer. Brats and sauerkraut. Cheese. These are obvious and significant draws when considering visiting this city, but there's much more to the place than that. Midwest style is the real deal, and Milwaukee's got it seeping from its sweaty pores. It's a real blue collar town: warehouses, factories, industries, steel bridges, train yards and smokestacks, and on good days the smell of the breweries. Faded ads on the sides of brick buildings from the 20s to the 50s, architecture from the 60s, condensed sans-serif type mixed with hand painted script lettering. To a designer or illustrator, Milwaukee will provide all the visual inspiration that one would expect from a place whose pop-culture exports include *Laverne and Shirley*, *Happy Days*, Miller Beer, and Harley Davidson.

The city lies alongside Lake Michigan, where the three rivers of the Menomonee, the Kinnickinnic and the Milwaukee meet. The weather is typical of Wisconsin. Brutally cold and snowy in the winter. Calm, sunny, and relaxing in the summer, with tons of outdoor festivals celebrating everything from music to ethnicity to food. Milwaukee is definitely a place that sits tight in the winter and then celebrates every moment of warm weather.

It's an easy city to navigate, as it's mostly laid out on a grid-system. Neighborhood-wise, check out Bayview, the cool south-side neighborhood where the hipsters live these days; the East Side, where the hipsters used to live and the home of University of Wisconsin Milwaukee, and the Third Ward, with its old warehouses and its public market. All of these areas are tucked along the mighty Lake Michigan.

Milwaukee won't try to impress you. It doesn't talk very loudly and has something of an inferiority complex. If you want to find what's good about it, you might have to dig a bit – but I promise it's worth it. You might just get hooked on its charm and realize why so many of us end up staying a while.

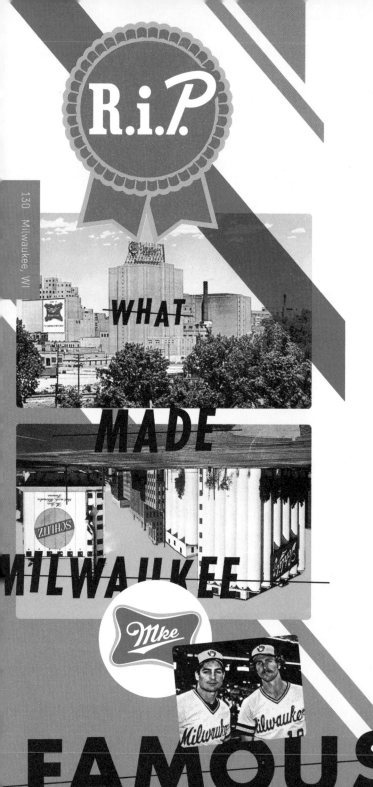

R.i.P.

WHAT MADE MILWAUKEE FAMOUS

Mke

IRON HORSE This place is "new" (actually really old) and real cool. An old warehouse with lots of motorcycles all over the place. Seeing as Milwaukee is the birthplace and headquarters of Harley Davidson, it makes sense. The people who put it together seem to know something about design. 500 West Florida St, Milwaukee, WI 53204, www.theironhorsehotel.com

PFISTER Old-school Milwaukee style. Tradition and money stay here. If Bruce Springsteen plays, or a celebrity visits for some unknown reason, they're probably at the Pfister. The place is allegedly haunted, so watch yourself. Ghosts love Milwaukee. Seriously. 424 East Wisconsin Ave, Milwaukee, WI 53202, www.thepfisterhotel.com

HOTEL METRO A middle-ground between the traditional Pfister and the hip Iron Horse. Classy but a little style-y too. 411 East Mason St, Milwaukee, WI 53202, www.hotelmetro.com

THE PALOMINO A Bayview fixture. The vibe is funky/gritty diner meets hipster bar. Great jukebox and great food – such as deep fried corn bread balls served with crazy sauces. The decor is faintly western. Somehow it all adds up. This place is by far one of our favorites. 2491 South Superior St, Milwaukee, WI 53207, www.myspace.com/palominobar

BEANS & BARLEY A deli, a restaurant, a mini-grocery store, a cool goods shop. Eat brunch here on a weekend morning, but make sure you're not in a hurry. Everybody eats brunch here. Milwaukee people love brunch. 1901 East North Ave, Milwaukee, WI 53202, www.beansandbarley.com

COMET A certain cable network featured Comet recently and made a big deal of its penchant for bacon, but locals know this East Side venue has a lot more going for it than swine. This is a 'slow food' kind of place. They aren't going to rush your meal, but they're going to make it good. Try the meatloaf and mashed potatoes. Reasonable prices and great vibe. 1947 North Farwell Ave, Milwaukee, WI 53202, www.thecometcafe.com

KOPPA'S Locally owned grocery store with Fulbeli Deli serving legendary sandwiches like The Bread Favre, the Oogle Noogle, and the Deli Lama. May the kraut be with you. Kind of silly, totally Polish, totally Milwaukee. Fans of artsy Midwest-style design will dig this place. 1940 North Farwell Ave, Milwaukee, WI 53202, www.koppas.com

CRAZY WATER This place doesn't scream "Milwaukee," but sometimes that's a good thing. I've heard it described as 'European bistro style', whatever that means. 839 South 2nd St, Milwaukee, WI 53204, www.crazywatermilwaukee.com

CAFE LULU Back to Bayview. Lulu is another one of those really good, really reasonably priced places. Visit in the summer when the front of the joint is wide open to the lively scene on Kinnickinnic Ave (don't even try to pronounce it – just call it "KK" – we'll understand). 2265 South Howell Ave, Milwaukee, WI 53207, www.lulubayview.com

TRANSFER Pizza, deformed and delicious. Milwaukee has some great joints for pizzas, but this place is new and hot on the scene. 101 West Mitchell St, Milwaukee, WI 53204, www.transfermke.com

CACTUS CLUB

QUALITY NEIGHBOR HOOD

SINCE 1867

Bay View
Bay View
Bay View
Bay View
Bay View
Bay View

HOLLER HOUSE

BUCKLE YOUR RUST BELT

AT RANDOM In this place it's still 1957. Famous for exotic ice cream drinks served out of large fishbowl-esque glasses complete with paper umbrellas. Highly recommended for the retro-loving designer, although it's not even technically retro, because it never let go of the past. 2501 South Delaware Ave, Milwaukee, WI 53207

BARNACLE BUD'S You do like Jimmy Buffet, right? Yeah, us neither. But Barnacle Bud's needs to be mentioned for the sick thrill of almost feeling like you're in Key West when in fact you're in Milwaukee. It's attached to a marina. Boats go by as you sip rum drinks. Weird times. 1955 South Hilbert St, Milwaukee, WI 53207, www.barnacle-buds.com

BURNHEARTS This bar is owned by the local indie band, Decibully, and aims to please the musicians of Milwaukee. If there's a national band in town, there's a good chance they'll end up here after their gig. Like Spoon. 2599 South Logan Ave, Milwaukee, WI 53207, www.myspace.com/burnhearts

THE SAFE HOUSE A Milwaukee legend. Kinda *Spy vs Spy* clubhouse meets prohibition era speakeasy. You need a password to get in or else they humiliate you in front of all the patrons. Good luck. 779 North Front St, Milwaukee, WI 53202, www.safe-house.com

TONY'S TAVERN A secret gem in the Fifth Ward of Milwaukee. Untouched since the late 1800s – except for the addition of a jukebox from the 60s. No one understands why U2's 'Mysterious Ways' is the only post-1960s song in the rotation. 12 South 2nd St, Milwaukee, WI 53204

VALUE VILLAGE A thrift store across the street from The Domes (see Go). Mike scored a sweatshirt with a large deer head and three other shirts: one with a howling wolf head, one with a snow owl, and one with a duck. It's just that kind of Wisconsin thrift store. 729 South Layton Blvd, Milwaukee, WI 53215

ATOMIC RECORDS Closed in 2009 but deserves mention due to its 24 years as Milwaukee's best source for independent music. Hard to find vinyl, rare cds, collector ephemera, and in-store performances. You can still buy the famously awesome Atomic Records T-shirt off their website, as seen on celebs like Dave Grohl, Frank Black, and Mike Krol. RIP Atomic. www.atomic-records.com

YELLOWJACKET Great vintage clothing store on Brady Street in Milwaukee's East Side. The owners bought an old house and put their store right inside. Check out all of Brady St while you're at it. You'll like the area. 1237 East Brady Street, Milwaukee, WI 53202, www.yellowjacketvintageclothing.com

SPARROW COLLECTIVE AND OWL EYES Two different collectives on KK in Bayview selling handmade clothing, jewelry, music, and zines by independent and local designers and craftsters. This place is exactly what you think it is. Both at: 2224 S Kinnickinnic Ave, Milwaukee, WI 53207, www.myspace.com/owleyes

TWO MILLION WISCONSINITES CAN'T BE WRONG

MILWAUKEE ART MUSEUM We blackmailed Calatrava and he designed an addition to our art museum. It's pretty amazing. Definitely a must-see if you are an art type. In fact, it's a must-see, period. 700 Art Museum Dr, Milwaukee, WI 53202, www.mam.org

CACTUS CLUB Your classic hole-in-the-wall punk/alternative/rock club that gets solid local stuff and underground acts. It's kind of like seeing a show in your basement. Or in a shed. Next door to The Palomino. 2496 South Wentworth Ave, Milwaukee, WI 53207, www. cactusclubmilwaukee.com

EISNER MUSEUM OF ADVERTISING AND DESIGN One of the few museums in the world devoted to, well, advertising and design. It's pretty small, but cheap to get into and usually has something worth checking out. We are proud to have had work displayed here. 208 North Water St, Milwaukee, WI 53202, www.eisnermuseum.org

ART VS CRAFT Milwaukee's first DIY indie market happens once a year around November. It has a reputation for showcasing the best art/design/handmade crafts from the Midwest and beyond. www.artvscraftmke.com

THE ORIENTAL Old movie theater where, on certain nights, a weird dude plays the pipe organ before your movie starts. Terrifying. Totally haunted. 2230 North Farwell Ave, Milwaukee, WI 53202, www.landmarktheatres.com

THE PABST/THE RIVERSIDE/TURNER HALL Suddenly we have three interrelated and totally amazing music venues where we get pretty much every show worth seeing. Andy loved seeing Grizzly Bear at the Pabst in 2009, but Krol doesn't like Grizzly Bear. It's criminal and ridiculous to go to a show at the Pabst and not drink tallboy cans of Pabst Blue Ribbon. Got that? Criminal and ridiculous. 144 East Wells St, 116 West Wisconsin Ave, and 1034 North 4th St, respectively, www.pabsttheater.org

BAYVIEW BOWL Milwaukee is famous for bowling. Did you know that? There are several bowling alleys in the Milwaukee area, but this one is geared towards 20 and 30-somethings who like to party and discuss art while they roll. 2416 South Kinnickinnic Ave, Milwaukee, WI 53207

THE DOMES (MITCHELL PARK CONSERVATORY) The Domes are awesome. They are what you think: big domes, but with special floral gardens and jungle vegetation and stuff. They've never been updated and have a very 60s vibe. Actually, that's not entirely true – they were recently updated with new state-of-the-art LED lights, so they light up at night like the Eiffel Tower. Whatever. Domes, you are still very 60s looking to us. 524 South Layton Blvd, Milwaukee, WI 53215, www.milwaukeedomes.org

THIRD WARD WALK They used to call Milwaukee "Cream City" because of all the cream colored bricks that were used to make the awesome old buildings in this area. Industrial architecture, faded ads on sides of buildings, large sans-serif steel type — you get the idea. This area also houses lots of little shops and stores: skateboards, vinyl toys, upscale clothes, fancy stuff for your pet, and a nice Design Within Reach studio.

MILLER PARK Does your baseball stadium have a roof? Yes? Well, does it MOVE? Our does. Sometimes it even moves when it's not supposed to. Our major league baseball team, the Brewers, is not great, but we have giant two-legged sausage beasts who race around the field during the seventh inning. 201 South 46th St, Milwaukee, WI 53214, www.brewers.mlb.com

LAKE DRIVE FROM WHITEFISH BAY TO MILWAUKEE ART MUSEUM Milwaukee people aren't exactly beach-type people (mostly due to the list of bars and restaurants previously mentioned). But we kind of have a beach that sometimes people use. Whether you use it or not, drive along the lake and see Milwaukee's biggest old houses and the lake. And maybe avert your eyes from the people on the beach.

VIOLENT FEMMES

LARGEST
4-SIDED
CLOCK
IN THE ★
WORLD

ADAM TURMAN'S MINNEAPOLIS Minn.

Bars, bikes, & beers

MINNEAPOLIS, MINNESOTA BY ADAM TURMAN

Minneapolis is the largest city in Minnesota, although it's quite small when compared to larger cities on the east and west coasts of the US. But size isn't everything, it's what's inside that counts, and man, this city has a ton of heart.

Minneapolis was historically known as the 'Mill City' because of all the flour milling companies that took advantage of the power that the Mississippi and Minnesota rivers could provide. To this day, the milling industry of Mpls is alive and well, and the Milling District is one of the most beautiful and historic areas of the city.

There are a bunch of other communities and neigborhoods worth visiting as well, each with its own character. Nordeast was traditionally where the mill workers lived, and is still considered a working-class community, with tons of bars and churches alongside each other. It also has great theaters and restaurants and a fantastic Arts District. Uptown is the unofficial hipster hangout – a great place to shop, eat, and people watch. Then there's Midtown – a lot of ethnic neighborhoods and cultural color make it interesting, and the annual No Coast Craft-o-Rama in December is a must for anyone interested in handmade goodies. It's also home to one of the best commuter/recreational bicycle trails in the United States – the Midtown Greenway. Finally, Downtown you'll find the Business District with Nicollet Mall running through its middle. It's pedestrian/bicycle friendly with shops, restaurants, and pubs for the weary traveler, and a cluster of good theaters.

The Lakes that Minnesota is so famous for border Uptown on the west side and are great to bike, run, walk, or sit and watch the sailboats. The three that are closest are: Lake of the Isles, Lake Calhoun, and Lake Harriet. Many of the lumber and milling barons have built castle-like homes here, and beautiful architecture abounds.

I love Minneapolis. It's one of those towns that once you get to know it, it doesn't feel very big. No one seems to be separated by more than one degree. There's a lot of diversity, and a lot of things to do, including an amazing music scene and great art, food, beer, and cycling. One final note: you may have heard Minneapolis supposedly has a twin called Saint Paul. However, if you're a local to either city, this is not a theory you would endorse. We'll leave Saint Paul for another time.

ALOFT HOTEL A cool boutique hotel with a super hip bar, right in the heart of the Milling District. It's one block off the Mississippi River, and overlooks the Gold Medal Flour Mill. 900 Washington Ave South, Minneapolis, MN 55415, www.starwoodhotels.com

THE DEPOT MINNEAPOLIS This used to be one of the main railroad depots in Minneapolis, and it's been renovated and updated with an ice rink and water park. I know what you're thinking, but honestly, it's cool. It's fun with or without kids. 225 3rd Ave South, Minneapolis, MN 55401, www.thedepotminneapolis.com

LE MÉRIDIEN CHAMBERS MINNEAPOLIS High-end and super-fancy with chic modern rooms and amazing furniture. The food at the lower level restaurant is fantastic. Plus it's located on Hennepin Ave, right in the heart of Downtown. Definitely worth checking out (even if you don't check in). 901 Hennepin Ave, Minneapolis, MN 55403, www.starwoodhotels.com

W MINNEAPOLIS – THE FOSHAY
The W is cool for a few reasons, but mostly it's awesome because it's inside the Foshay Tower – which was the tallest building in Minneapolis when it was built in 1929. The W has preserved the exterior and made the interior all sleek and modern. 821 Marquette Ave South, Minneapolis, MN 55402, www.whotels.com

EAT STREET If variation is what you're after, Eat Street is the place to go. There's everything from Asian to Mexican and vegan to BBQ. Asia, Jasmine Deli, Salsa Ala Salsa, and Black Forest are a few of my faves. Nicollet Ave, North of Lake St, Minneapolis, MN 55408

CAKE EATER BAKERY Cake Eater is a small bakery tucked into a quiet neighborhood, but it has loads of personality... and the pastries are to die for. 2929 East 25th St, Minneapolis, MN 55406, cakeeaterbakery.com

RED STAG SUPPER CLUB The Red Stag is awesome. It hosts live performances from local bands and draws a nice crowd. Great atmosphere, delcious food. 509 1st Ave Northeast, Minneapolis, MN 55413, www.redstagsupperclub.com

NYE'S POLONAISE Everyone who visits Minneapolis needs to go to Nye's. Seriously. Grab some pierogis and eat them in the glittery gold booths to the sound of Sweet Lou Snider at the piano, or dance the polka to the World's Most Dangerous Polka Band in the bar. Good times! 112 East Hennepin Ave, Minneapolis, MN 55414, www.nyespolonaise.com

CAFE 28 You'll find Cafe 28 in Linden Hills, a really nice neighborhood near Lake Harriet. It's a bistro with a commitment to sustainable agriculture, and the food speaks for itself. Plus they serve Surly – the best beer in the country. I'll take any excuse to eat here. 2724 West 43rd St, Minneapolis, MN 55410, www.cafetwentyeight.com

PIZZA LUCÉ The best pizza in the city hands down in my opinion. They have mashed potato pizza with bacon, I mean come on! Lucé has been kicking ass since 1993, with new locations popping up throughout the Twin Cities. It's one of those places that you might end up in after a long night of partying, chilling, biking – whatever. They're open til the wee hours of the morning. 119 North 4th St, Seward, 2200 East Franklin Ave, and 3200 South Lyndale Ave, www.pizzaluce.com

TOWN TALK DINER Town Talk is uniquely daring with its combinations of flavors. Get Frickles – fried pickles... I know, I didn't think so either, but they're awesome! The drinks are also great – names like Hair of the Lion, Mexican Pine Cone and Bacon Manhattan will hook you right away. You can get a 40 of Highlife in a wine chiller with two champagne glasses. 2707 East Lake St, Minneapolis, MN 55406, www.towntalkdiner.com

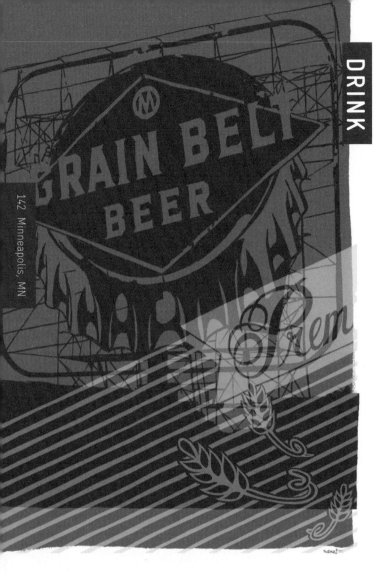

PRACNA ON MAIN Pracna is right on the banks of the mighty Mississsippi. Have a glass of wine or a pint outside, and play with some lego at your table. They also serve food. 117 Southeast Main St, Minneapolis, MN 55414, www.stanthonymain.com

MATT'S BAR All I have to say about this place is that it's the home of the Juicy Lucy... you'll have to take my word for it. If you go on a Friday or Saturday night, you'll want to wear comfy shoes to stand in line. 3500 Cedar Ave South, Minneapolis, MN 55407, www.mattsbar.com

BRIT'S PUB A taste of English style in Downtown Minneapolis. Have a pint and go lawn bowling upstairs on a sunny day. 1110 Nicollet Mall, Minneapolis, MN 55403, www.britspub.com

FIRST AVENUE & THE 7TH STREET ENTRY The home of Prince for crying out loud! It still hosts great bands before they get big, and I've seen some of my all-time favorite performances there. 701 North 1st Ave, Minneapolis, MN 55403, www.first-avenue.com

TRIPLE ROCK SOCIAL CLUB The Triple Rock is owned by one of the members of Minneapolis's best punk rock bands, Dillinger Four. Plus it has food. And we're not talking your average bar food, we're talking po'boy sandwiches that ooze out the sides like crazy. 629 Cedar Ave, Minneapolis, MN 55454, www.triplerocksocialclub.com

SURLY BREWERY TOUR Surly is one of the most popular breweries in Minnesota and the Midwest, and they offer a fun tour most Friday evenings. Make sure to sign up really early – they always fill up. 4811 Dusharme Dr, Minneapolis, MN 55429, www.surlybrewing.com

I LIKE YOU I Like You is run by two super-cool chicks who sell locally handmade products including stuff by yours truly. 501 1st Ave Northeast, Minneapolis, MN 55413, www.ilikeyouonline.com

MITREBOX Great frame shop with a large assortment of fun cards and a lot of gorgeous letterpressed stuff. 213 North Washington Ave, Minneapolis, MN 55401, www.mitreboxframing.com

SHUGA RECORDS Vinyl records! Lots of awesome stuff jammed into a small space in a cool locale. 165 13th Ave Northeast, Minneapolis, MN 55413, www.shugarecords.com

WHO MADE WHO Local Mpls poster designers produce and showcase their work in this space in the heart of Nordeast's Arts District. 158 13th Ave Northeast, Minneapolis, MN 55413, www.whomadewho.etsy.com

ONE ON ONE BIKE STUDIO Run by Gene-O, you can hang out, get a cuppa joe, check out some awesome bicycles, and visit the infamous basement for odd and obscure bikes parts. 117 North Washington Ave, Minneapolis, MN 55401, www.oneononebike.com

CRAFTY PLANET Are you crafty? This place has every shade of wool you can imagine, and everything you might need to make the most efficient use of a yard of fabric. Plus classes for crafters in the making. 2833 Johnson St Northeast, Minneapolis, MN 55418, www.craftyplanet.com

RAGSTOCK AND STEEPLE PEOPLE Two shops in Uptown selling vintage clothing. Ragstock is more selective with some high-end vintage and new stock, whereas Steeple People is more your traditional thrift store, with some great bargains if you have the eye. **RAGSTOCK:** 433 West Lake St, Minneapolis, MN, 55408, **STEEPLE PEOPLE:** 2004 South Lyndale Ave, Minneapolis, MN 55405

SHOP

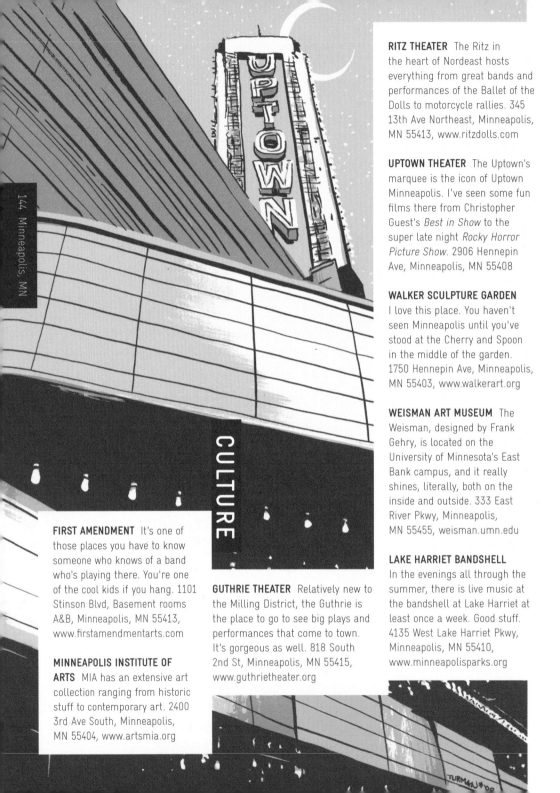

CULTURE

RITZ THEATER The Ritz in the heart of Nordeast hosts everything from great bands and performances of the Ballet of the Dolls to motorcycle rallies. 345 13th Ave Northeast, Minneapolis, MN 55413, www.ritzdolls.com

UPTOWN THEATER The Uptown's marquee is the icon of Uptown Minneapolis. I've seen some fun films there from Christopher Guest's *Best in Show* to the super late night *Rocky Horror Picture Show*. 2906 Hennepin Ave, Minneapolis, MN 55408

WALKER SCULPTURE GARDEN I love this place. You haven't seen Minneapolis until you've stood at the Cherry and Spoon in the middle of the garden. 1750 Hennepin Ave, Minneapolis, MN 55403, www.walkerart.org

WEISMAN ART MUSEUM The Weisman, designed by Frank Gehry, is located on the University of Minnesota's East Bank campus, and it really shines, literally, both on the inside and outside. 333 East River Pkwy, Minneapolis, MN 55455, weisman.umn.edu

LAKE HARRIET BANDSHELL In the evenings all through the summer, there is live music at the bandshell at Lake Harriet at least once a week. Good stuff. 4135 West Lake Harriet Pkwy, Minneapolis, MN 55410, www.minneapolisparks.org

FIRST AMENDMENT It's one of those places you have to know someone who knows of a band who's playing there. You're one of the cool kids if you hang. 1101 Stinson Blvd, Basement rooms A&B, Minneapolis, MN 55413, www.firstamendmentarts.com

MINNEAPOLIS INSTITUTE OF ARTS MIA has an extensive art collection ranging from historic stuff to contemporary art. 2400 3rd Ave South, Minneapolis, MN 55404, www.artsmia.org

GUTHRIE THEATER Relatively new to the Milling District, the Guthrie is the place to go to see big plays and performances that come to town. It's gorgeous as well. 818 South 2nd St, Minneapolis, MN 55415, www.guthrietheater.org

TURMAN #08

CYCLE MINNEAPOLIS

minn.

CHAIN OF LAKES Minneapolis is home to tons of lakes. Many of them in the major metropolitan area have walking/biking trails around them, plus they link together. In the summer there's swimming and in the winter there's ice skating. The three that are closest are: Lake of the Isles, Lake Calhoun, and Lake Harriet. Lake Harriet is wooded and peaceful with a beautiful rose garden and a bandshell. Calhoun is busy but fun with a nice three-mile walking trail, and Lake of the Isles quieter and good for fishing, canoeing and kayaking.
www.minneapolisparks.org

GRAND ROUNDS Minneapolis is a great place for bicycle enthusiasts, and if you're a really keen cyclist, you should try the Grand Rounds (or part of it). It's a linked circuit of parks that go all the way through the city, with over 50 miles of bike paths. It includes the Downtown riverfront, the Mississippi Gorge, Minnehaha, the Chain of Lakes, Theodore Wirth Park, Victory Memorial, and a path through Nordeast. It's the best example of a scenic urban byway in the country.

MIDTOWN GREENWAY A six-mile, traffic-free bicycle highway that cuts right the way through Minneapolis and takes you within a mile of pretty much everywhere you need to go in the city. It used to be a train track, so it's completely flat, and it's been really well maintained, with a smooth, level surface that's even plowed in winter. There's a bike shop and cafe halfway along. You gotta love it.
www.midtowngreenway.org

FRESH WHITE CORN
PRESERVATION HALL
RIPE SWE NECTARIN
ByWATER RESTAURANT
Boudin
KREWE OF KOSMIC DEBRIS
SEA FOODS
FRENCH MARKET
café du monde
MEAT PHONE 531-0031 PO BOYS
NICE & RIPE
tom varisco's
new orleans

NEW ORLEANS, LOUISIANA BY TOM VARISCO

A lot has happened to the New Orleans area in the past few years. First Hurricane Katrina and then the BP oil spill. You could be forgiven for thinking that New Orleans is now floating belly up in a pool of filthy muck. For the record, this is not so. Most of the residents are back, and there is a new sense of optimism flooding the hearts and minds of the locals and the new young do-gooders who moved here to help clean up the city that care forgot and its surrounding waterways. It's an exciting time to live in the Big Easy.

It's hard for me to capture the nature of today's New Orleans in brief. Don't worry, the old New Orleans is still here. The French Quarter, or simply the Quarter to us locals, remains our number one attraction, with Bourbon Street in particular drawing the most visitors. I used to live on Bourbon Street, but I quickly grew tired of the strip club, midway atmosphere. These days I think the bars, clubs, bookstores, coffee houses, markets, and neighborhoods in the Marigny and Bywater Districts are the most interesting. They're still sleepy areas, but now there is also a new feeling. There is live music, vintage clothing, antiques, inexpensive and diverse cuisine, and a healthy, friendly mix of hipsters, artists, and performers of all ages, as well as the exciting new St Claude Avenue art gallery scene. Like the rest of the city, a lot has changed here for the better, but the essence of it remains the same as it ever was.

New Orleans is often referred to as the most European of American cities. If it is, it's a small version. The city proper only occupies about 350 square miles, and a first visit should take you no more than three or four days. It's not a difficult city to get your head round, but you might just find that once you've left its memory lingers on, and like me, you may just want to stay indefinitely in this singular pearl at the mouth of the Mississippi River, where 50 per cent of its land is below sea level, where celebrating anything is encouraged, where happy hour usually means all afternoon, where you can get a po-boy in at least 1,000 locations, where you won't need a coat eight months of the year, and where you'll experience the most tolerant citizenry with a unique sense of identity and humor. This place is open for anything. Something to drink about.

WINDSOR COURT HOTEL This is the upper end of posh. On two luxuriant occasions I've stayed there myself, and I have fond memories of teddy-bear soft towels, bathrobes, crisp bedsheets, mini bar, etc, etc.... There's fine dining in the Grill Room and fine dancing in the Polo Lounge. That name alone should tell you something about the price you will pay to stay. Worth it. 300 Gravier St, New Orleans, LA 70130, www.windsorcourthotel.com

EDGAR DEGAS HOUSE This grand house was once home to its painterly namesake, and is sure to make an impression (sorry about that). As a B&B, it has maintained its original floor plan, and has high ceilings and a lovely balcony. It's located Mid-City between the Quarter and City Park, and is a bit of a hike to get to either – so if you don't have a car, you'll have to learn the bus route. 2306 Esplanade Ave, New Orleans, LA 70119, www.degashouse.com

MARIGNY MANOR HOUSE You're only a short walk away from the Quarter in this 19th Century B&B with its friendly staff and plantation-life feel. There's a classic New Orleans patio and courtyard, lots of antiques, and it's quiet. Ideal for an inexpensive, authentic stay. 2125 North Rampart St, New Orleans, LA 70116, www.marignymanorhouse.com

MELROSE MANSION A very large house on the corner of Burgundy (pronounced BurGUNdy). Friends of mine stayed here a few years ago and loved the high ceilings and antique furnishings. I like the name and location – at the edge of the Quarter and the beginning of the Marigny District. Plus, it's reasonably priced. 937 Esplanade Ave, New Orleans, LA 70116, www.melrosegroup.com

INTERNATIONAL HOUSE I think this is the best designed medium-sized hotel in the city with a spectacularly slick, contemporary lobby. It's in a good Downtown location a couple blocks from Canal Street. Have a cocktail at the decadent, one-of-a-kind bar, Loa. 221 Camp St, New Orleans, LA 70130, www.ihhotel.com

Why you're here may determine where you stay

edgar degas house

windsor court hotel

melrose mansion

marigny manor house

international house

the joint
august
bayona
everyone has an opinion about where to eat and they are all right
parkway tavern
irene's cuisine
domilise's
cochon

This is the hardest section to write about. Where once New Orleans was all neighborhood restaurants serving every dish with thick sauces, the last 20 years has seen a foodie boom, with hundreds of fine restaurants popping up, serving dishes made with fresh, local ingredients in a cuisine sometimes called 'Southern Regional'. Eating here has never been better.

THE JOINT This town does not boast a lot of great barbeque places, but this is it for great pulled pork and ribs at very decent prices. 801 Poland Ave, New Orleans, LA 70117, www.alwayssmokin.com

CAFE RECONCILE This place in the Lower Uptown area, offers young, at risk 16-22 year-olds a chance for a positive turnaround by letting them prepare and serve home cooked meals. Smothered chicken with greens is always a favorite. The prices are very reasonable. It gets crowded, so get there before noon. 1631 Oretha Castle Haley Blvd, New Orleans, LA 70113, www.cafereconcile.com

IRENE'S CUISINE This restaurant in the Quarter serves such dependable, home cooked French Provincial and Italian food that locals don't mind waiting an hour to be seated, and that's very unusual here. My favorite is pollo rosemarino – very juicy marinated chicken pieces with garlic accents that linger and linger. This may sound corny, but I love the way this place sounds. Lots of laughter. Try it. You'll be back. 539 St Philip St, New Orleans, LA 70116

BAYONA Chef Susan Spicer is an old friend of mine, whose surname is remarkably apt. She was one of the first chefs here to re-think the cooking and presentation of local cuisine, and the result is deceptively simple, elegant dishes in a casual, comfortable setting. Try the grilled shrimp with black bean cake. 430 Dauphine St, New Orleans, LA 70112, www.bayona.com

PO'BOYS This sandwich is similar to the gyro, but is uniquely New Orleans. The bread is flaky inside with a hard outer-shell and the main ingredients are traditionally juicy roast beef, fried shrimp, oysters, or soft shell crab. There are literally thousands of places to buy Po'boys. The best are Johnny's in the Quarter, Parasol's in the Irish Channel area Uptown, Parkway Tavern and Bakery in Mid-City, which has the very best (and biggest) roast beef po-boy in town, and Domilise's. This last one is possibly my favorite – it just feels like New Orleans to me. Sit at the small bar and sip a Barq's root beer or a Dixie beer while you wait. Nothing like the smell of fried shrimp in the morning.... **JOHNNY'S:** 511 St Louis St, New Orleans, LA 70130, **PARASOL'S:** 2533 Constance St, New Orleans, LA 70130, **PARKWAY TAVERN AND BAKERY:** 538 Hagan St, New Orleans, LA 70119, **DOMILISE':** 5240 Annunciation St, New Orleans, LA 70115

COCHON I'm originally from Lafayette, Louisiana, the 'hub of Acadiana', and I can tell you that this is the best example of Cajun food in New Orleans, and it tops most of what you might find in the Bayou towns of Cajun Country. Chefs Donald Link and Steve Stryjewski offer a cauldron of choices from pork cheeks (my favorite) to meat pies to a killer oyster and bacon sandwich. Take your time, eat up... then take a nap. 930 Tchoupitoulas St, New Orleans, LA 70195, www.cochonrestaurant.com

RESTAURANT AUGUST If it's high end, fancy cuisine with a distinctly Southern flair that you're after, you can't go wrong here. To quote from their menu, their dishes "represent our peasant roots as well as our refined tastes". It's old world charm meets contemporary attitude, and the sugar and spice duckling with ground grits is not to be missed. 301 Tchoupitoulas St, New Orleans, LA 70130, www.restaurantaugust.com

snug harbor
d.b.a.
saturn
yuki
all way
one eyed jacks
if there's really such a thi
as happy hour,
it must be
between 2 and 6pm

New Orleans has the friendliest dive bars anywhere, and most of them have live music (it's difficult to separate music and drinking in this town). Most of my recommendations are away from Bourbon Street — too many rowdy tourists.

D.B.A. d.b.a. (lowercase intended) is to me the most welcoming place in a city where almost every bar feels warm. It's on happening Frenchmen Street, in the Marigny section behind the Quarter, and it has the best beer selection – plus, if you're lucky you'll get to listen to Gal Holiday's rockabilly with a bite. 616 Frenchmen St, New Orleans, LA 70195, dbabars.com/dbano

SNUG HARBOR A few doors down from d.b.a, this place may not be the most comfortable venue, but its laid back, clumsy setting is part of its appeal. Sit upstairs at the rail and look down at the likes of trumpet player Terence Blanchard. If you like jazz, this is it. 626 Frenchmen St, New Orleans, LA 70116, www.snugjazz.com/site

YUKI IZAKAYA A hybrid of sorts that opened after Hurricane Katrina. Izakaya means 'tavern' in Japanese, and it is that. You can eat Japanese tapas here while you sit on very tiny seats. The front bar holds no more than 20 people. Most Wednesday nights, a great local country band called By and By plays. 525 Frenchmen St, New Orleans, LA 70116

ALLWAYS This lounge and theater is situated in the heart of the burgeoning St Claude art scene. You can catch local bands in the smoky bar area at the front, or head to the rear to see anything from one acts to readings or something called Radical Faeries Ball. Across the street is the Hi Ho Lounge, another worthwhile drinking den. 2240 St Claude Ave, New Orleans, LA 70117, www.marignytheatre.org

ONE EYED JACKS If you're going to visit a bar in the Quarter, this is the one to choose. It used to be an independent movie theater, and it attracts a too-hip-to-grip clientele. You can sometimes catch national music darlings like Bonnie Prince Billy or Meat Puppets. 615 Toulouse St, New Orleans, LA 70130, www.oneeyedjacks.net

DRINK+MUSIC

THE MAPLE LEAF BAR Up near the river in Carrollton, is this old stand-by with a dance floor. Have a drink and listen to crazy traditional music like Rebirth Brass Band. Usually lots of late night dancing. 8316 Oak St, New Orleans, LA 70118, www.mapleleafbar.com

CHICKIE WAH WAH Despite being named after an annoying local song, this cozy Mid-City venue offers up terrific music from Anders Osborne on Tuesday nights and maybe even Germain Bazzle. He writes and plays haunting, angry blues, she is a local jazz songstress who rarely performs. It is also the only local bar I know that is smoke free. 2828 Canal St, New Orleans, LA 70119, www.chickiewahwah.com

VAUGHAN'S LOUNGE Home to Kermit Ruffins and his Barbeque Swingers. Great music, decor, and a ping pong table. 800 Lesseps St, New Orleans, LA 70117

SAINTS

lagniappe

a cross between Scarlett o'hara and blanche dubois a manipulative flirt dependent upon the kindness of strangers

who dat

DRINK

Now for what I would call BAR bars, where you would not go to hear music necessarily, but should visit anyway.

THE COLUMNS A hotel, bar, rehearsal hall, front porch get–together that looks like part of a plantation tour, but it has that certain mystery about it. Lots of nooks and secret places to hide in or sit on the steps outside and watch the streetcars go by. 3811 St Charles Ave, New Orleans, LA 70115, www.thecolumns.com

SATURN BAR This used to be a local bar for oldsters, but these days it's part of a new Marigny scene, with dance parties drawing in the desperately arty crowd. The interior still looks like an old stage set. Great neon. It's fun. 3067 St Claude Ave, New Orleans, LA 70117

MARKEY'S BAR A working man's bar. No nonsense, television, free pool. Just feels right. 640 Louisa St, New Orleans, LA 70117

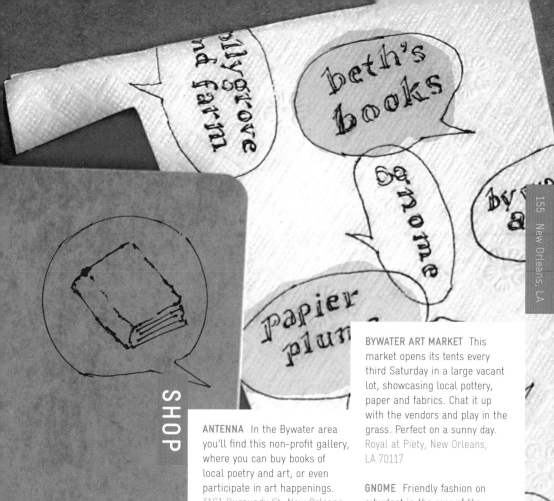

SHOP

ANTENNA In the Bywater area you'll find this non-profit gallery, where you can buy books of local poetry and art, or even participate in art happenings. 3161 Burgundy St, New Orleans, LA 70117

FARMERS' MARKETS There are many farmers' markets here, but I like these two best. Crescent City Farmers' Market is open Saturdays from 8am, selling fresh everything inside and out. Hollygrove Market and Farm is in its own indoor space, selling a generous and reasonably priced selection of locally grown fruit and veg. **CRESCENT CITY:** 700 Magazine St, New Orleans, LA 70130, **HOLLYGROVE:** 8301 Olive St, New Orleans, LA 70118

BETH'S BOOKS Used and new books, comics and magazines including *Esopus*. This place just feels cozy and right. Tristen, a great guy with a great beard, is the very knowledgeable manager. This book would be welcome there. 2700 Chartres St, New Orleans, LA 70117

BYWATER ART MARKET This market opens its tents every third Saturday in a large vacant lot, showcasing local pottery, paper and fabrics. Chat it up with the vendors and play in the grass. Perfect on a sunny day. Royal at Piety, New Orleans, LA 70117

GNOME Friendly fashion on a budget in the rear of the Quarter. Wooden floors, casual displays and nice stock. 1301 Decatur St, New Orleans, LA 70116

FAULKNER HOUSE BOOKS A jam-packed, beautifully appointed haven for books by and about Mr Faulkner (who did indeed live here), along with local and current releases. Rosemary James and Joe DeSalvo, the owners, have done wonders with such a small space. 624 Pirates Alley, New Orleans, LA 70116, www.faulknerhousebooks.net

Well, uh, there is this thing called Mardi Gras that happens every year in February, sometimes in early March. Billed as the "greatest free show on earth," you need to see and feel it to believe it... at least once. Apart from that these are my favorites:

JAZZ FEST From its humble beginnings in 1970, when a few hundred folks showed up to cheer on local bands, this has grown to a massive two-weekend affair at the end of April/beginning of May, featuring local, national and international acts and food. The acoustics are perfect, and the acts actually start on time.

CONTEMPORARY ART CENTER The CAC is housed in a former drugstore and drugstore warehouse with really cool spaces that are worth a visit in their own right. They have great permanent installations and a neat cafe. 900 Camp St, New Orleans, LA 70130

ST CLAUDE STREET GALLERIES To see the hottest local and regional talent, check out the galleries that line St Claude from Elysian Fields (behind the Quarter) all the way to the Press Street rail tracks. Before you come, visit www.scadnola.com for all of the latest on St Claude happenings, including the Fringe Festival and the Backstreet Cultural Museum.

ZEITGEIST INTERDISCIPLINARY ARTS CENTER Thanks to filmmaker/owner Rene Broussard, New Orleans has a unique venue for viewing and presenting local and international independent film on a regular basis (sometimes with bands playing afterwards). It's in a peculiar spot that could be called Uptown but feels distinctly its own universe. Also features the occasional Pecha Kucha night. 1618 Oretha Castle Haley Blvd, New Orleans, LA 70113, www.zeitgeisttheater.wordpress.com

THE PRYTANIA The only single-screen movie theatre in town. It's family run (Robert Brunet and his dad) and located in a nice Uptown neighborhood. The projection is state of the art, but the setting is cozy and they screen current releases as well as the occasional indie film. What could be better? 5339 Prytania St, New Orleans, LA 70115, www.theprytania.com

A GALLERY FOR FINE PHOTOGRAPHY Exactly what it says it is. Owner Josh Pailet has established a truly world-class photo gallery here in the Quarter. He has all the greats from Ansel Adams to EJ Belocq to Helmut Newton, and often shows local talents like Josephine Sacabo and Louviere & Vanessa. Not to be missed. 241 Chartres St, New Orleans, LA 70130

OGDEN MUSEUM OF SOUTHERN ART A relatively new upstart in a beautifully designed building across from the CAC, specializing in Southern art. 925 Camp St, New Orleans, LA 70130

CULTURE

ower ninth ward
garden district
the quarter
mid-city
9th ward
lakeview
where y'at
irish channel
uptown
by water
warehouse district
mississippi rive

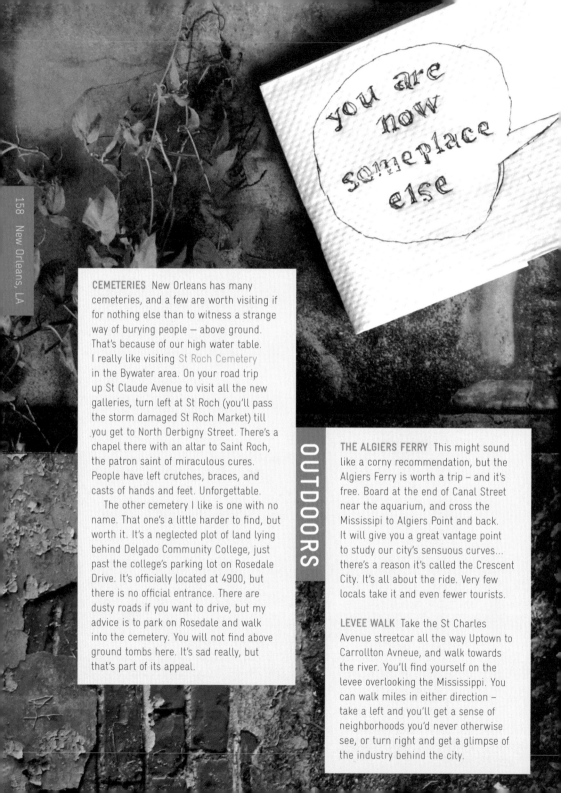

you are now someplace else

CEMETERIES New Orleans has many cemeteries, and a few are worth visiting if for nothing else than to witness a strange way of burying people — above ground. That's because of our high water table. I really like visiting St Roch Cemetery in the Bywater area. On your road trip up St Claude Avenue to visit all the new galleries, turn left at St Roch (you'll pass the storm damaged St Roch Market) till you get to North Derbigny Street. There's a chapel there with an altar to Saint Roch, the patron saint of miraculous cures. People have left crutches, braces, and casts of hands and feet. Unforgettable.

The other cemetery I like is one with no name. That one's a little harder to find, but worth it. It's a neglected plot of land lying behind Delgado Community College, just past the college's parking lot on Rosedale Drive. It's officially located at 4900, but there is no official entrance. There are dusty roads if you want to drive, but my advice is to park on Rosedale and walk into the cemetery. You will not find above ground tombs here. It's sad really, but that's part of its appeal.

OUTDOORS

THE ALGIERS FERRY This might sound like a corny recommendation, but the Algiers Ferry is worth a trip – and it's free. Board at the end of Canal Street near the aquarium, and cross the Mississipi to Algiers Point and back. It will give you a great vantage point to study our city's sensuous curves... there's a reason it's called the Crescent City. It's all about the ride. Very few locals take it and even fewer tourists.

LEVEE WALK Take the St Charles Avenue streetcar all the way Uptown to Carrollton Avneue, and walk towards the river. You'll find yourself on the levee overlooking the Mississippi. You can walk miles in either direction – take a left and you'll get a sense of neighborhoods you'd never otherwise see, or turn right and get a glimpse of the industry behind the city.

comeback

shotgun

creole cottage

town house

the architecture of the quarter is as much Spanish as it is french

CAMILLIA BENBASSAT'S

NYC

//AVEC

NEW YORK CITY, NEW YORK

BY CAMILLIA BENBASSAT

The thing I love most about New York is its relentless energy. You feel it as you walk down the street, as you fall asleep at night, when you wake up in the morning. The city is literally pulsating and you feel its reverb as you go through your day. On some days it carries you as you walk down the street, and on others it's like a wind in your face. It's potent and inspiring and is constantly challenging you to hope and ask for more. You feel like you can achieve whatever you want and find whatever it is you're looking for. It's electric. Coming from California, I grew up with a very different vibe. There, the sun greets you daily and the day spreads out before you. Here, the sun can be fleeting and everything comes alive at night. You'll find yourself sitting at the bar at 4am, completely wide awake and wondering where the time went.

Visually, the inspirations are endless. Iconic images that you've seen a million times in movies are so much more potent in the flesh. Worn brick buildings framed by fire escapes, the Statue of Liberty, the lights of Times Square – nothing about New York ever becomes a cliché. I still love seeing a fleet of yellow cabs fill the street, and I hold my breath as I cross the Williamsburg Bridge and catch a glimpse of the city at night – the Empire State all aglow.

In the end, there really is no other city like New York, and compiling this list of where to go, what to see, and (most importantly) where to eat, was not a simple task. I live in Williamsburg, an area of Brooklyn that has seen so much development over recent years that it's like another town to the one I moved to. Nonetheless it's an area I love and which offers a welcome respite from the madness of Manhattan, so I've included a number of my local favorites. I've stuck to what I know, but I encourage you to keep exploring... the city changes much faster than anyone can manage to keep up with, and it's up to you to keep looking around each corner – to try and harness that crazy, buzzing energy and to somehow keep pace with this incredible, inspiring city.

STAY

ACE HOTEL Newly opened in 2009, this is the place to spot some rockstars, and then retreat to your loft-style room. The lobby feels like a cozy study hall or library with one wall covered from floor to ceiling with an installation of graffiti tag stickers. The hotel restaurant, The Breslin, is top notch (the guys who run it also have a great restaurant in the West Village called the Spotted Pig). The brunch is particularly fantastic. 20 W 29th St, Midtown West, www.acehotel.com

COOPER SQUARE HOTEL The Cooper Square Hotel rises above the Bowery dressed in glass. Dark 'tree lined' hallways lead you to light-filled rooms with floor-to-ceiling windows that actually open (a rarity in NY). My friend stayed here and was impressed by the contrast between the minimalist interiors and the carefully selected furniture and vintage art books. Actually, I designed the hotel's identity, so at the very least go and pick up a business card! 25 Cooper Sq, East Village, www.thecoopersquarehotel.com

BOWERY HOTEL This place has one of my favorite hotel bars. Antique furniture, plush sofas, and cozy fireplaces. Order a whisky on the rocks and settle in for some good celebrity sightings. 335 Bowery, Noho, www.theboweryhotel.com

GRAMERCY PARK HOTEL This hotel is a famous NY fixture and a sleek, trendy hotspot (I love its dripping logo). Walk through the heavy wrought-iron doors into a lobby that welcomes you with huge fireplaces. The overall vibe is plush, ornate, and bohemian. 2 Lexington Ave, Gramercy, www.gramercyparkhotel.com

JANE HOTEL With a range of prices, this is the most affordable in the boutique set. Podlike rooms set up like a ship allow for a cheap yet trendy overnight stay. Many of the larger rooms overlook the Hudson. The bar is a super-trendy NY hotspot. It's tricky to get in, but fun to try! 113 Jane St, West Village, www.thejanenyc.com

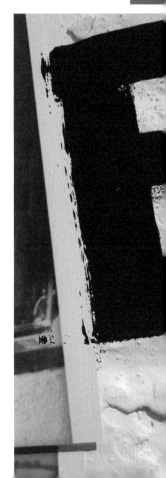

LATIN RESTAURANTS Caracas is a Venezuelan restaurant that serves arepas, lovely corn tortillas stuffed with various combinations of meat, cheese, and vegetables. Being from California, I am very picky about Mexican food, but Barrio Chino manages to exceed all expectations. The food is awesome, and the margaritas are even better (my favorite is the jalapéno). For a delicious Cuban brunch and a little star sighting, head to the forever packed Café Habana. On the high-end, for amazing tequilas and a great atmosphere go to La Esquina. The door marked 'Employees Only' is a secret entrance to the VIP den. If you can't manage to talk yourself past the bouncer, don't worry. The taqueria upstairs is delicious as well. Make sure to get the corn on the cob. **CARACAS:** 91 E 7th St, East Village or 291 Grand St, Williamsburg, Brooklyn, **BARRIO CHINO:** 253 Broome St, Chinatown, **CAFÉ HABANA:** 17 Prince St, Nolita, **LA ESQUINA:** 114 Kenmare St, Soho

MARLOW & SONS This is by far my favorite restaurant in NY. The menu changes daily, with specials based on farm fresh ingredients. The oysters are phenomenal – many of my oyster-doubting friends were converted here. Make sure to order the chocolate caramel tart for desert. If you are there late enough, you can help yourself to one of the brown bags that sit on the counter – leftover pastries from the cafe in the morning. Next door you'll find Diner, which shares a kitchen. Both places are excellent for brunch. 81 and 85 Broadway, Williamsburg, Brooklyn, www.marlowandsons.com

MOMOFUKU I have to confess to having recurring dreams about the pork buns at this minimalist noodle bar in the East Village. The name means 'lucky peach' in Japanese, and they have several branches within a few blocks of each other, each with slightly different menus. The best is the 12-course set menu at Momofuku Ko (or so I hear – I haven't yet managed to get through the impossible online reservation system). Momofuku Ssam has a milk bar attached serving weird and wonderful sweet meets savory concoctions. Try the crack pie or compost cookie. **MOMOFUKU NOODLE BAR:** 171 1st Ave, East Village, **MOMOFUKU KO:** 163 1st Ave, East Village, **MOMOFUKU SSAM:** 207 2nd Ave, East Village

EAT

ITALIAN RESTAURANTS When I tasted Italian food in New York, I realised I was on a whole new level with food. The first time I fell in love with my dinner was at Inoteca, and soon discovered a whole host of Italian restaurants that fill the East Village and Lower East Side. Luckily, they are all equally good and reasonably priced, so you can't go wrong: Lil Frankies, Supper, Frank, and Frankies Spuntino are all fantastic. Another great spot is Al di La in Park Slope, it's always packed, and you'll know why as soon as you try the food. **INOTECA:** 91 Rivington St, Lower East Side, **LIL FRANKIES:** 19 1st St, East Village, **SUPPER:** 156 E 2nd St, East Village, **FRANK:** 88 2nd Ave, East Village, **FRANKIE'S SPUNTINO:** 17 Clinton St, Lower East Side, **AL DI LA:** 248 5th Ave, Park Slope, Brooklyn

PIZZA For the late night slice, go to Artichoke, where the line for the counter (it's take out only) weaves down the block anytime after 1am, and the thick, bready, artichoke-doused pizza is well worth the wait. Grimaldi's and Lombardi's are sit down whole-pie only places, but make sure you're feeling zen, as you'll be waiting in line for a while there as well. **ARTICHOKE BASILLE'S PIZZA & BREWERY:** 328 E 14th St, East Village, **GRIMALDI'S PIZZERIA:** 19 Old Fulton St, Dumbo, Brooklyn, **LOMBARDI'S:** 32 Spring St, Nolita

BURGERS I never loved burgers like I do since coming to New York. If it's summer, visit the Shake Shack in Madison Square Park. The line will probably be winding down the block, but at least it's beautiful in the park while you wait. The burger that changed everything was from Dumont Burger in Williamsburg. Get it with the brioche bun, caramelized onions and manchego cheese. Corner Bistro also stands with the best. Come here in the afternoon, grab a McSorley's pint and enjoy the tavern feel. Don't order anything but the Bistro Burger. **SHAKE SHACK:** Madison Ave at 23rd St, Madison Square Park, and 366 Columbus Ave, Upper West Side, **DUMONT BURGER:** 314 Bedford Ave, Williamsburg, Brooklyn, **CORNER BISTRO:** 331 W 4th St, West Village

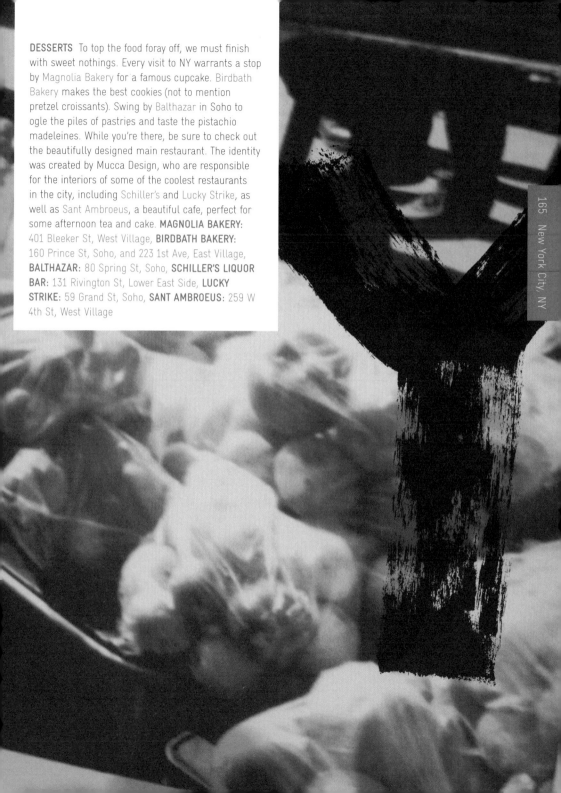

DESSERTS To top the food foray off, we must finish with sweet nothings. Every visit to NY warrants a stop by Magnolia Bakery for a famous cupcake. Birdbath Bakery makes the best cookies (not to mention pretzel croissants). Swing by Balthazar in Soho to ogle the piles of pastries and taste the pistachio madeleines. While you're there, be sure to check out the beautifully designed main restaurant. The identity was created by Mucca Design, who are responsible for the interiors of some of the coolest restaurants in the city, including Schiller's and Lucky Strike, as well as Sant Ambroeus, a beautiful cafe, perfect for some afternoon tea and cake. **MAGNOLIA BAKERY:** 401 Bleeker St, West Village, **BIRDBATH BAKERY:** 160 Prince St, Soho, and 223 1st Ave, East Village, **BALTHAZAR:** 80 Spring St, Soho, **SCHILLER'S LIQUOR BAR:** 131 Rivington St, Lower East Side, **LUCKY STRIKE:** 59 Grand St, Soho, **SANT AMBROEUS:** 259 W 4th St, West Village

SPEAKEASIES Speakeasies have become the hidden gems of the NY bar scene. Amazing cocktails made by famous mixologists coupled with gorgeously designed interiors. Most have a host of rules, and you usually have to pass through a doorman or, at PDT you actually have to pick up the phone in an old telephone booth – in a hot dog joint, no less – to be granted permission to pass through. Usually though, this is more about seating than anything else – no standing allowed. Visit Death & Co, then walk down the road to the tiled, south-of-the-border styling of Mayahuel with their tequila-based cocktails. Little Branch and East Side Company make all their drinks from fresh ingredients. For a bit of Asian influence, climb the stairs that lead you above and through the adjacent sushi restaurant to find Angel Share. Milk & Honey is the quietest of the bunch, mostly for members, but you can call their number (discreetly listed below) and make a reservation to have a drink before 9pm. **PDT:** 113 St Marks Pl, East Village, **DEATH & CO:** 433 E 6th St, East Village, **MAYAHUEL:** 304 E 6th St, East Village, **LITTLE BRANCH:** 20 7th Ave South, West Village, **EAST SIDE COMPANY BAR:** 49 Essex St, Lower East Side, **ANGEL SHARE:** 6 Stuyvesant St, 2nd Fl, East Village, **MILK & HONEY:** 134 Eldridge St, Lower East Side, [212 625 3397]

WILLIAMSBURG BARS My local in Williamsburg is Larry Lawrence. Besides loving the owners and bartenders, the interior is dimly lit and beautifully designed with gorgeous, luscious wood. As is typical with NY bars, there is no sign outside, so look for a large wooden door and walk down the long corridor to the bar hidden at the back. Down the road is the lovely Rose Bar which features great live jazz and interiors covered in rose patterned wallpapers. You can also head downstairs for a bite to eat at Vutera. Around the corner is the Spuyten Duyvil, which serves beers from around the world, complete with a perfect summer garden. Hotel Delmano is in an old tattoo parlor and is totally Brooklyn. Amazing cocktails, patina paint, tattooed hipsters, good music, and very cool tiling in the bathrooms. **LARRY LAWRENCE:** 295 Grand St, Williamsburg, **ROSE BAR/ VUTERA:** 345 Grand St, Williamsburg, **SPUYTEN DUYVIL:** 359 Metropolitan Ave, Williamsburg, **HOTEL DELMANO:** 82 Berry St, Williamsburg

LOWER EAST SIDE When I first moved to NY, I spent most of my days hanging out in the Lower East Side. The bars here have the dirty, seedy feel that you expect (and want) from New York. Drinks are cheap too. If you're lucky you can catch the burlesque dancer in the window at Motor City. For something a bit different, check out The Back Room, tucked away beyond a sign for a toy store. Walk through the alley to the back and enter a speakeasy that harkens back to the prohibition era. You'll have to sip your drink from teacups and the beers are actually served in brown bags. My favorite though is 151, dark and underground with fantastic music, and the same bartenders that have been there since forever. **MOTOR CITY:** 127 Ludlow St, Lower East Side, **THE BACK ROOM:** 102 Norfolk St, Lower East Side, **151:** 151 Rivington St, Lower East Side

BROOKLYN Head out to Brooklyn for some neighborhood charm. Flatbush Farm in the summer is so lovely: huge, rustic tables fill a backyard strung with fairy lights. Sit at the bar and enjoy the top notch jukebox at Brooklyn Social. If you manage to make it down to Red Hook, do not miss Fort Defiance. By day it's a lovely cafe where the light spills in, and at night it turns into a cozy, welcoming cocktail bar. **FLATBUSH FARM:** 76 St Marks St, Park Slope, **BROOKLYN SOCIAL:** 335 Smith St, Carroll Gdns, **FORT DEFIANCE:** 365 Van Brunt St, Red Hook

124 RABBIT CLUB This is my favorite bar. It's a bit unexpected as I am usually a cocktail girl, but this beer and wine bar hidden off a crazy, drunk filled street, is a respite in the city. Friendly, awesome bartenders remember you every time you walk in. Dark, barely lit, exposed brick, small perfect. 124 MacDougal St, West Village

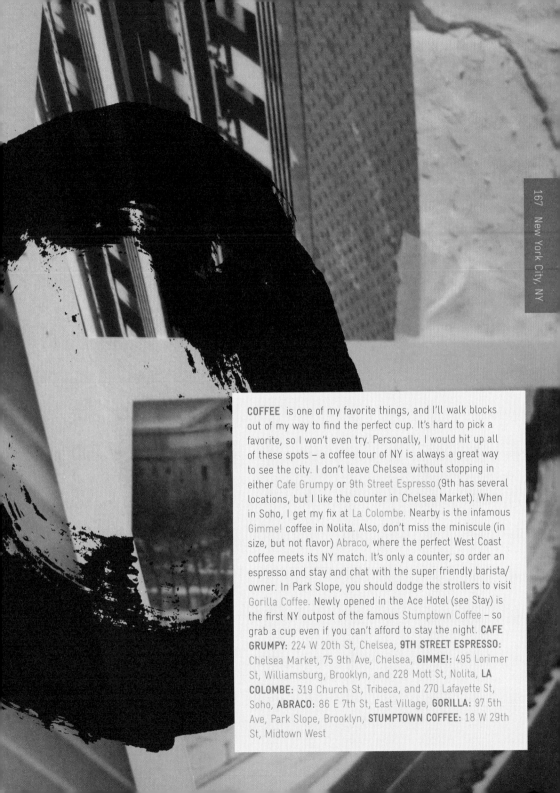

COFFEE is one of my favorite things, and I'll walk blocks out of my way to find the perfect cup. It's hard to pick a favorite, so I won't even try. Personally, I would hit up all of these spots – a coffee tour of NY is always a great way to see the city. I don't leave Chelsea without stopping in either Cafe Grumpy or 9th Street Espresso (9th has several locations, but I like the counter in Chelsea Market). When in Soho, I get my fix at La Colombe. Nearby is the infamous Gimme! coffee in Nolita. Also, don't miss the miniscule (in size, but not flavor) Abraco, where the perfect West Coast coffee meets its NY match. It's only a counter, so order an espresso and stay and chat with the super friendly barista/owner. In Park Slope, you should dodge the strollers to visit Gorilla Coffee. Newly opened in the Ace Hotel (see Stay) is the first NY outpost of the famous Stumptown Coffee – so grab a cup even if you can't afford to stay the night. **CAFE GRUMPY:** 224 W 20th St, Chelsea, **9TH STREET ESPRESSO:** Chelsea Market, 75 9th Ave, Chelsea, **GIMME!:** 495 Lorimer St, Williamsburg, Brooklyn, and 228 Mott St, Nolita, **LA COLOMBE:** 319 Church St, Tribeca, and 270 Lafayette St, Soho, **ABRACO:** 86 E 7th St, East Village, **GORILLA:** 97 5th Ave, Park Slope, Brooklyn, **STUMPTOWN COFFEE:** 18 W 29th St, Midtown West

SHOP

DESIGN BOOKSHOPS There are some amazing design-minded bookshops scattered throughout the city. One of my favorites is the New Museum bookstore with its collections of beautifully designed art and artists books (the museum itself is beautiful architecturally as well). After gallery hopping in Chelsea, be sure to stop by Printed Matter, a non-profit bookshop lined with small, contemporary publications created by artists. Dashwood Books is devoted almost exclusively to photography, while the Moma Design and Bookstore offers not just books but a collection of modern objects so well curated that it could live within the museum walls. **NEW MUSEUM:** 235 Bowery, Soho, **PRINTED MATTER:** 195 10th Ave, Chelsea, **DASHWOOD BOOKS:** 33 Bond St, Noho, **MOMA DESIGN AND BOOKSTORE:** 11 W 53rd St, Midtown West and 81 Spring St, Soho

LUDLOW STREET Ludlow Street in the Lower East Side is filled with cool shops. I always stop by Dolce Vita – they have great clothes and even better shoes. For menswear, check out Assembly. You'll find great jeans around the corner at Earnest Sewn Co. **DOLCE VITA:** 149 Ludlow St, Lower East Side, **ASSEMBLY:** 174 Ludlow St, Lower East Side, **EARNEST SEWN CO:** 90 Orchard St, Lower East Side

CLOTHES It goes without saying that Bloomingdales is a must visit, but I simply love the NY boutiques. My favorite is OAK, with gorgeous men and women's pieces in the standby designer colors of gray and black. Visit the avant-garde boutique Opening Ceremony, which features designers from a different country every year. For menswear, check out Odin and the J Crew concept store in Soho, decorated as a hipster liquor bar with reclaimed wood and vintage fixtures. For his all-important hipster slash hunter gear, there's also Freeman's Sporting Club, complete with an old-fashioned barbershop tucked away in the back. After shopping, grab a bite at the taxidermy-filled Freeman's restaurant down the back of the adjacent alley. **OAK:** 28 Bond St, Noho, and 208 N 8th St, Williamsburg, Brooklyn **OPENING CEREMONY:** 35 Howard St, Soho, **ODIN:** 328 E 11th St, East Village; 199 Lafayette St, Soho, and 750 Greenwich St, West Village, **J CREW MEN'S SHOP AT THE LIQUOR STORE:** 235 W Broadway, Soho, **FREEMAN'S SPORTING CLUB/FREEMAN'S:** 8 Rivington St/Freeman's Alley, Lower East Side

MARKETS Visit Brooklyn Flea for vintage furniture, clothing, collectibles, and antiques, as well as new jewelry, art and crafts by local artisans, plus delicious food. Every weekend check out the Union Square Farmers' Market. Expect crowds, but finagle your way to each booth for the fresh eats, fruits, and flowers. Take a walk through Chelsea Market and you'll find a beautiful space littered with bakeries (Amy's Bread is awesome), fish and produce, and Buon Italia – a great little Italian grocery. Don't forget to grab a coffee from 9th Street Espresso after your stroll (see Drink). **BROOKLYN FLEA:** 176 Lafayette Ave, Fort Greene and 81 Front St, Dumbo, Brooklyn, **UNION SQUARE FARMERS' MARKET:** Union Square, **CHELSEA MARKET:** 75 9th Ave, Chelsea

CUTLURE

MOMA You'll already know about MoMA, but it's still worth a mention, because its collection is fantastic, its architecture is amazing and because it never ceases to inspire. 11 W 53rd St, Midtown West, www.moma.org

COOPER HEWITT The only museum in the USA dedicated solely to contemporary and historical design, conveniently located on the Upper East Side within 'museum mile'. Particularly worth a visit if the Design Triennial is on. 2 E 91st St, Upper East Side, www.cooperhewitt.org

NEUE GALERIE I have a fondness for this gallery, which is devoted to German and Austrian art, because they hold pieces by one of my favorite artists, Egon Schiele. 1048 5th Ave, Upper East Side, www.neuegalerie.org

THE MUSEUM OF ARTS AND DESIGN This used
to be called the American Craft Museum, but
it has jazzed up its image with a new name, a
new identity (designed by Pentagram), and a new
premises on Columbus Circle. 2 Columbus Circle,
Upper West Side, www.madmuseum.org

CHELSEA GALLERIES I highly recommend
wandering through the tree-lined streets of
Chelsea, dropping in and out of the multitude of
galleries that line the streets. One of my favorites
is the Paula Cooper Gallery, which exhibits a
lot of work by installation artist Sophie Calle.
My other go-tos are Zwirner & Wirth and the
infamous Gagosian Gallery. **PAULA COOPER:** 534
W 21st St, Chelsea, **ZWIRNER & WIRTH:** 525 W
19th St, Chelsea, **GAGOSIAN GALLERY:** 555 W 24th
St, Chelsea

OUT OF TOWN GALLERIES If you have time to head out of the city, one of the best day trips is to the Dia: Beacon. Take an 80-minute train trip along the river and through the Hudson Valley and see this striking museum in a converted printing factory. The collection features sculptures, installations, drawings, and paintings from some amazing artists including Richard Serra, Bruce Nauman, and Sol LeWitt – and the grounds are breathtaking. Other artistically inclined day trips include The Cloisters, which is the uptown branch of the Metropolitan Museum, and the 500-acre sculpture garden that is the Storm King Art Center and Sculpture Park. **DIA: BEACON:** 3 Beekman St, Beacon, **THE CLOISTERS:** 99 Margaret Corbin Dr, Fort Tryon Park, **STORM KING:** Old Pleasant Hill Rd, Mountainville

MUSIC

MUSIC VENUES If you want to experience the New York nightlife, there is no end of clubs and music venues to explore. My favorites are the smaller ones, such as the Mercury Lounge, the Bowery Ballroom and the Music Hall of Williamsburg. They often host big names but allow for an intimate setting. Next on my list is Glasslands for some grunge or punk, or Union Hall and Fontanas for some gentler on the ears rock. **MERCURY LOUNGE:** 217 E Houston St, Lower East Side, **BOWERY BALLROOM:** 6 Delancey St, Lower East Side, **MUSIC HALL OF WILLIAMSBURG:** 66 N 6th St, Williamsburg, Brooklyn, **GLASSLANDS:** 289 Kent Ave, Williamsburg, Brooklyn, **UNION HALL:** 702 Union St, Park Slope, Brooklyn, **FONTANA'S:** 105 Eldridge, Lower East Side

JELLY POOL PARTIES Alas the pool in this case is no longer a reality, but this is another New York summer essential. Every Sunday in the East River Park in Williamsburg you'll find half-clad hipsters playing dodgeball and sliding down a slip n' slide, while up-and-coming bands play on the backdrop of the New York City skyline. Grab some food and beer and sit on the grass, or join the throngs of fans pushed up against the stage. And all this for free. East River Park between N 8th and N 9th St on Kent Ave, Williamsburg, Brooklyn, www.thepoolparties.com

CENTRAL PARK You can't come to NY and miss Central Park. With a city that moves at this pace you need some respite, and this park with its endless winding pathways is it. If it's warm, head to Sheep Meadow with your Frisbee, or take some cheese and wine and listen to a free summer concert by the NY Philharmonic while you stare up at the stars. From June to August, famous bands play every Sunday afternoon on Summerstage. Come early or you might not get in. www.centralparknyc.org, www.nyphil.org, www.summerstage.org

DUMBO One of my favorite spots in the entire city is in Dumbo. Step off the train and walk down cobblestone streets underneath the hulking overpass of the Manhattan Bridge. Just that interplay of light and shadow is inspiring. Turn the corner and you'll find yourself at the waterfront park between two of the city's iconic bridges, staring at a view of lower Manhattan. Breathtaking is an understatement.

PROSPECT PARK This is New York's 'other park', in Park Slope. It's pretty big and includes everything from carousels to botanical gardens and the Brooklyn Art Museum. If you're there in spring, check out the festival while the pink cherry blossoms float down on you. There are free summer concerts at the bandshell. www.prospectpark.org

THE HIGH LINE This is a long promenade built on the train tracks that rise above the West Village and Chelsea. The park is a work in progress and has been tastefully designed with understated elements, such as parts of the railway appearing and vanishing again. Grab a seat on one of the wooden lounge chairs facing the Hudson and relax. The chairs roll along the tracks, so you can move closer to one another if you so wish. Gansevoort St to 34th St, Chelsea, www.thehighline.org

THE FLOATING POOL This is one of our more bizarre, but of course super-cool, New York attractions. It's a swimming pool that rests on the East River at the edge of the Brooklyn shore. Every summer the pool floats to a new spot on the river, so be sure to look up its location. Tip: check the website to avoid 'kids' playtime'. www.nycgovparks.org

OUTDOORS

Katie Hatz's

PHIL
ADEL
PHIA

PHILADELPHIA, PENNSYLVANIA BY KATIE HATZ

Founded by William Penn in 1701, Philadelphia is now the sixth most populous city in the United States. You wouldn't think it to live here, though; it's common to hear Philadelphians talk about how small the city feels, due, most likely, to the fact that we tend to stick to the same few neighborhoods all the time and run into the same batch of people. I myself am guilty of this, as evidenced by the fact that there are no West Philly attractions in this chapter.

Another thing you'll hear Philadelphians say is that we love our city for its "grittiness and personality." This is referring to the fact that Philly (sometimes affectionately called "Philthy") has a reputation for being dirty, smelly, and unsafe, but we love it anyway. There's an element of thrill to it, really. Stick to the good neighborhoods and you'll be fine (at least that's what they tell you, maybe a little too enthusiastically)!

Speaking of neighborhoods, there are a lot of them; and each has its own unique culture and vibe. Wikipedia's list of Philadelphia neighborhoods provides a pretty good breakdown. Olde City, the historic center, has lots of pretty little green spaces, and decent food and shopping, but is often overrun by tourists. Society Hill, just south of Olde City, is laid back and somewhat residential, but still has a lot of good places to hang out. The area right around South Street has a lot of bars, shops catering to punk and hip hop fashion, and tattoo and piercing parlors. Rittenhouse, the more fancypants area of town, is great for people watching, shopping, and eating swanky meals. A bit further north and east, Northern Liberties (NoLibs) and Fishtown are the trendier parts of town; NoLibs is a bit more established (ie. pretty and pricey), while Fishtown is more up-and-coming, favored by artists and students.

Philly's public transportation is neither the best, nor the worst. Two main subway lines cross at City Hall; the orange line runs north-south along Broad Street, and the blue line (also known as the El, because part of it is elevated) runs east-west along Market Street, before heading on a northeast diagonal. There are also buses, trolleys, and a regional rail system. For more transportation information, check out www.septa.org.

STAY

If I were, through some unforeseeable turn of events, rendered simultaneously filthy rich and homeless, I would gladly live in any of the following.

SEVENTH STREET B&B This B&B is basically like staying with a friend in town, except that your friend happens to have a beautifully decorated, immaculate house, and also happens to stay out of your way unless he's making you food or giving you advice on where to go in the city, and also happens to be a guy named Steve. My point is that that staying here will provide you with a much closer approximation of what it would be like to actually live in Philly, which is pretty awesome. 702 South 7th St, Philadelphia, PA 19147, http://mysite.verizon.net/lu72

MORRIS HOUSE HOTEL Built in 1787, the Morris House Hotel is a lovingly preserved slice of history with a private garden that plays host to many small weddings, barmitzvahs, and other such celebrations, which means you just might get to spy on a stranger's party! Oh please, you'd do it too. I bet you'd even bring binoculars. Weirdo. 225 South 8th St, Philadelphia, PA 19106, www.morrishousehotel.com

HOTEL PALOMAR PHILADELPHIA Not only is Hotel Palomar new, clean, modern, dog-friendly, and advantageously located; it's also the only LEED registered hotel in Philadelphia, which means they've had to meet incredibly rigorous third-party-imposed standards to prove their eco-friendliness. 117 South 17th St, Philadelphia, PA 19103, www.hotelpalomar-philadelphia.com

PENN'S VIEW HOTEL This cozy Olde City gem boasts the world's largest wine preservation and dispensing system, allowing its onsite restaurant, Ristorante Panorama, to keep 120 open wine bottles without compromising the wine's vitality. Apparently it's something to do with inert nitrogen gas. So apart from the old world charm of the place you also get over 800 wines a year available by the glass! 14 North Front St, Philadelphia, PA 19106, www.pennsviewhotel.com

THE RITTENHOUSE Located right on Rittenhouse Square, this place is consistently ranked as the best, fanciest, most luxurious, prettiest, most super amazing hotel in Philadelphia and/or the universe. I haven't spent a night there (yet), but I have had the pleasure of enjoying Sunday brunch at their restaurant, Lacroix, and I have to say, it did not disappoint. The staff is friendly, knowledgeable, and not at all snooty. I totally thought they'd be snooty. Sorry, guys! 210 West Rittenhouse Sq, Philadelphia, PA 19103, www.rittenhousehotel.com

If you feel the need commemorate your Philly experience with a cheesesteak, go right ahead. Just save room for the good food, upon which topic I will now enlighten you.

MODO MIO Ask any Philadelphian where to find the best Italian food in town, and chances are they'll send you to Fishtown's Modo Mio. It's a tiny place in huge demand, so be sure to make a reservation. It's also BYOB, a common occurrence in PA, where liquor licenses are hard to come by. 161 West Girard Ave, Philadelphia, PA 19123, www.modomiorestaurant.com.

MEMPHIS TAPROOM A little off the beaten path, but totally worth the trip — I always leave this place happy. Described in the *Philadelphia Inquirer* as "regional pub food," the fare at Memphis Taproom is unique and delicious. And omigod the brunch. That is all. 2331 East Cumberland St, Philadelphia, PA 19125, www.memphistaproom.com

EKTA When it comes to Indian takeout, nothing tops Ekta (except maybe sometimes Tiffin, which is right down the street and pretty much the same). Everything there is delicious, but the chicken korma is my go-to dish. 250 East Girard Ave, Philadelphia, PA 19125, www.ektaindianrestaurant.com

GOLDEN EMPRESS GARDEN Yes, Philly does have a whole Chinatown section. I just happen to love this place right off South Street – and once you try their vegan orange duck, you'll be right there with me. A dish made of beancurd skins may not sound particularly appetizing, but this stuff is a work of art. 610 South 5th St, Philadelphia, PA 19147

HONEY'S SIT 'N EAT Featuring delicious Southern comfort food fused with Jewish home cooking in a cozy, rustic setting, Honey's is hands-down the most popular brunch spot in NoLibs. Just be sure to arrive early on weekends if you don't want to stand in line for what feels like an eternity when you're hungry. 800 North 4th St, Philadelphia, PA 19123, www.honeys-restaurant.com

HORIZONS MODERN VEGAN CUISINE If you tend to shy away from vegan cuisine, this is the place that will change your outlook. Once a more casual cafe several miles north of the city, Horizons moved Downtown a few years ago and really kicked things up a notch. Their new digs are breezy, comfortable and upscale, and the menu now includes a fine assortment of organic wines and beers. 611 South 7th St, Philadelphia PA 19147, www.horizonsphiladelphia.com

CREPERIE BEAU MONDE This is my favorite place to eat around South Street. Lavishly decorated with dark wood, murals and velvet draperies, it serves up some of the most delicious crepes around. They also mix up a mean Bloody Mary. 624 South 6th St, Philadelphia, PA 19147, www.creperie-beaumonde.com

I mostly prefer bars that have food at least as delicious as can be found in decent restaurants. Lucky for me, Philly has a lot of those, for when Scotch just isn't enough (sacrilege, I know).

ROYAL TAVERN Royal Tavern is down on Passyunk (pronounced 'Pash-unk'), a bit further south than my other picks. Good music, tasty nachos, and a dark, cozy ambiance make this a great place to pass a relaxed evening with friends. While you're there, check out The Dive, another fun bar on the same block. 937 East Passyunk Ave, Philadelphia, PA 19147, www.royaltavern.com

TRIA So named for its delectable offerings of wine, cheese, and beer, Tria has two prime locations, a great menu of local and imported fare, outdoor seating, and tasting classes, making it a local favorite. 123 South 18th St, Philadelphia, PA 19103 and 1137 Spruce St, Philadelphia, PA 19107, www.triacafe.com

KRAFTWORK Not to be confused with Kraftwerk the band, this is one of Fishtown's newest hotspots. Highlights include an extensive list of craft beers on tap, tasty food, handmade tables, and tons of custom metalwork decor. 541 East Girard Ave, Philadelphia, PA 19125

BOB & BARBARA'S A Philadelphia institution, Bob & Barbara's made *Details* magazine's list of the best dive bars in America. Special events at the PBR-themed hole-in-the-wall include drag shows, drunken spelling bees, live jazz, and more. Ask for the house special, and a mere three bones will buy you a Pabst and a shot of Jim Beam. Not for the faint of heart or the overdressed! 1509 South St, Philadelphia, PA 19146

BAR FERDINAND With its prime Northern Liberties location, swanky-yet-cozy decor and extensive wine and tapas menu, Bar Ferdinand is a great place to go for drinks, but then accidentally get stuffed on tiny portions of excellent food. My favorite is the Manchego Frito and Tempranillo. Lots of Tempranillo. 1030 North 2nd St, Philadelphia, PA 19123, www.barferdinand.com

JOHNNY BRENDA'S Not exactly Fishtown's best-kept secret, Johnny Brenda's has gained enormously in popularity in recent years as people have begun to deem this part of Girard 'safe'. JB's boasts local beers on tap, amazing (albeit pricey) burgers, and a great music venue upstairs. 1201 Frankford Ave, Philadelphia, PA 19125, www.johnnybrendas.com

GOOD DOG BAR AND RESTAURANT You know when you're in a bar and your friend gets up to use the bathroom/smoke a cigarette/talk to someone attractive, and you're in a place so slick and stark that there's nowhere to rest your eyes without staring awkwardly at the other patrons, so you pretend to play with your phone until your friend comes back? Here, you don't have to do that, because there are photos of cute dogs all over the walls. Furthermore, the beet salad has big fried goat cheese balls in it. 224 South 15th St, Philadelphia, PA 19102, www.gooddogbar.com

MOSTLY BOOKS This is my favorite of Philly's many used bookstores. Conveniently located a block from South Street, Mostly Books is a great place to go for interesting postcards, old photographs, used records, and, of course, books. Don't let its tiny, cramped interior fool you; a doorway in the back opens into a cavernous back room with even MORE books! It's a bibliophile's wet dream. 529 Bainbridge St, Philadelphia, PA 19147, www.mostlybooksphilly.com

ARTSTAR Part boutique, part gallery, ArtStar sells quality handmade work by emerging artists all over the world. It also hosts Craft Bazaar, Philadelphia's largest annual outdoor craft fair, every May. 623 North 2nd St, Philadelphia, PA 19123, www.artstarphilly.com

LOST & FOUND Reasonable prices, interesting style, and a mix of vintage and modern pieces make Lost & Found one of my favorite shops on North 3rd Street (there are many!). 133 North 3rd St, Philadelphia, PA 19106

WILBUR A good curator is what separates the great vintage shops from the sea of mediocre ones, and Dan Wilbur is up to the challenge, selling an excellent selection of vintage clothes, consignment pieces and jewelry in a cozy, approachable space. 716 South 4th St, Philadelphia, PA 19147, www.wilburvintage. blogspot.com

READING TERMINAL MARKET When Reading Terminal Market first opened in 1892, it was the largest indoor market in the country. Today, it remains a huge, bustling center, full of tons of local and international produce, spices, handicrafts, books, plants, and more. My favorite treat is the ham, egg, and cheese pretzel roll-up from Miller's Twist. It's a breakfast sandwich AND a pretzel. I can't even think about it right now. 12th St and Arch St, Philadelphia, PA 19107, www.readingterminalmarket.org

AIA BOOKSTORE AND DESIGN CENTER The AIA Bookstore and Design Center has tons of really cool art, architecture, and design books, and since it's less than a block from Reading Terminal Market and the Fabric Workshop and Museum, you can get more visual and mental stimulus than you know how to handle, all in one little stroll! 1218 Arch St, Philadelphia, PA 19107, www.aiabookstore.com

HEADHOUSE FARMERS' MARKET The Headhouse Farmers' Market is set up under a permanent roof that runs the length of a cobblestone block of 2nd Street. Open weekends 2nd St and Lombard St, Philadelphia, PA 19147, www.thefoodtrust.org

There's a lot to do in Philly for anyone with a healthy interest in the arts. It may not all be air conditioned, but let's face it: neither is most of Europe, and people hang out there all the time.

WAGNER FREE INSTITUTE The Wagner Free Institute provides free science education to Philadelphians. Take a gander at the interesting architecture, amazing historic lecture hall, and huge collection of meticulously catalogued critters, preserved forever (kind of) through the miracle of taxidermy. 1700 West Montgomery Ave, Philadelphia, PA 19121, www.wagnerfreeinstitute.org

LANDMARK RITZ THEATRES Perhaps it's a little weird that they're packed so closely together, but whatever the reason, Philly has three Ritz theatres within a few blocks of each other. Between Ritz Five, Ritz at the Bourse, and Ritz East, our independent and foreign film needs are taken care of. **RITZ FIVE:** 125 South 2nd St, **RITZ EAST:** 214 Walnut St, **RITZ AT THE BOURSE:** 400 Ranstead St, Philadelphia, PA 19106, www.ritzfilmbill.com

FLUXSPACE AT ART MAKING MACHINE STUDIOS A gallery started in 2007 by some friends of mine from undergrad, who turned a Kensington warehouse into dozens of studios, wood and metal shops, and a gallery. It's a bit of a hike from Downtown, but it's worth it for FLUXspace's awesome shows, movie nights, and events. 3000 North Hope St, Philadelphia, PA 19133, www.artmakingmachine.com, www.thefluxspace.org

FLEISHER ART MEMORIAL A community-oriented art institution offering classes, workshops, and exhibitions to Philadelphians from all walks of life. Be sure to check out the Romanesque-revival sanctuary, a beautiful music and performance space. 719 Catharine St, Philadelphia, PA 19147

AMERICAN PHILOSOPHICAL SOCIETY MUSEUM Established over 260 years ago, this is the city's newest contemporary art venue, which also exhibits old maps, books, manuscripts, and scientific specimens and curiosities. A truly intriguing experience. 104 South 5th St, Philadelphia, PA 19106, www.amphilsoc.org

EASTERN STATE PENITENTIARY Once home to the likes of Willie Sutton and Al Capone, Eastern State Penitentiary is now a popular destination for those interested in prisons or (surprise!) contemporary art. Every year, ESP grants space and funding for site-specific installations. 2027 Fairmount Ave, Philadelphia, PA 19130, www.easternstate.org

THE PIAZZA AT SCHMIDT'S AND LIBERTIES WALK Two relatively new destinations in Northern Liberties, which are now home to a plethora of galleries, shops and restaurants. The center of the Piazza is a huge cobblestone space with a stage and a massive LED screen, which shows everything from sports to art films. It's Philly's answer to Rome, plus a giant TV. North 2nd St, between Girard and Poplar, www.atthepiazza.com

THE FABRIC WORKSHOP AND MUSEUM An institution in the Philly art world, the Fabric Workshop's all-encompassing mission is to create "new work in new materials and new media", and it's a great place to see some really innovative contemporary art. My favorite piece ever was Tristin Lowe's beautiful life-sized felt whale, with barnacles and everything. 1214 Arch St, Philadelphia, PA 19107, www.fabricworkshopandmuseum.org

THE CRANE ARTS BUILDING Founded in 2004, the Crane is home to numerous artist studios and the enormous Ice Box Gallery, as well as hosting loads of interesting events. Plus, the building itself is really cool and old. Check out the photos on their website – I kind of want to live there. 1400 North American St, Philadelphia, PA 19122, www.cranearts.com

PENN TREATY PARK Perched at the edge of Fishtown on the banks of the Delaware River, Penn Treaty Park has plenty of sun, shade, rolling hills, and a panoramic view of New Jersey. Who could ask for anything more?

FAIRMOUNT PARK At 9,200 acres, Fairmount Park is the world's largest landscaped urban park. It includes 63 neighbourhood and regional parks, the Philadelphia Zoo, a collection of outdoor sculptures, and a huge art museum (yes, the Philadelphia Museum of Art is technically in Fairmount Park too). It's big.

WISSAHICKON CREEK PARK Although it's technically part of Fairmount Park, this deserves its own entry. The main path through the park is Forbidden Drive, a wide, scenic gravel road running parallel to Wissahickon Creek, on which cars are forbidden (hence the name), and runners, cyclists and strolling families abound. From Forbidden Drive, one can access a number of hiking trails, as well as the Valley Green Inn, which is adorable.

LIBERTY LANDS PARK Run by the Northern Liberties Neighbors Association, Liberty Lands is almost always hopping with activity, including a free summer movie series, which takes place on Tuesday nights. 700 North 3rd St, Philadelphia, PA 19123

RITTENHOUSE SQUARE Rittenhouse Square is one of the smaller green spaces – more about ambiance than sprawl. Smack in the middle of one of Philadelphia's nicest neighborhoods, it's is a great place to meet up with friends for a picnic around the fountain. There's also a free summer concert series; so get there early on a Wednesday night, bring a blanket and some snacks, and brace yourself for the (weirdly civilized) crowds. 18th St and Walnut St, Philadelphia, PA 19103

One of my favorite things about Philly is its bikeability (which, I am aware, is not a word according to the stodgy old dictionary, but just ask the internet!). With over 200 miles of bike lanes and 50 miles of trails, Philadelphia has the greatest number of bicycle commuters per capita of the nation's most populated cities, according to a 2008 survey by the US Census Bureau. Usual rules of the road apply, stay off the sidewalk, and try riding through the 5th Street tunnel at night while yelling. Trust me.

WESTWARD HO

.phx

JON ASHCROFT'S

(PHOENIX)

PHOENIX, ARIZONA BY JON ASHCROFT

The greater Phoenix area, or the Valley of the Sun, as it is often referred to, is an island of human habitation surrounded by wilderness that varies from mountain ranges to low-lying desert flats. It is made up of a series of interlinked cities including Phoenix, Scottsdale, Tempe, Chandler, Mesa, Gilbert, Peoria, and dozens of other smaller communities. Together they make one of the nation's fastest growing metropolitan areas, and one if its largest in land area. Most of my reviews will be centered around central Phoenix, Tempe and Scottsdale because those are the places I live, play, and work.

Phoenix is often thought of as being absurdly hot. This is true (believe me it's true), but only for four months of the year. The rest of the time the weather is fantastic, with temperate winters, and an almost guaranteed breathtaking sunset every night. One advantage of being geographically isolated is that we are surrounded by hundreds of miles of the great outdoors. World-class mountain biking, hiking trails, climbing routes and camping are right on the city's doorstep. Only a few hours separate urban Phoenix from the Grand Canyon, the mountains in Flagstaff and the rocks of Sedona. All of this makes Phoenix the perfect urban destination for anybody who enjoys the city life, but doesn't want to sacrifice the wonders of the great outdoors.

Culturally, however, Phoenix suffers something of an identity crisis. For all its size, diversity and potential, it has always lacked a cultural core. However, I truly believe that this is now changing. A thriving tech industry means business for an art/design scene, and the city has become one of the top destinations for young professionals and creatives like myself. This fresh blood is shaping a new cultural scene that is reversing the momentum of growth – slowing the sprawl and focusing instead on the revitalization of Downtown and the more densely populated areas. A new emphasis has been placed on community and creativity, and I believe that the next decade will see Phoenix rise from its artistic ashes, and assume a position as a cultural capital.

STAY

THE CLARENDON HOTEL The Clarendon is a trendy, modern hotel in Phoenix's Midtown Museum District. It features an oasis pool complete with an Italian mosaic and thousands of LEDs that make the water look like a night sky. But the highlight of the hotel is the rooftop bar and lounge which offers great views of the Phoenix skyline and is one of the best places to experience the awesome Arizona sunsets. 401 West Clarendon Ave, Phoenix, AZ 85013, www.goclarendon.com

HOTEL VALLEY HO Located in Downtown Scottsdale, alongside all the art galleries, shopping, and fine dining, this is a great example of mid-century modern architecture. Built in 1956 and restored in 2005, it includes restaurants, a spa, and floor-to-ceiling windows that offer panoramic views of Camelback Mountain. It's not cheap, but if you're into that era, it's worth the price. 6850 East Main St, Scottsdale, AZ 85251, www.hotelvalleyho.com

MARICOPA MANOR A unique B&B in the heart of historic North Central Phoenix. It's a kind of miniature gated community made up of four separate historic homes within landscaped grounds. It's all very plush, and is minutes from Downtown Phoenix and the newly built light rail. 15 West Pasadena Ave, Phoenix, AZ 85013, www.maricopamanor.com

EAT

CORNISH PASTIES CO I am a newcomer to pasties, but I knew it was love from the first flakey bite. The Cornish Pasty Co offers delicious pasties filled with everything from peanut butter and jelly to lamb vindaloo. Great atmosphere too, with a mining themed interior and booths made of old church pews. 1941 West Guadalupe, Suite 101, Mesa, AZ 85202, www.cornishpastyco.com

THE ORANGE TABLE My colleagues and I love this place. It has a relaxed vibe that really allows you to wind down. Their sandwiches and burgers are massive and delicious. Highly recommended. 7373 East Scottsdale Mall, Scottsdale, AZ 85251, www.orangetable.net

MATT'S BIG BREAKFAST Matt's Big Breakfast is a classic diner that's all about simplicity and quality. Located in the heart of Downtown Phoenix in a tiny space, the food is made using fresh, quality ingredients. Don't come expecting anything too crazy though – Matt's sticks to basics and does them better than your beloved grandma. 801 North 1st St, Phoenix, AZ 85004, www.mattsbigbreakfast.com

GALLO BLANCO CAFE Located in the very hip Clarendon Hotel (see Stay), this cafe/bar is famous for its tacos – but has an amazing menu that doesn't disappoint. The contemporary decor and artwork adds to the experience. 401 West Clarendon Ave, Phoenix, AZ 85013, www.galloblancocafe.com

CAROLINA'S MEXICAN FOOD This is not a restaurant for the faint hearted. To get there you have to drive through one of seediest parts of town only to arrive at an old, beaten down building riddled with bullet holes. The interior isn't much better and it certainly isn't the cleanest of places. "So why eat here?", you ask. Because the sign reads "The Best Tortillas in Town" and it isn't lying. Packed with delicious Mexican ingredients, these are award winning tortillas at rock bottom prices – and as a result the place has a buzzing atmosphere. Lots of fun. 1202 East Mohave St, Phoenix, AZ 85034, www.carolinasmex.com

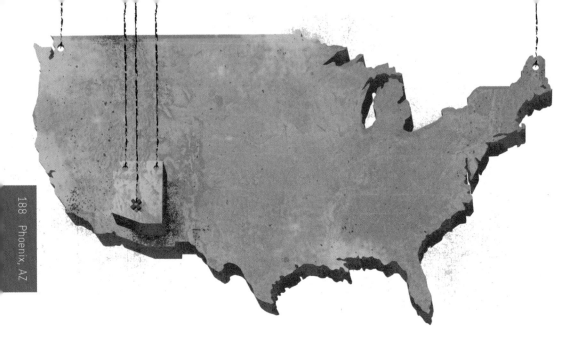

THE LOST LEAF Located in a non-descript 1920s bungalow in the Roosevelt Arts District, The Lost Leaf is possibly my favorite hangout. The bar also functions as a commission-free art gallery for local artists and a music venue featuring great local bands and live jazz every Thursday night. 914 North 5th St, Phoenix, AZ 85004, www.thelostleaf.org

CASEY MOORE'S OYSTER HOUSE Casey Moore's, or just Casey's as locals like to call it, is located within a tree-lined neighborhood of historic Tempe, near Arizona State University. Most of the seating is situated on a huge wrap-around patio that makes for a great place to relax on cool Arizona nights. The bar features a huge selection of draught beers, and I hear that their oysters are pretty delicious too, if you're into that kind of thing. 850 South Ash Ave, Tempe, AZ 85281, www.caseymoores.com

THE ROSE AND CROWN One of my favorite late night spots in central Phoenix, The Rose and Crown is located in Heritage Square, across from the famous Pizzeria Bianco and within walking distance of the light rail. A billiards table, cornhole set, jukebox, and front patio are just some of the highlights. On the downside, drinks aren't exactly cheap, and the patio can get overcrowded at times. 628 East Adams St, Phoenix, AZ 85073, www.myspace.com/roseandcrownpub

THE ROOSEVELT TAVERN I'm a huge fan of bars like this one that are well integrated within a neighborhood, rather than out in some strip mall. Nestled in the Roosevelt Arts District, you'd think this was just another residential bungalow if you didn't know better. The bar has a pleasant, relaxed atmosphere and it serves up a good selection of regional craft brews and boutique wines. 816 North 3rd St, Phoenix, AZ 85004

FOUR PEAKS BREWERY My love for Four Peaks is rooted in the fact that they are the creators of my all time favorite beer, Kilt Lifter Scottish-Style Ale. The brewery also features a great food menu which includes the best green chilli cheeseburger in town. The only downside is that everybody else has cottoned on, so it's almost impossible to get a seat without having to wait half an hour. 1340 East 8th St, Tempe, AZ 85281, www.fourpeaks.com

BUNKY BOUTIQUE I'm not sure what the term 'Bunky' means, but it is somehow fitting for this cool little shop. Conveniently located Downtown next to the Roosevelt Tavern, Bunky sells a meticulous selection of clothes, accessories, and handmade goods. Nice staff and good tunes make shopping fun. 812 North 3rd St, Phoenix, AZ 85004, www.bunkyboutique.com

MACALPINES Inside a 1920s drug store you'll find this retro soda bar, restaurant and vintage store. The restaurant features the original bar, and the rooms coming off it are packed with everything from vintage furniture, to clothing, jewelry and vinyl – none of which are too expensive. Staff dress in their best vintage threads, and oldies pour from the speakers as you sip your malt shake. 2303 North 7th St, Phoenix, AZ 85006, www.macalpines1928.com

FRANCES Frances is a great little vintage shop in central Phoenix that is named after the owner's grandmother. The inventory is definitely geared more towards the ladies, with a large selection of vintage dresses, purses, and jewelry that my wife can't seem to get enough of. There's also some men's clothing, cool paper goods, and random retro gadgets for the guys. 10 West Camelback Rd, Phoenix, AZ 85013, www.francesvintage.com

DOWNTOWN PHOENIX PUBLIC MARKET The Downtown Phoenix Public Market is a growing program by Community Food Connections, where you can buy fresh, locally grown and produced food and goods. It's got a great community atmosphere and is easily accessible by light rail or bike. 14 East Pierce/721 North Central, Phoenix, AZ 85004, www.foodconnect.org/phoenixmarket

BARDS BOOKS One of the few indie bookshops that has survived in Phoenix, thanks to its open, community-focused vibe. It's not just a retail outlet, but also a social center, hosting workshops, readings, and many other events. The selection of new and used books is pretty great too. 3508 North 7th St #145, Phoenix, AZ 85014, www.bardsbooks.com

STINKWEEDS RECORD EXCHANGE Stinkweeds is an independently owned record store that has been meeting the valley's music needs for nearly 20 years. With a great stock of new and used CDs, vinyl, books, and magazines, it's long been a central hub for music geeks of all description. They also sell tickets to local gigs, and sometimes host their own. 12 West Camelback, Phoenix, AZ 85013, www.stinkweeds.com

SHOP

THE ICEHOUSE The Constable Ice Storage Facility was built in 1910 to manufacture the 300lb ice blocks required for transporting produce from California to the East Coast. It was later used by the police as a huge storeroom for criminal evidence. Its latest incarnation is as an arts center, which hosts lots of events and large-scale exhibits. The historic red brickwork makes for an atmospheric backdrop. 429 West Jackson St, Phoenix, AZ 85003, www.theicehouseaz.com

PHOENIX ART MUSEUM The Phoenix Art Museum has been around since 1959 and has rotating travelling exhibitions as well as a pretty impressive permanent collection of art from around the world. My favorite is the collection of surrealistic Victorian-themed paintings by Phillip C Curtis, the museum's founding director. 1625 North Central Ave, Phoenix, AZ 85004, www.phxart.org

CULTURE

FRACTAL PHOENIX A multi-use space in an old pie factory in Downtown Phoenix. Depending on the time of day, Fractal is a design studio with freelance rental space, a multi-media gallery, a design mentoring center for underprivileged youth, a community bike collective, a social outreach center, a place to lounge and catch up friends, or all of the above. Whenever you go it's always fun and worthwhile. 1301 Northwest. Grand Ave, Phoenix, AZ 85007, www.fractalphx.com

THE MONORCHID A revamped 1937 warehouse at the heart of the central Phoenix Arts District. It's a vast space with exposed wood trusses, industrial styling, and some of the most innovative exhibits the Valley has to offer. It also functions as a collaborative creative space, with artists taking up residence in the building's unique loft spaces. 214 East Roosevelt St, Phoenix, AZ 85004, www.monorchid.com

THE EYE LOUNGE This contemporary art space, run by an artists' collective, is an important venue for both established and emerging artists. Lots of restaurants and bars in the immediate area make it great for a quick culture fix on an evening out. 419 East Roosevelt St, Phoenix, AZ 85004, www.eyelounge.com

TEMPE CENTER FOR THE ARTS This arts center is on the shore of Tempe Town Lake in a beautiful building designed by Tempe-based Architekton, and the award wining Barton Myers Associates. Its roof has a fragmented surface with jagged geometric shapes protruding from its glass façade. At sunset, its reflection in the lake is a sight to behold. The contents are not bad either – it's a great place to catch the Tempe Symphony, some theater and other cultural events. 700 West Rio Salado Pkwy, Tempe, AZ 85281, www.tempe.gov/tca

VALLEY ART THEATRE A great little one-screen, classically-styled movie theater on the ever-happening Mill Avenue. It's the place to catch indie/arthouse films, as well as poetry readings, comedy gigs, and other live performances. Top-notch concession bar to boot. 509 South Mill Ave, Tempe, AZ 85281, www.millavenue.com

FIRST FRIDAY ART WALK A self-guided art outing that takes place on the first Friday night of every month. It was the first and is still the largest event of its kind, and should definitely be experienced if you get the chance. Several streets in Downtown are closed to traffic, dozens of galleries open their doors to the public, and street vendors sell everything from hot dogs to oil paintings. www.artlinkphoenix.com

MILL AVENUE DISTRICT Downtown Tempe, or Mill Avenue as it's more often referred to, is home to the Valley's most vibrant night life. Adjoined to ASU's main campus and Tempe Town Lake and Beach Park, Mill Avenue is lined with restaurants, bars, clubs, shops and buskers. The light rail offers good transport links to Phoenix and Mesa. www.millavenue.com

FRANK LLOYD WRIGHT ARCHITECTURAL TOUR Frank Lloyd Wright lived in the Valley of the Sun in his later life and is responsible for a number of amazing buildings sprinkled around the place. The jewel in the crown is Taliesin West. Built in 1937, it was FLW's winter home, studio and architectural campus. It's now the Frank Lloyd Wright Foundation's international headquarters, and holds a truly impressive collection of his work. It's also a good starting point for a tour of his buildings, which include houses, churches and public buildings that you can visit free of charge. It's worth taking a driving tour around all of them. 12621 Frank Lloyd Wright Blvd, Scottsdale, AZ 85259, www.franklloydwright.org

LOVE IT OR LEAVE IT

BRIAR LEVIT'S PORT LAND

ALSO KNOWN AS: STUMPTOWN, CITY OF ROSES, BRIDGE TOWN, RIP CITY, P-TOWN, *AND* PDX

PORTLAND, OREGON BY BRIAR LEVIT

Portland is a city of people who do it themselves: commute by bicycle, get in to the wilderness regularly, make art, and live sustainably. The population of the city has been steadily growing as places like California and New York become too expensive for young professionals and creative types. Here, it's possible to live comfortably on a meager income and still have money and time to work on your personal projects (music, art, sustainability, activism, etc). Almost everyone here has something creative going on outside of their day job.

Portland (also known as PDX, City of Roses, Stumptown, and Rip City to basketball fans) was established in 1841, and grew steadily through the years, particularly the war years, with an economy based on its seaport (initially the only one in the Pacific Northwest). In the 1970s, it began to really devote itself to its own infrastructure, investing in public transport, parks, and neighborhood renewal, and we're still reaping the benefits of that today.

Geographically, Portland is a river city. Its five sections all relate to the Willamette River, which bisects the city from west to east, and Burnside Street, which divides it from north to south. The Downtown area (SW) and the recently developed Pearl District (NW) have traditionally been where most of the galleries and restaurants are located, but that's all changing as shabbier areas on the east side of the river have started to offer less slick and often friendlier alternatives.

Whilst the input of the creative industries means that Portland's urban appeals are constantly developing and changing, the surrounding wilderness has always been a draw. Within minutes, you can find yourself deep in the woods of Forest Park or in just a half an hour, you can get to the Columbia River Gorge, a lush area boasting two rivers, waterfalls and a plethora of hiking trails. If you're willing to travel just a little further (about 90 minutes) you'll reach the coast. Roughly the same distance to the east, you'll find the majestic Mount Hood (visible from all over Portland). There are more lakes, skiing, and hiking than you can shake a stick at — a true haven of Pacific Northwest recreation.

ACE HOTEL The Ace is a sign of the growing creative class of Portland. Each room features a mural by a local artist, as well as a turntable and a decidedly Pacific Northwest design aesthetic. The hotel is home to the delicious Clyde Common restaurant (see Eat) as well as a gallery, The Cleaners, offering something different nearly every week. 1022 Southwest Stark St, Portland, OR 97205, www.acehotel.com/portland

JUPITER HOTEL Just across the river, The Jupiter Hotel offers a great alternative to traditional city center hotels. It shares a complex with the Doug Fir Lounge, one of the best music venues and bars in town, and is a must for the rock n' roll traveler. Think log-cabin-modern. 800 East Burnside St, Portland, OR 97214, www.jupiterhotel.com

HOTEL DELUXE For a more upscale experience, try the Art Deco Hotel Deluxe. Its website calls it "a contemporary tribute to the Golden Era of Hollywood filmmaking". Check out the glamorous Driftwood Room, a bar that always makes me feel like I'm stepping back in time. 729 Southwest 15th Ave, Portland, OR 97205, www.hoteldeluxeportland.com

THE KENNEDY SCHOOL The Kennedy School is a project by McMenamins, a couple of guys who have bought up old, derelict buildings around the city and revamped them for use as hotels, bars, theaters, etc. This particular hotel was once an elementary school. Choose the bar that suits you (the Honors Bar or the Detention Bar), go for a swim in the soaking pool or enjoy the courtyard restaurant in the former cafeteria. 5736 Northeast 33rd Ave, Portland, OR 97211, www.kennedyschool.com

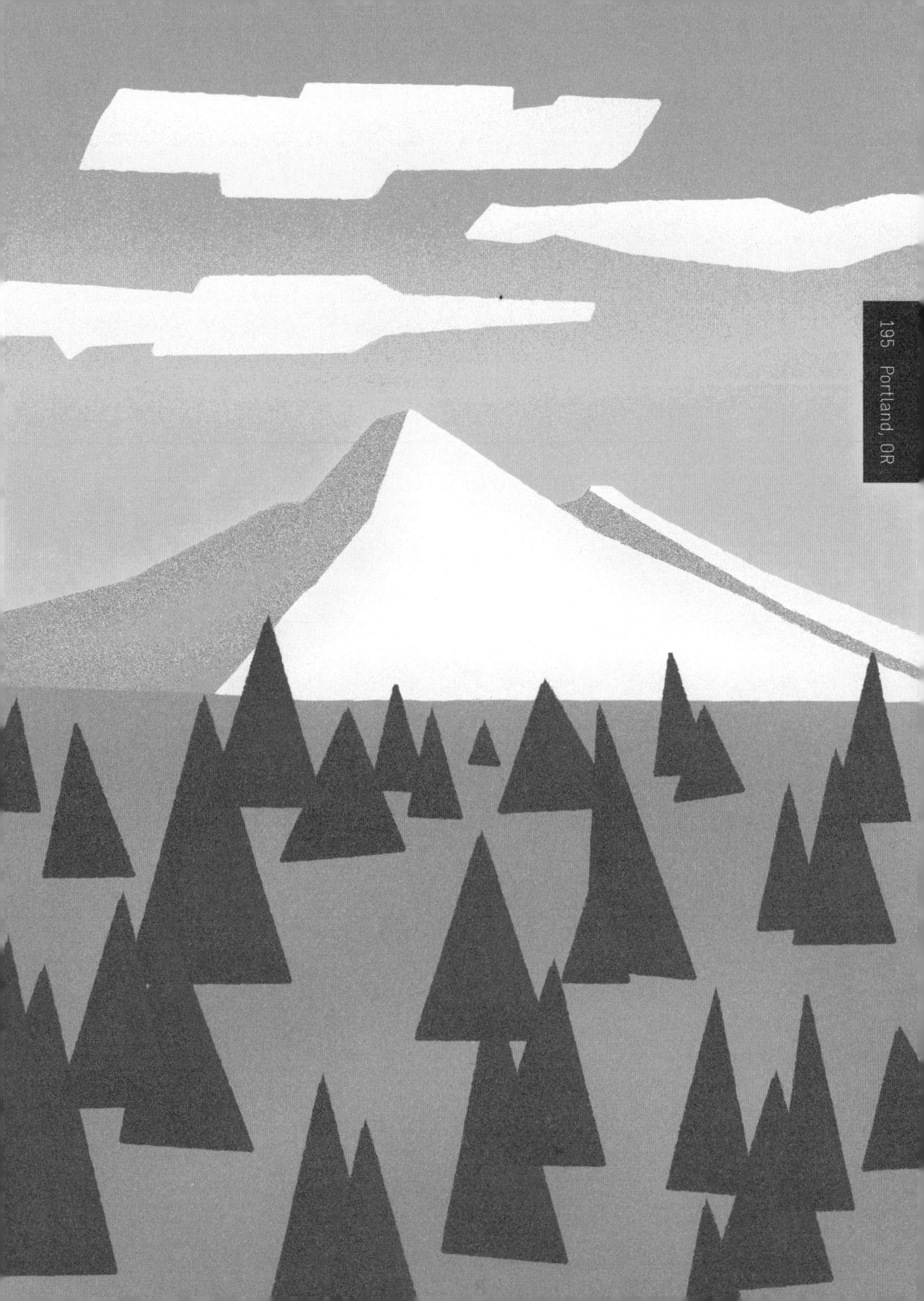

LE HAPPY Original Portland Frenchy Style — or at least that's how they describe themselves. This is one of my favorite places to bring people from out of town. A tiny, dimly lit restaurant serving delicious crepes until 2:30am. Try the Faux Vegan, packed with crème fraiche and goat cheese, or Le Trash Blanc — bacon, cheddar, and a Pabst Blue Ribbon. 1011 Northwest 16th Ave, Portland, OR 97209, www.lehappy.com

BEAST One of the growing number of young, chef-owned restaurants in Portland, Beast has made a splash serving a six-course, prix-fixe meal that focuses on, as you might have guessed, meat! Seating is communal and the food is cooked in sight of the table. A unique experience. 5425 Northeast 30th Ave, Portland, OR 97211, www.beastpdx.com

FOOD CARTS While food carts exist across the country, there's been a real renaissance for this mobile meal format in Portland. Sure, we have your typical taco trucks and burger guys, but we've also got carts making fantastic food ranging from Turkish to Hawaiian to Peruvian. Individual carts are popping up like wildflowers, but if you want a selection to choose from, then check out the food cart clusters at SW 10th and Alder, and SW 5th and Stark. www.foodcartsportland.com

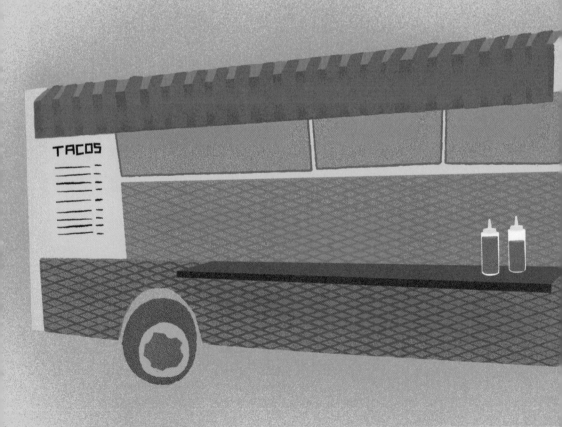

BLOSSOMING LOTUS For the health nut, there's Blossoming Lotus, serving only raw, vegan food. As a omnivore, I was skeptical, but it only took one meal for me to fall in love with this place. Flavorful soups, 'live' pizza and pastas as well as fresh juices and smoothies make this place a great break from all the heavy food you find yourself eating on vacation. The clean, modern atmosphere is equally refreshing. 1713 Northeast 15th Ave, Portland, OR 97212, blpdx.com

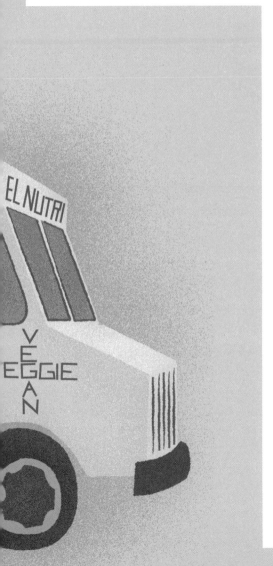

FARM One of the first restaurants in the area to feature local and organic farm-to-table ingredients, Farm is now an institution. The warm surroundings contrast with the elegant dishes and food presentation. The menu changes constantly. You can't help but love this place. 10 Southeast 7th Ave, Portland, OR 97214, www.thefarmcafe.com

PINE STATE BISCUITS A hugely popular, closet-sized restaurant, Pine State Biscuits serves hearty buttermilk biscuit sandwiches. The menu isn't extensive — but from a simple egg and cheese biscuit to one with shitake mushroom gravy, there's something for everyone. 3640 Southeast Belmont St, Portland, OR 97214, www.pinestatebiscuits.com

POK POK For a town impacted with Thai food — lots of really good Thai food, mind you — Pok Pok stands out. For one thing, don't count on finding the traditional American favorites like Pad Thai – it's all authentic food from the homes and streets of Southeast Asia. The setting is cozy and relaxed, literally in the house of the chef. 3226 Southeast Division St, Portland, OR 97202, pokpokpdx.com

KENNY & ZUKES Just up the block from The Ace Hotel, Kenny & Zukes offers great NYC-style sandwiches, hearty soups, latkes, blintzes and other tasty Jewish deli treats that are hard to find anywhere else in the city. 1038 Southwest Stark St, Portland, OR 97205, www.kennyandzukes.com

COURIER COFFEE ROASTERS This is where I grab a bite after a long bout of browsing at Powell's Books and Reading Frenzy. The menu is simple, but the coffee (their own roasted beans which are delivered to other local cafes via bicycle) is good, as are their homemade vegan desserts. 923 Southwest Oak St, Portland, OR 97205, www.couriercoffeeroasters.com

CLYDE COMMON This restaurant/bar, which is connected to the Ace Hotel, offers a mixture of American and European cuisine in elegant surroundings. A foodie's delight. 1014 Southwest Stark St, Portland, OR 97205, www.clydecommon.com

THE BYE AND BYE This place considers itself a biker bar in the Portland sense of the term, and the front is lined with fixed gear bikes. It might seem a bit heavy on the hipster front, but this spacious place is actually very laid back and is one of the few fully vegan bars in town. Great for non-vegans too! 1011 Northeast Alberta St, Portland, OR 97211, www.myspace.com/byeandbyeportland

SARAVEZA This is my new favorite bar! The owner, a Wisconsin transplant, decided to recreate a little piece of the Midwest, decorating this place with wood paneling and vintage beer ads. It's warm and cozy, and you can buy beers to take back with you from a selection of over 200 in the fridge that lines the wall. 1004 North Killingsworth St, Portland, OR 97217, www.saraveza.com

THE LIBERTY GLASS A truly Portland bar, The Liberty Glass is in an old, pink house, complete with chairs on the porch (and usually a lazy old dog), that sits just off bustling Mississippi Street. Pick from a comfort menu of mac n' cheese, tater tots, and Triscuit nachos – all criminally delicious. 938 North Cook St, Portland, OR 97227

THE DOUG FIR LOUNGE The Doug Fir Lounge is conveniently located across the courtyard from the Jupiter Hotel. It offers great happy hour deals on food and drink in a cozy cabin/disco environment. 830 East Burnside St, Portland, OR 97214, www.dougfirlounge.com

AMNESIA BREWING Like most towns in the US, breweries are popping all over Portland in order to quench the new microbrew thirst of beer connoisseurs. Most here are pretty standard including Hopworks, Henry's, and Dechutes. But for a more Portland-style experience, head over to Amnesia Brewing Company after some shopping on Mississippi and enjoy the homemade beer, tasty sausage-heavy menu, and open-air dining. 832 North Beech St, Portland, OR 97227

DRINK

HOLOCENE Holocene is a smallish dance venue, with a clean, modern aesthetic that focuses mainly on DJs and electronic acts. It definitely owns this niche, as most of Portland caters to the burgeoning indie-rock scene. 1001 Southeast Morrison St, Portland, OR 97214, www.holocene.org

THE WONDER BALLROOM A medium-sized music venue, The Wonder Ballroom hosts a huge percentage of the well-known bands that come through town. Heads-up: This place is all-ages, so watch out for the tweens. 128 Northeast Russell St, Portland, OR 97212, www.wonderballroom.com

GROUND KONTROL For the geek in you, Ground Kontrol is a massive video arcade filled with over 90 vintage games from the 70s, 80s, and 90s. And the icing on the cake? They serve beer! 511 Northwest Couch St, Portland, OR 97209, www.groundkontrol.com

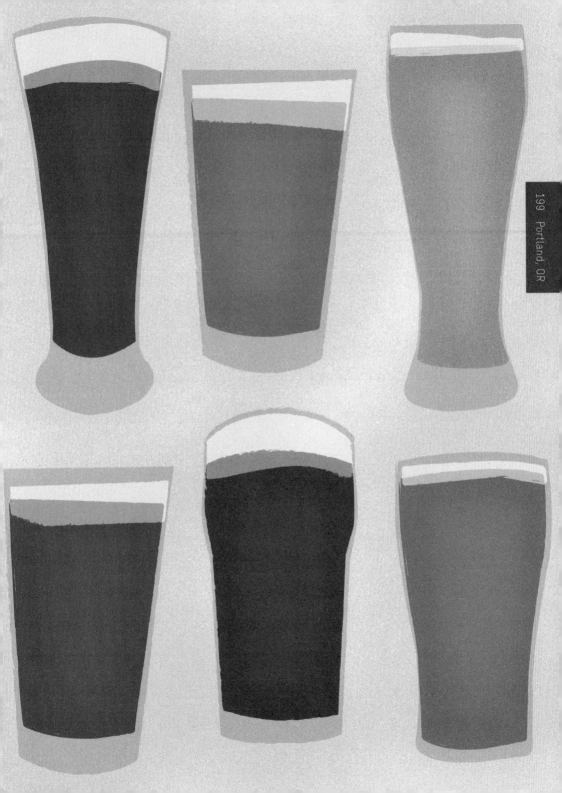

MISSISSIPPI The Mississippi area is one of the more recently developed parts of town. Formerly a quiet residential street, it is now home to a selection of great bars, restaurants, and little shops. Some of the more interesting: Pistils Nursery, a cozy plant shop for the urban farmer, She Bop, the most modern and stylish sex shop you'll find (female owned and operated), and Land Gallery, which is in the headquarters of BuyOlympia.com, one of the first online shops for handmade goods (WAY before Etsy, y'all). North Mississippi and Fremont Sts

23RD STREET This northwest area of the city (sometimes called 'Trendy Third') is home to the more upscale boutiques as well as a sprinkling of some of the less offensive chain stores (think Kiel's and Restoration Hardware). It's a great area to find unusual clothing and gifts and have a nice lunch along the way. Northwest 23rd at Burnside to Thurman

POWELL'S CITY OF BOOKS There's quite a lot to check out Downtown, but Powell's is probably the biggest draw, and certainly the most famous store in Portland. A full city block's worth of books – new and used – they literally have printed maps at the front to help you navigate. That said, this is NO mega-chain. Powell's is independently owned and operated, and the vibe of the store reminds you of that. After you hit Powell's, check out nearby Everyday Music and Reading Frenzy, and then grab a quick snack at Courier Coffee (see Eat). 1005 West Burnside, Portland, OR 97209, www.powells.com

HAWTHORNE Hawthorne Street is great for lots of different kinds of shopping, but it really stands apart when it comes to vintage clothing and homewares. I've probably furnished half my house with affordable finds from Hawthorne Vintage, Lounge Lizard and House of Vintage. For clothing, check out Red Light Clothing Exchange and Buffalo Exchange. You'll also find used and new music at Jackpot Records. And last but not least, if you didn't get enough of Powell's Books Downtown, you'll find another branch here, as well as a separate shop devoted solely to house and garden books! Southeast Hawthorne and 39th Ave

READING FRENZY One of the first shops in the USA to sell zines, Reading Frenzy deserves historic status to many zinesters and designers. In addition to books, zines and locally-made crafts, Reading Frenzy uses its walls for gallery space. Take this opportunity to pick up some amazing (and amazingly affordable) art. 921 Southwest Oak St, Portland, OR 97205, www.readingfrenzy.com

GRASS HUT A small, artist-run gallery, Grass Hut is another great place to go for art books, zines, prints, and original art (shows rotate monthly). Conveniently located across the street from The Doug Fir and The Jupiter Hotel. 811 East Burnside, Portland, OR 97214, www.grasshutcorp.com

CONTEMPORARY MUSEUM OF CRAFT The Contemporary Museum of Craft was founded in 1937, and has just moved into a new state-of-the-art space in a central Downtown location. This institution is constantly expanding the definition of craft and what it means to craft something. 724 Northwest Davis St, Portland, OR 97209, www.museumofcontemporarycraft.org

PORTLAND ART MUSEUM The Portland Art Museum is the oldest museum on the West Coast. It has great collections of art by native North American peoples as well as English silver and graphic arts. 1219 Southwest Park Ave, Portland, OR 97205, www.pam.org

TOGETHER GALLERY Another small, charming, artist-run space, the Together Gallery mostly features the work of emerging artists from the Pacific Northwest. 2916 Northeast Alberta St, Portland, OR 97211, www.togethergallery.com

CRAFTY WONDERLAND Once a small event, Crafty Wonderland has expanded and grown, and is now a super sale of handmade goods by local artists and designers that happens twice a year. Everything from stationery, to jewelry, clothing and more. Check the website for dates and location. www.craftywonderland.com

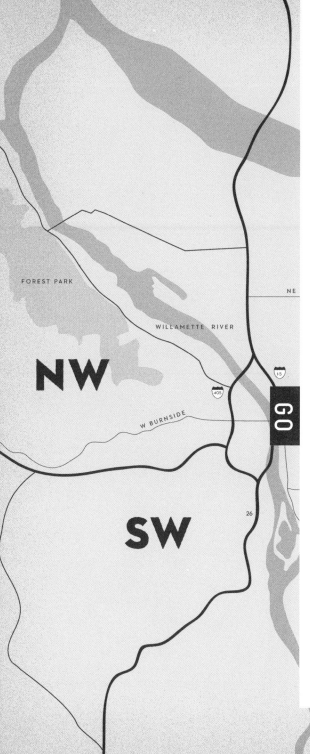

FOREST PARK

WILLAMETTE RIVER

NW

W BURNSIDE

SW

NE

GO

FOREST PARK Minutes from Downtown is Forest Park, a densely wooded, vastly trailed park offering hiking, cycling, and horseback riding. A gem in Portland's crown of green spaces. Northwest 29th Ave and Upshur St to Newberry Rd

MULTNOMAH FALLS Multnomah Falls are a sight. Located in the nearby Columbia River Gorge, the falls never run dry, even in the peak of summer. Walk to the top and reward yourself by wading in the river on a hot day, or for those who can't make it that far, the paved trail will take you to Benson Bridge, where you can get a stunning view. Be warned, this area gets very crowded in the summer. Located off of Highway 84 East. Take exit 28

EASTBANK ESPLANADE The Eastbank Esplanade runs 1.5 miles along the Willamette River, extending north from the Hawthorne Bridge to the Steel Bridge, with connections to East Side neighborhoods as well as across the river to the Waterfront Park. It's a great place to rent bikes and get a little closer to the water. Walkers beware – cyclists sort of own this area. Southeast Water Ave and Hawthorne Blvd

THE GROTTO This might be my favorite spot in Portland. I don't go here every day or even every month, but when I do, I feel a calm come over me. This 62-acre Catholic shrine and botanical garden is a great place to walk and contemplate or chat with friends. Perhaps the most impressive feature is Our Lady's Grotto, a rock cave shrine carved into the base of 110ft cliff. While I'm not religious myself, the way the church has worked its sculpture, shrines, and architecture into the natural landscape is refreshing and always peaceful. 8840 Northeast Skidmore St, Portland, OR 97220, www.thegrotto.org

adam lucas'

PROVIDED

PROVIDENCE, RHODE ISLAND BY ADAM LUCAS

I've always been drawn to cities that are defined by their geography.
First it was Baltimore, snuggled in the arm of the Chesapeake Bay; then
Portland, bordered by Forest Park to the east, and eight miles of ridgeline
to the west; and now Providence, Rhode Island, which nestles in the
mouth of the Providence River at the head of Narragansett Bay.

Much like Portland, Providence's geography contains the city,
and prevents it from expanding much beyond its original footprint.
The river runs along the eastern edge of Downtown, creating an east/
west side dynamic. The West Side includes the primary commercial
zone and its adjacent neighborhoods, and the East Side is home to the
university campuses – Brown and Rhode Island School of Design (RISD).
I like the manageable size of Providence – it means that no matter
which part you're in, the entire city is accessible by bike and/or public
transportation, and the Downtown is especially pedestrian friendly.

Similar to many other Eastern seaboard cities, which developed prior
to the automobile, the roads here are dense and chaotic. If you get lost,
try to find Westminster Street, a primary east-west artery, which runs
through Downtown and is the focal point for Providence's mercantile
district, known as 'Downcity'. This neighborhood is where you'll find much
of the city's most interesting architecture, including its tallest structure –
the Art Deco Bank of America building, and the Westminster Arcade – the
oldest enclosed shopping mall in the US (built in 1828).

Providence is one of the original 13 colonies, and perhaps my
favorite aspect of the city is that many of its streetscapes and residential
areas look like they did almost a century ago – sometimes because of
efforts at restoration and preservation, but often simply due to a lack of
development. This is, in my eyes, the key to much of Providence's charm.
There is a grittiness to it, both in appearance and in what it offers its
creative community. Music venues, art galleries, performance spaces,
and community studios are everywhere, catering to the diverse crowd
of artists, designers, students, and art lovers that live and visit here.

STAY

PROVIDENCE BILTMORE A reasonably priced, classic, historical hotel located in Kennedy Plaza in the heart of Downtown. Elegant rooms and great views. 11 Dorrance St, Providence, RI 02903, www.providencebiltmore.com

OLD COURT BED & BREAKFAST A charming, classic B&B on the East Side, just outside the RISD campus. 144 Benefit St, Providence, RI 02903, www.oldcourt.com

MOWRY NICHOLSON HOUSE INN Actually this has the best prices out of the three places listed here and it is where Obama stayed during his primary campaign in February 2008. 11 West Park St, Providence, RI 02908, www.providence-inn.com

MY APARTMENT Although I live with two roomates, we have a huge couch and an air mattress. We will cook the best food you will ever eat anywhere, and we will throw a dance party. Promise.

EAT

APSARA PALACE / RESTAURANT Excellent Chinese, Vietnamese, Thai, and Cambodian food for cheap and a BYO policy. I've been told that the original Apsara Restaurant on the West Side is a bit better, but I can't taste the difference. I think your best bet is whichever one is closer so the trip back home on a full stomach of noodles is shorter. 783 Hope St, Providence, RI 02906, and 716 Public St, Providence, RI 02907, www.apsara-palace.com

CLASSIC CAFE From the outside, this corner cafe looks like any other mediocre breakfast joint, but looks can be deceiving. One bite of their homemade corned beef hash, you'll know what's up. 865 Westminster St, Providence, RI 02903, www.ourclassiccafe.tripod.com

AL FORNO RESTAURANT The most expensive food on this list but also the top quality. If you want a big city, 5-star dining experience for Providence prices, go to Al Forno. 577 South Main St, Providence, RI 02903, www.alforno.com

THE RED FEZ A favorite spot of mine for the food, drinks, and atmosphere. They serve an eclectic but delicious selection, from the best pulled pork plate I've ever had to duck quesadillas, in a funky, hip setting. Plus they use all local fare! 49 Peck St, Providence, RI 02903

JULIAN'S Another excellent restaurant and bar with all local, organic menu options. They're especially choice for breakfast and weekend brunch, but can get busy at those times. It's worth the wait though. The staff are superb... and so is the Bloody Mary. 318 Broadway, Providence, RI 02909, www.juliansprovidence.com

LA LUPITA Top-notch, authentic Mexican food – and the cheapest restaurant on this list. Located in Olneyville on the West Side, La Lupita offers some of the best burritos and tacos I've ever had, using the freshest ingredients. 1950 Westminster St, Providence, RI 02909

LOCAL 121 Not quite as upmarket as Al Forno, but definitely on the fancier end of the spectrum. This restaurant is situated on the first floor of the newly refurbished historic Dreyfus Hotel, and serves all local, organic cuisine. 121 Washington St, Providence, RI 02903, www.local121.com

DRINK

THE RED FEZ This place not only serves great food, but an excellent drink selection as well. There are two bars: the upstairs is a bit more funky and dive-ish and the downstairs is classier. It's the only place in Providence where you can get a Dark n' Stormy for $4 or a Schlitz tall-boy for $2. 49 Peck St, Providence, RI 02903

THE SCURVY DOG The diviest of dive bars. The constant explosion of thrash metal from implanted car speakers impedes any worthwhile conversation, there are no windows, and any elbow room is limited to a foot-wide buffer zone around the billiards table — watch for the cue sticks. In the end, the absence of these luxuries is only an absence of distractions for getting another round of whiskey shots. 1718 Westminster St, Providence, RI 02909, www.scurvydogbar.com

THE HOT CLUB This might sound like a beach club in Miami, but actually it's situated on the eastern banks of the Providence River, with great views of the city and the best karaoke in town. 575 South Water St, Providence, RI 02903

THE E&O TAP I would place this bar in between the Red Fez and the Scurvy Dog — funky, cheap, good drink selection, but still a bit divey. A billiards table and arcade games make it extra fun, although as it's in a residential area, doors close at midnight. 289 Knight St, Providence, RI 02909

THE WILD COLONIAL TAVERN Located on the East Side, this place has a pool table and darts boards, but is by no means a dive bar. It has a spacious interior and serves pricier drinks. 250 South Water St, Providence, RI 02903

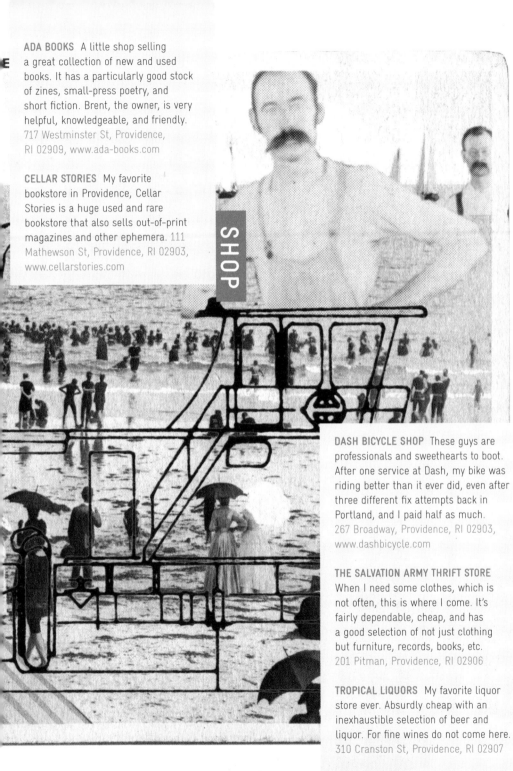

SHOP

ADA BOOKS A little shop selling a great collection of new and used books. It has a particularly good stock of zines, small-press poetry, and short fiction. Brent, the owner, is very helpful, knowledgeable, and friendly. 717 Westminster St, Providence, RI 02909, www.ada-books.com

CELLAR STORIES My favorite bookstore in Providence, Cellar Stories is a huge used and rare bookstore that also sells out-of-print magazines and other ephemera. 111 Mathewson St, Providence, RI 02903, www.cellarstories.com

DASH BICYCLE SHOP These guys are professionals and sweethearts to boot. After one service at Dash, my bike was riding better than it ever did, even after three different fix attempts back in Portland, and I paid half as much. 267 Broadway, Providence, RI 02903, www.dashbicycle.com

THE SALVATION ARMY THRIFT STORE When I need some clothes, which is not often, this is where I come. It's fairly dependable, cheap, and has a good selection of not just clothing but furniture, records, books, etc. 201 Pitman, Providence, RI 02906

TROPICAL LIQUORS My favorite liquor store ever. Absurdly cheap with an inexhaustible selection of beer and liquor. For fine wines do not come here. 310 Cranston St, Providence, RI 02907

AS220 AS220 is many awesome things all at once, but above all, it is a non-profit community arts space that includes a print shop (letterpress, silkscreen, intaglio, offset litho), live/work spaces, a darkroom, and other resources for creativity. It also has a restaurant, music venue, art gallery, and a bar with a nice beer and cocktail selection. If you come to Providence, you will need to come to AS220 one way or another, so check out their website to find out what's on. 9115 Empire St, Providence, RI 02903, www.as220.org

FIREHOUSE 13 Similar to AS220, this is a multi-use arts space. The first floor is primarily a performance venue, the second floor is a communal artist-in-residence living space, and the third floor is an open live/work studio for long-term rental. 41 Central St, Providence, RI 02907, www.firehouse13.org.

CULTURE

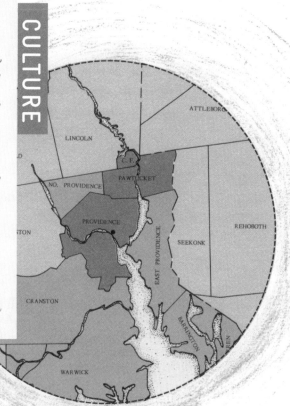

PROVIDENCE WITHIN ITS SPHERE OF INFLUENCE

WEST SIDE ARTS AND NEW URBAN ARTS
West Side Arts is a space for a collective of local artists, activists, and appreciators of art who share a concern about the world we live in. Next door you'll find New Urban Arts — a nationally recognized interdisciplinary arts studio for high school students and emerging artists. 743-745 Westminster St, Providence, RI 02903, westsidearts.org, www.newurbanarts.org

THE STEEL YARD / RECYCLE-A-BIKE The Steel Yard is an interior and exterior space that is utilized as a studio, metal shop, classroom, and a space for workshops, performances, and exhibitions. It also houses Recycle-a-Bike, a volunteer-run bike education and maintenance collective. 27 Sims Ave, Providence, RI 02909, www.thesteelyard.org, www.recycleabike.org

RISD MUSEUM OF ART Rhode Island School of Design (RISD) is home to the state's leading museum of fine and decorative art, housing a collection of 84,000 objects of international significance. The permanent collection and rotating exhibits are always top quality. 224 Benefit St, Providence, RI 02903, www.risdmuseum.org

WOODS GERRY GALLERY The main exhibition venue for RISD undergraduate students. Free and open to the public. 62 Prospect St, Providence, RI 02906

SOL KOFFLER GRADUATE STUDENT GALLERY
The primary exhibition space for RISD's graduate students, it is also free and open to the public. 169 Weybosset St, Providence, RI 02903

GELMAN GALLERY This is where any RISD student-curated group show is exhibited. 20 South Main St, Providence, RI 02903

PROVIDENCE ART CLUB GALLERIES The Providence Art Club, one of the oldest in the country, has two galleries — the Maxwell Mays and the Dodge House Gallery — both of which exhibit work by local painters. 11 Thomas St, Providence, RI 02903, www.providenceartclub.org

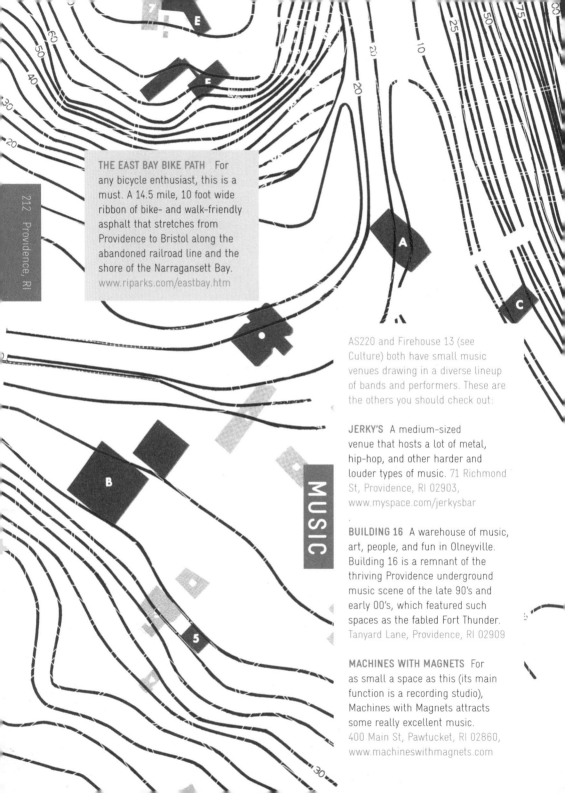

THE EAST BAY BIKE PATH For any bicycle enthusiast, this is a must. A 14.5 mile, 10 foot wide ribbon of bike- and walk-friendly asphalt that stretches from Providence to Bristol along the abandoned railroad line and the shore of the Narragansett Bay. www.riparks.com/eastbay.htm

MUSIC

AS220 and Firehouse 13 (see Culture) both have small music venues drawing in a diverse lineup of bands and performers. These are the others you should check out:

JERKY'S A medium-sized venue that hosts a lot of metal, hip-hop, and other harder and louder types of music. 71 Richmond St, Providence, RI 02903, www.myspace.com/jerkysbar

BUILDING 16 A warehouse of music, art, people, and fun in Olneyville. Building 16 is a remnant of the thriving Providence underground music scene of the late 90's and early 00's, which featured such spaces as the fabled Fort Thunder. Tanyard Lane, Providence, RI 02909

MACHINES WITH MAGNETS For as small a space as this (its main function is a recording studio), Machines with Magnets attracts some really excellent music. 400 Main St, Pawtucket, RI 02860, www.machineswithmagnets.com

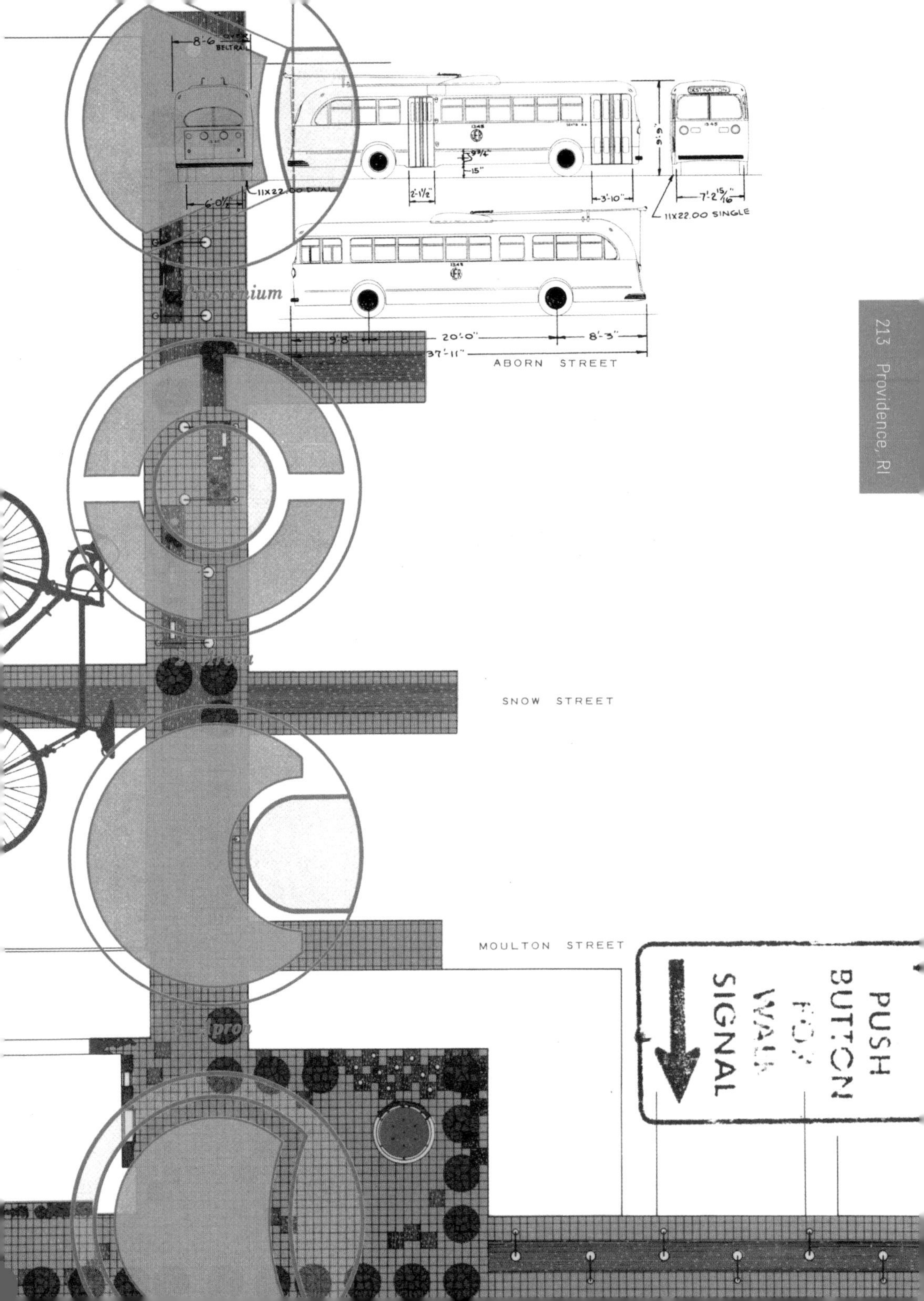

8'-6"
BELTRAIL

6'-0½"

11X22.00 DUAL

9¾"
15"

2'-1⅛"

3'-10"

9'-6"

EXTRA FARE

7'-2¹⁵/₁₆"

11X22.00 SINGLE

3'-8"

20'-0"

8'-3"

37'-11"

ABORN   STREET

SNOW   STREET

MOULTON   STREET

PUSH
BUTTON
FOR
WALK
SIGNAL

Cameron Ewing's

SAN
FRANCISCO

SAN FRANCISCO, CALIFORNIA

BY CAMERON EWING

San Francisco is often referred to as the most European of American cities, and for good reason. It's highly pedestrian friendly with a great metropolitan vibe. Most of it is walkable, and there's tons happening by way of music and art. Victorian, Modern, and Art Deco architecture lend it a sense of history, and everywhere you look you'll find iconic monuments such as the Golden Gate, Alactraz, and Giants Stadium, as well as sweeping views of the Pacific Ocean. Just don't call it 'Frisco' or we're going to have words.

The two essentials to bring if you come here are walking shoes (because the hills are silly really), and plenty of layers. The late afternoon fog brings a real chill, and you can always spot the tourists rocking tacky overpriced souvenir jumpers because they left the hotel underdressed. Mark Twain once said that 'the coldest winter I ever spent was a summer in San Francisco'. You've been officially warned. On the other hand, if you do happen to catch the city on a hot streak (usually late summer/early fall), you're in for a massive treat.

San Francisco has a rich history, most of which you probably know already. It started off as a gold rush town, and then grew as a major port city, particularly during the World Wars. It really gained notoriety in the late 60s as the heart of the cultural revolution and the home of the Summer of Love. Its reputation as a center of liberal expression and activism has never really gone away, and there is still a refreshing, anarchic vibe that I can't get enough of. I have lived in New York, Los Angeles, London, and Minneapolis, but somehow San Francisco just keeps calling me home.

Many of my recommendations are in the Mission District (or just 'the Mission' to locals), an area that was traditionally quite Latino working class, and now very trendy, but still a nice mix. But my advice to you is to make San Francisco your own. Stray off that beaten path and you'll be hard pressed not to have a great time.

STAY

THE CLIFT HOTEL The Clift is super swank, but a great spot to crash if can afford to live it up. The crowd is posh but cool – more fun to gawk at than to laugh at. Belly-up to the Redwood Room Bar for some lush cocktails (see Drink) 495 Geary St, San Francisco, CA 94102, www.clifthotel.com

PHOENIX HOTEL The Phoenix Hotel is a self-professed rock n' roll joint. It's got that mid-century, updated motel feel about it and if you happen to be in town during a rare warm spell it's got a dope pool for hanging out and sipping drinks served up at the Bambuddha Bar. 601 Eddy St, CA 94109, www.jdvhotels.com/phoenix

W HOTEL Located in the heart of Downtown, the W is next door to San Francisco's MoMA and within walking distance of most of the city's central locations. It's on the high-end, trendy side of the spectrum. 181 3rd St, San Francisco, CA 94103, www.starwoodhotels.com

THE GOOD HOTEL The Good Hotel is not only green, but is also the hippest of the set. It's cozily decorated using reclaimed and recycled materials, and contributes to a range of philanthropic organizations on behalf of each room. It's centrally located in SOMA, and offers free bike rentals and tours of the city. 112 7th St, San Francisco, CA 94103, www.jdvhotels.com/hotels/good

ST FRANCIS FOUNTAIN This retro diner is the 'it' breakfast spot in the Mission. Super hip staff, and a menu that will set you right after a big night out. Get there before 11am to beat the rush. I recommend the huevos rancheros, but seriously, everything is amazing. 2801 24th St, San Francisco, CA 94110 www.stfrancisfountainsf.com

MISSION STREET FOOD This is a hot little tip for Mission fine-dining. For five days of the week it operates as a mediocre Chinese restaurant, but on Thursdays and Saturdays it's transformed into a rad BYOB food extravaganza! Every week a different chef curates the menu with themes ranging from Mexiterranean to Ameritalian. Yeah, I said it. Come at 5pm to put your name in, and grab a glass of wine across the street at Corner until you're called. 2234 Mission St, San Francisco, CA 94110, www.blog. missionstreetfood.com

CHARANGA A Cuban dining spot that feels like you're stepping into a sweet little bodega in the heart of Havana. They serve amazing cocktails and delicious small plates for sharing. 2351 Mission St, San Francisco, CA 94110, www.charangasf.com

SLOW CLUB The Slow Club is a dope little speakeasy tucked in between the Mission and Portrero Hill. Totally urban-chic, it has an ever-changing weekly menu of delicious, sophisticated and surprisingly affordable meals. Plus amazing cocktails served up with much dramatic flair. 2501 Mariposa St, San Francisco, CA 94110, www.slowclub.com

EL PAPALOTE There's an ongoing debate about the best burritos in the Mission. As you can imagine similar debate is also raging about the best tacos. For my money, the best fish tacos/ burritos are being slung at El Papalote. The fish is fresh as f#$%, the salsa is spicy and divine, the chips are thick and they keep 'em coming as you wait for your dish. 3409 24th St, San Francisco, CA 94110, www.papalote-sf.com

EAT

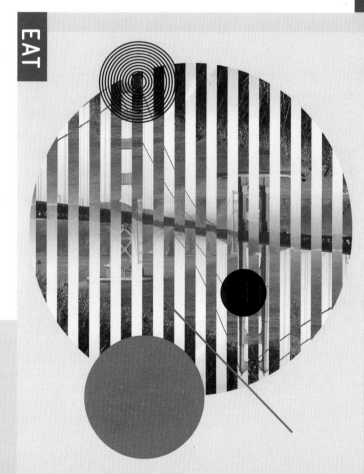

DRINK

THE RITE SPOT In a quiet corner of the Mission District, The Rite Spot has live music nightly and a very down-home atmosphere. If you're lucky enough to come on a night when they're serving their homemade pies, be sure to get one – they're delicious. 2099 Folsom St, San Francisco, CA 94110, www.ritespotcafe.net

CORNER Also in the Mission, this wine bar is great for posting up and watching the world stroll by. Corner has lots of great small plates for nibbling or sharing, but I'd recommend this place based on its polished yet cosy interior and their vast selection of rather delicious vino. 2199 Mission St, San Francisco, CA 94110, www.thecornersf.com

BERETTA Tucked cosily in the Mission, Beretta serves up a nasty array of cocktails including the Rangoon Gin Cobbler, the Airmail, and house specialty, the Snakebite – a delicious citrus laden ditty. The food here is also fantastic – mostly small sharing dishes. Great for easing into a big night on the town. 1199 Valencia St, San Francisco, CA 94110, www.berettasf.com

REDWOOD ROOM Located in the luxurious Clift Hotel, this bar was built in 1934 and had a massive makeover a few years ago. It's on the posh side of watering holes, but great for people watching and sipping fine cocktails. Make this a night-starter rather than a final destination. 495 Geary St, San Francisco, CA 94102, www.clifthotel.com

THE ATTIC At the opposite end of the spectrum from the Redwood Room lies The Attic. This place is dark, dank, and all about hard booze and cheap American beer. Come here to get wasted, period. There's usually someone spinning hip tunes, and the clientele take their getting booze pretty seriously, so contribute or get outta the way. 3336 24th St, San Francisco, CA 94110

SHOP

HAYES VALLEY Super cute corridor of shops and cafes in is what is otherwise a very residential part of San Francisco. It runs along Hayes Street from about Franklin to Webster and is great for hanging out in the afternoon to grab a coffee, a stroll and maybe a meal. Shops range from high-end shoes to casual travel wear. A nice, local scene. Hayes St, San Francisco, CA 94102

UNION SQUARE If you're a tourist in San Francisco, you're going to hit Union Square anyway, but it must be said that the shopping there's not bad. It's best to go there with a purpose – have a coffee and visit a couple shops as part of an afternoon out – rather than getting caught up in the throngs of skyline-gazing tourists. Union Sq, San Francisco, CA 94102

FORCE OF HABIT This is the greatest little record shop in the city and makes Amoeba look like a cheap big-box. Located in the Mission, this rock slanted hole-in-the-wall is the place for any vinyl enthusiast. There are bargains to be had in the $2 bins – everything from Chicago to Richard Hell and the Voidoids. Best leave the shopping list at home – the inventory is small but dotted with gems. 3565 20th St, CA 94110, www.forceofhabit.com

Where cable cars climb halfway to the stars.
And the morning fog may chill the air.

I left my heart in San Francisco
High on a hill it calls my name.

CAL ACADEMY OF SCIENCE: NIGHTLIFE This is what you get when you mix one part culture, one part science, and two parts SF nightlife. A good night out every time, Nightlife offers up mixed cocktails, witty conversation, and creative museum programming for the very hip. It's on the first Thursday of every month from 6-10pm, but if you miss it, the Exploratorium is still worth checking out in the daylight. 55 Music Concourse Dr, San Francisco, CA 94118, www.calacademy.org/events/nightlife

BALMY ALLEY For you fans of street art, Balmy Alley in the Mission is a block of political murals dating back to the 80s. If you're a total mural geek, Patricia Rose offers guided tours on the weekends, but to be honest, you'll probably get just as much out of the experience by strolling around on your own. 3007 24th St, San Francisco, CA 94110, www.balmyalley.com

THE AUDIUM The Audium is a little-known San Francisco classic, a sound sculpture built in the 50s, comprising 169 speakers that play a piece of music composed specifically for the space. It holds around 50 visitors a night, and over the course of the show creates a virtual labyrinth of sound. Prepare to have your mind blown. 1616 Bush St, San Francisco, CA 94109, www.audium.org

THE WAVE ORGAN The Wave Organ is a magical little spot, where you can hear the tides play a melodic siren's serenade on a series of concrete tubes and man-made rock caverns. Drive out as far as you can along 1 Yacht Road, park at the parking lot, and then stroll to the very tip of the jetty. Best to visit this spot in the early morning. 1 Yacht Rd, Marine Blvd, CA 94123

WHITE WALLS AND SHOOTING GALLERY I hate the term urban art, but that's what these two adjacent galleries show. Local and national artists making art that's just this side of cliché, sometimes tiptoeing into edgy. If art of the now is your bag, they're your best bet. Located in the notorious Tenderloin, the openings are pretty well attended, frequented by the city's hip set – and they're BYOB, so don't get caught out. 835 and 839 Larkin St, San Francisco, CA 94109, www.whitewallssf.com and www.shootinggallerysf.com

FECAL FACE GALLERY Located just down the road from White Walls and the Shooting Gallery, Fecal Face is another one of the younger galleries that are doing it well. The space is big and open and usually gets in work by hot, up-and-coming photographers, painters, illustrators, and graphic visionaries. 66 Gough St, San Francisco, CA 94102, www.fecalface.com/SF

SF MOMA The definitive contemporary art spot in SF. 'Nough said. This is the big one in town and worth a visit if you're in need of some inspiration. The space is great, the rotating exhibitions are almost always excellent, and the cherry on top is the new rooftop sculpture garden. Grab a coffee in the upstairs cafe, put your feet up, and take in some fresh air amongst some challenging sculptural installations. 151 3rd St, San Francisco, CA 94103, www.sfmoma.org

ALCATRAZ NIGHT TOUR Everyone tells you about Alcatraz Island, its history, and the films that have been shot there. What they don't tell you is that you can visit this place at night. It's a super spooky experience, offering up great views of the night skyline. It's popular, so be sure to book well in advance, and definitely take the audio-guide option – the recreations of sounds will scare you right out of your pants! www.parksconservancy.org/visit/alcatraz, www.alcatrazcruises.com

GOLDEN GATE FORTUNE COOKIE FACTORY
Locals tend not to go to Chinatown very often, but when they do it's mostly for the tea shops or for this amazing fortune cookie factory. It's tucked halfway down a rather shady alley, banging out hot fortune cookies right off the presses all day long. Totally authentic – and it's said that their fortunes are more accurate than most. 56 Ross Alley, San Francisco, CA 94108

RED BLOSSOM TEA TASTING Red Blossom is a rad little tea house in the heart of Chinatown. They import hundreds international teas, and are more than happy to walk you through the elaborate tea tasting rituals. I'd recommend opting for the roll your own tea filters, rather than the hardware. It makes the brewing process way more fun, and lets you steep your favorite leaves in your mug all day. 831 Grant Ave, San Francisco, CA 94108, www.redblossomtea.com

SKY GARDEN, FEDERAL BUILDING
The Federal Building is a 'green' building, designed by the architectural studio Morphosis in 2007. With its concrete and steel-meshed façade jutting out at all angles, it's a total architectural spectacle. And the best part is that the 'nook' is open to the public. Just go to the main entrance and tell the guards you're going to the Sky Garden. You'll have to put your bags through a scanner, and then take the elevator to the 11th floor. I recommend bringing a packed lunch up and enjoying it with the most incredible view of both north and south San Francisco. 90 7th St, San Francisco, CA 94103, www.morphopedia.com/projects/san-francisco-federal-building

SAILING ON THE BAY If you're itching to get out on the water while you're visiting San Francisco there are tons of options. The more pedestrian version is taking the ferry to Alameda, while the slightly more chic, but still pretty affordable option is to go sailing under the tutelage of the San Francisco Sailing Company. Make sure you've checked the weather before you book, because the San Francisco Bay can get rough. www.eastbayferry.com and www.sailsf.com respectively

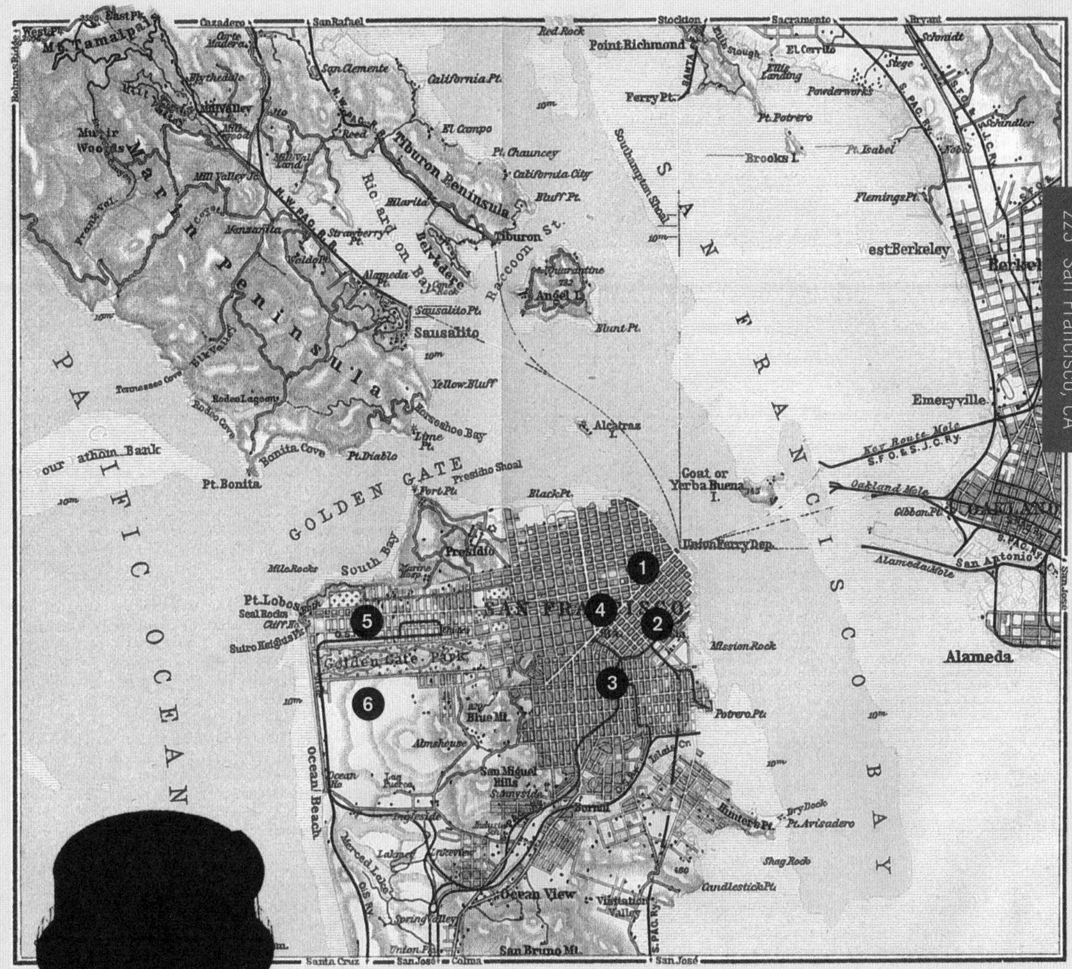

1. Downtown
2. SOMA
3. The Mission
4. The Tenderloin
5. The Sunset
6. The Richmond

TWIN PEAKS If you're mobile (read: have access to a car) charge up to the highest peak in the city. Twin Peaks affords one of the most spectacular views of the city and is home to the iconic Sutro Tower Antenna. The view at night is arguably more spectacular than that had by day, but you'll have to share it with car-loads of teeny-boppers getting into late-night trouble.

TANK HILL Everyone knows about Twin Peaks, but who ever talks about Tank Hill? Exactly. This spot offers up some of the most beautiful views in San Francisco, but is so small it doesn't even figure on some maps. It was designated a public space in 1977, when the eponymous water tank was made redundant. To get there, drive to the southern end of Stanyan Street, then turn left onto Belgrave Avenue and follow it to the end. Look for the short path to the left of the dead end. You'll need a car of course… and if you're driving already, you may as well check out Twin Peaks and tick it off your bucket list. Tank Hill, Belgrave Ave, San Francisco, CA 94117

GOLDEN GATE PARK Most tourists don't make it out to this part of town, but if you like a slice of the outdoors plus a good bit of adventure, this is not a bad place to start. I recommend visiting on a Sunday, as the main road that runs down the middle of the park is shut to traffic. For a great bike ride or a nice stroll, start at the 'Panhandle' and make your way west towards the Pacific Ocean. Check out the Japanese Tea Garden, the De Young Museum of Art, and the Conservatory of Flowers on your way. If you've worked up an appetite by the time you reach the coast, grab a bite at the Beach Chalet or the historic Cliff House Restaurant. www.sfgate.com/neighborhoods/sf/goldengatepark

SUTRO BATHS The Sutro Baths are an excellent place for an adventure at the city's edge. More of a scramble than a walk, the ruins of what were once San Francisco's only Victorian-era indoor salt water baths give way to a series of tide pools and trails at the edge of the ocean. A beautiful historic location, this merits a visit no matter what the weather. Point Lobos Ave and Merrie Way, San Francisco, CA 94121, www.sutrobaths.com

Many thanks to contributors: Mauri Skinfill, Justin Kerr, Matthew Ladra, Chrissy Loader, Terry Ashkinos, and Kimi Recor.

BJORN SONESON'S

SE
AT
TLE

SEATTLE, WASHINGTON BY BJÖRN SONESON

I grew up on the flatlands of the Midwest in Iowa, and I was drawn to Seattle for lots of reasons, but first and foremost for the dramatic landscape, which is everywhere you look – inside the city and around it – permeating its soul. Snuggled inside the Puget Sound, between Portland and Vancouver, it is surrounded by water and grand mountain ranges, with a temperate climate – mild grey winters and warm sunny summers. Inside the city you can explore the great parks, or experience the city from the water, and a short drive will take you to the heart of the Cascade Mountains, where you'll be surrounded by a lush, green, temperate rain forest that feels a million miles from any urban center.

Of course this attracts its fair share of sandal-wearing outdoorsy folk who complement their local-sustainable-fairtraide-organic-vegan vittles with the latest roast of coffee or seasonal micro-brew, but also a certain brand of laid back, vintage-clad hipster, who keeps the vibrant cultural scene alive with great theater, music, and art. Bikes dominate the roads, and electric cars abound. In the summer, the water bustles with seaplanes, people riding ferries across Elliot Bay, kayaking on Lake Union, and sailing on Lake Washington. In the winter, the ski slopes are spitting distance away.

As far as locations to visit within the city, there is plenty to do Downtown, but I usually spend most of my time in the surrounding areas. With no formal boundaries, the districts are created generally by the hilly topography surrounding Lake Union. I recommend starting your explorations around Pike and Pine on Capitol Hill, Downtown Fremont, and Ballard Avenue in Ballard. There's a good bus system, but the routes can be a bit tricky to work out if you don't know your way around. Alternatively, you can rent a bike. The hills will give you a good workout, but it's the best way to really get to know this fantastic city I call home.

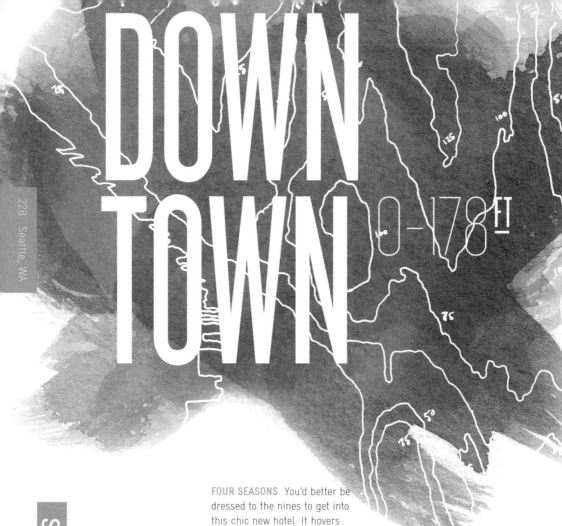

DOWN TOWN 0-178 FT

STAY

ACE HOTEL Hot illustrator Shepard Fairey (the one responsible for the Obama poster campaign), has one of his iconic Andre the Giant stencils on this old building turned hip hotel. Rooms are stylishly minimal, with an old-school science lab vibe. Pop into Rudy's Barber Shop around the corner to get more of a taste of Fairey's work. 2423 1st Ave, Seattle, WA 98121, www.theacehotel.com

FOUR SEASONS You'd better be dressed to the nines to get into this chic new hotel. It hovers above the waterfront, offering up endless views that are reflected in the interesting wall treatments and immaculate decor. 99 Union St, Seattle, WA 98101, www. fourseasons.com/seattle

HOTEL SORRENTO This boutique hotel is all old-world class, with dark wood and low light. I always feel like I should be wearing a top hat when I come here. Make like a millionaire and stay the night or just stop in for happy hour. 900 Madison St, Seattle, WA 98104, www.hotelsorrento.com

AURORA AVENUE MOTELS Although I do not recommend actually staying the night, Aurora Avenue is chock-full of mid-century, run-down roadside motels with great, kitsch neon signs. Anyone into vintage Americana will love it.

EAT

VOLTERRA This Tuscan restaurant brings flavors to your mouth that seem to have belonged there forever. Wonderful ingredients make their succulent pasta and meat dishes come to life. If French food is more your thing, try the excellent Bastille down the road. 5411 Ballard Ave, Seattle, WA 98107, www.volterrarestaurant.com

MOLLY MOON'S ICE CREAM Using ingredients you might expect to see in your entrée rather than your ice cream, Molly Moon's serves up wacky but delicious combos including my favorites, Balsamic Strawberry and Rosemary Meyer Lemon. It gets busy, but it's worth waiting for. 1622 North 45th St, Seattle, WA 98103, www.mollymoonicecream.com

AGUA VERDE CAFE AND PADDLE CLUB There's no better way of experiencing Seattle in the summer than from the water. Rent a kayak and paddle to Lake Union for a great view of Downtown, and then satisfy your hunger with the mouth-watering Mexican fare served up at the cafe next to the paddle club. 1303 Northeast Boat St, Seattle, WA 98105, www.aguaverde.com

PURPLE In the heart of Downtown, this dramatic restaurant features a winding spiral of wine that reaches from floor to ceiling. Small plates allow you to sample several of their delicious contemporary dishes. Be careful getting up because their chairs are really heavy… no joke. 1225 4th Ave, Seattle, WA 98101, www.thepurplecafe.com

MATT'S IN THE MARKET Overlooking Pike Place farmers' market, this amazing restaurant serves up gourmet combinations of local seafood, meats, and produce. Their lamb burgers are unbeatable, and their sandwiches offer an affordable way of experiencing their great food. 94 Pike St, Seattle, WA 98101, www.mattsinthemarket.com

LA SPIGA Wonderful Italian cuisine using market-fresh ingredients. Nice decor with modern lines complementing the rustic wood. 1429 12th Ave, Seattle, WA 98122, www.laspiga.com

SERIOUS PIE Tom Douglas is a Seattle institution. He's a chef and restauranteur with a handful of places around the city. This pizza joint serves up awesome pies straight from the wood-fired oven with adventurous toppings and delectable starters in a dark, intimate atmosphere. 316 Virginia St, Seattle, WA 98101, www.tomdouglas.com

PASEO The most delicious sandwich in Seattle – marinated and grilled pork, perfectly caramelized onions, garlic aioli, cilantro, jalapeños, topped with romaine on a toasted baguette. YUM. And it's cheap. Be prepared to wait in line with the locals. With limited seating, take it to go and enjoy it by the Fremont Canal down the road. 4225 Fremont Ave, Seattle, WA 98103, www.paseoseattle.com

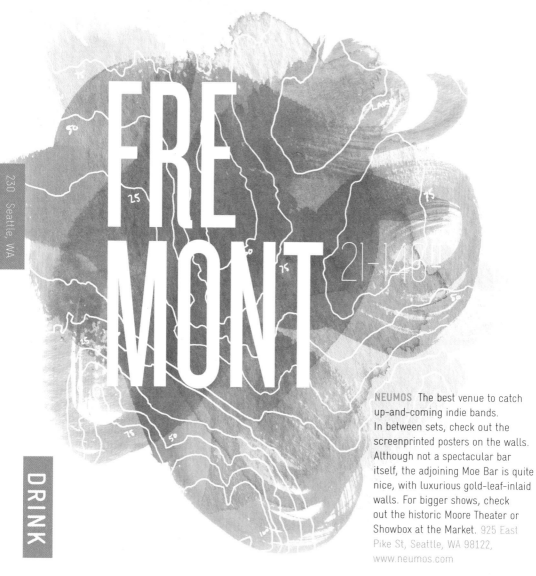

FRE MONT

21-146

DRINK

NEUMOS The best venue to catch up-and-coming indie bands. In between sets, check out the screenprinted posters on the walls. Although not a spectacular bar itself, the adjoining Moe Bar is quite nice, with luxurious gold-leaf-inlaid walls. For bigger shows, check out the historic Moore Theater or Showbox at the Market. 925 East Pike St, Seattle, WA 98122, www.neumos.com

BROUWER'S CAFE 64 beers on tap and hundreds of bottled options in a neo-medieval interior. They specialize in Belgian beers, but the knowledgeable bartenders can point you in the direction of plenty of local brews too. Their food is not bad either. 400 North 35th St, Seattle, WA 98103, www.brouwerscafe.com

KING'S HARDWARE King's in Ballard is all vintage cabin vibe, with a laid back atmosphere and the added bonus of skee-ball. It can get a bit rowdy on the weekends, but a pitcher of Rogue Hazelnut Brown on the patio is usually a real treat. If you dig the vibe, check out Linda's Tavern on Capitol Hill as well. 5225 Ballard Ave, Seattle, WA 98107, www.kingsballard.com

GARAGE BILLIARDS If there is such thing as a contemporary, cool bowling alley, this is it. Catering to the young Capitol Hill crowd, the place is decorated with modern/vintage furniture, and creepy doll parts on the walls. Kick back and relax, or play a game in the huge billiards hall. 1130 Broadway, Seattle, WA 98122, www.garagebilliards.com

BAUHAUS COFFEE A nice place to relax, browse the books that line the walls, or work on your latest project with the other young Seattlites hunched over their computers. Large windows offer up great views of the Space Needle and Olympic Mountains. 301 East Pine St, Seattle, WA 98122, www.bauhauscoffee.net

ZOKA COFFEE ROASTER & TEA COMPANY Off the beaten path in the sleepy area of Green Lake is a true neighborhood coffee shop and perhaps my favorite in Seattle. They serve full leaf teas, a great range of roasts brewed by the cup, and they pour their lattes the correct way. 2200 North 56th St, Seattle, WA 98103, www.zokacoffee.com

CUPCAKE ROYALE AND CAFE VÉRITÉ Leading the cupcake revolution is Cupcake Royale. Complement your gourmet cupcake with a cappuccino from Vérité Coffee (under the same roof), which is served in a dainty pastel pink cup that looks like it's come straight out of a teddy bear's tea party. Can't get enough? Stop by at the rival Trophy Cupcakes in Wallingford too. 2052 NW Market St, Seattle, WA 98107, www.cupcakeroyale.com

CAPITOL HILL

PETER MILLER BOOKS On the first floor of the Terminal Sales Building (where I happen to work) is Peter Miller Books, a must stop for any designer. You'll find a trove of architecture, design, and art books as well as a collection of design objects that will really get your blood pumping. Be sure to pick up an issue of *ARCADE*, the free quarterly journal of design and architecture in the Northwest. And if that still hasn't satisfied the aesthete in you, check out Paperhaus down the road for high end art supplies. 1930 1st Ave, Seattle, WA 98260, www.petermiller.com

METSKER MAPS From nautical to relief maps, Metsker has it all. Check out the local Northwest terrain or learn more about your next destination. 1511 1st Ave, Seattle, WA 98260, www.metskers.com

AREA 51 A goldmine for the eyes, featuring original Modern furniture design classics from Eames to Herman Miller. Vintage sign letters beg to be taken home and placed firmly on your desk to declare your love for typography. Most of it is pretty pricey, but there are some less expensive items there too. 401 East Pine St, Seattle, WA 98122, www.area51seattle.com

SONIC BOOM Seattle is a city that loves its music, and this is the record store that gives the musos their fix. They stock a fine selection, and have just opened a new store in Captiol Hill (the original is in Ballard). 1525 Melrose Ave, Seattle, WA 98101, www.sonicboomrecords.com

SHOP

FREMONT AND BALLARD MARKETS Seattle has more than its fair share of markets, and these two are particularly nice. They're both open on Sundays. Fremont Market is geared more towards artists, jewelry, vintage goods and street food, with a flea market vibe, while Ballard Market sells more produce and food-goods. A great way to start a Sunday, with plenty of people watching – especially in summer. **FREMONT:** North 34th St, Seattle, WA 98103, www.fremontmarket.com **BALLARD:** Ballard Ave, Seattle, WA 98107

THEO CHOCOLATE After the organic and fair trade beans make their way to Seattle, Theo turns them into intense and wonderful chocolate. Try something different with a coconut curry or a fig fennel almond bar. Mounds of samples to try before you buy. And the factory tour is really pretty fun. 3400 Phinney Ave North, Seattle, WA 98103, www.theochocolate.com

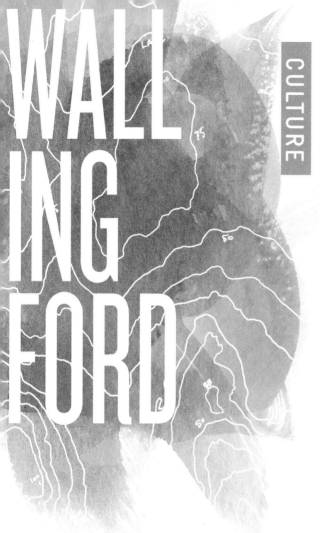

WALL ING FORD

SEATTLE ART MUSEUM (SAM) SAM has a really good permanent collection that ranges from historical to contemporary, as well as some cool exhibitions. The Australian Aboriginal collection is my favorite. They also host interesting events and have a great shop and cafe. To see the big pieces, head up 1st Avenue and explore the Olympic Sculpture Park. 1300 1st Ave, Seattle, WA 98101, www.seattleartmuseum.org

HENRY ART GALLERY On the University of Washington campus, the Henry is a contemporary art gallery which is especially strong on photography. Don't miss James Turrell's calming Skyspace. 15th Ave NE and NE 41st St, Seattle, WA 98105, www.henryart.org

UNIVERSITY OF WASHINGTON'S SUZZALLO LIBRARY READING ROOM If you're into the grand and Gothic, the Reading Room is the place for you. Row upon row of desks with low lights huddle underneath a towering Gothic ceiling. Red Square, Seattle, WA 98195, www.lib.washington.edu/suzzallo

SEATTLE CENTRAL PUBLIC LIBRARY A Rem Koolhaas designed building (with environmental graphics by Bruce Mau), this is one of my favorite pieces of architecture in Seattle. It's truly innovative design with some really spectacular highlights including a type-laden floor on the first level, chartreuse portal-like escalators, a floor that works as a kind of blood-vessel, and a view over Elliot Bay from the top level. Check out the Seattle Architecture Foundation for tours. 1000 4th Ave, Seattle, WA 98164, www.spl.org and www.seattlearchitecture.org

CHAPEL OF ST IGNATIUS Designed by Stephen Holl, this minimalist chapel on the Seattle University campus is immaculately designed down to the tiniest detail. Light filters and reflects, creating wonderful moods throughout the space. 901 12th Ave, Seattle, WA 98122

CENTER FOR WOODEN BOATS Seattle is surrounded by water, and its boating history runs deep in its veins. The Center for Wooden Boats is a kind of museum on water, where you can see all the different types of wooden vessels. You can rent one of them, or go for a free ride on Sunday afternoons. If you want to see something more modern, walk the docks of Fisherman's Terminal and check out Seattle's mighty fleet of fishing boats. 1010 Valley St, Seattle, WA 98109, www.cwb.org

GUM WALL AND PIKE PLACE MARKET Some find this disgusting, but the chewing gum mosaic tucked under Pike Place Market is pretty remarkable. It was started by bored people waiting in line for shows at the Market Theater. Buy a pack of gum and make your mark. And then go and explore the market above. Post Alley, Seattle, WA 98101

GREEN SPACES

KERRY PARK One of the best viewpoints over the city, hands down. You can capture the most amazing postcard snapshots of Mount Rainer and Elliot Bay, with the Space Needle in the foreground, and watch the airplanes as they fly up the Puget Sound. 211 West Highland Dr, Seattle, WA 98119

BALLARD LOCKS These locks, officially known as the Hiram M Chittenden Locks, connect the fresh waters of Salmon Bay and Lake Union with the salt water of the Puget Sound. Every boat that wants to cross from one to another must come through here, and it's the perfect place to see anything from huge fishing boats to pleasure yachts and tiny wooden boats. Apart from boat spotting it also offers a great view of the fish ladder, where the huge salmon of Seattle make their journey to spawn. 3015 Northwest 54th St, Seattle, WA 98107

GAS WORKS PARK Jutting out into Lake Union, Gas Works used to be the site of an old refinery that was transformed into a luscious green space. The industrial grandeur of the surrounds contrasts with the unparalleled views of the skyline. I like coming here with a picnic on a Tuesday evening in summer, when you can watch hundreds of sailboats dodging each other on the lake. Don't forget to bring your kite! 2101 North Northlake Way, Seattle, WA 98103

WASHINGTON PARK ARBORETUM With acres of trails, ponds, and beautiful flora, all very carefully laid out, this is a really romantic spot with something for everyone. Plus it's free to enter. 2300 Arboretum Dr East, Seattle, WA 98112

INNER CITY NATURE If you don't have access to a car, there are plenty of ways of exploring nature within the city. Discovery State Park has miles of trails, you can go for a run around Green Lake, relax at the beach at Golden Gardens, or rent a bike and cycle the 27-mile Burke Gilman Trail that cuts right through Seattle.

OUT OF TOWN If you have the time to rent a car and do some exploring, Seattle offers easy access to some of the most incredible nature. If you drive east on 90, you can hike miles and miles of trails in the Cascade Mountains. Northwards will take you to Deception Pass State Park and the majestic San Juan Islands, where you can hike alongside the water. A drive South will take you to the daunting Mount Rainier. If you come in winter, there are plenty of ski slopes all around.

BALL ARD

FREMONT SOLSTICE PARADE Every year on the summer solstice, the streets of Fremont are filled with crazy floats, costumes, and cyclists nude except for some body paint. A wonderful event of creativity and joy. www.fremontartscouncil.org

SEATTLE INTERNATIONAL FILM FESTIVAL Every May, Seattle plays host to film-goers from around the world. Spread across numerous theaters, it's a great way to see interesting films as well as Seattle's historic cinema architecture. www.siff.net

FIRST THURSDAY ARTWALK IN PIONEER SQUARE Pioneer Square, one of the oldest areas of the city, is now home to dozens of galleries and artist co-ops. On the first Thursday of every month, they all open their doors to the public. You can sometimes catch some great shows. It's also worth noting that most museums in town are free on first Thursdays. www.firstthursdayseattle.com

EVENTS

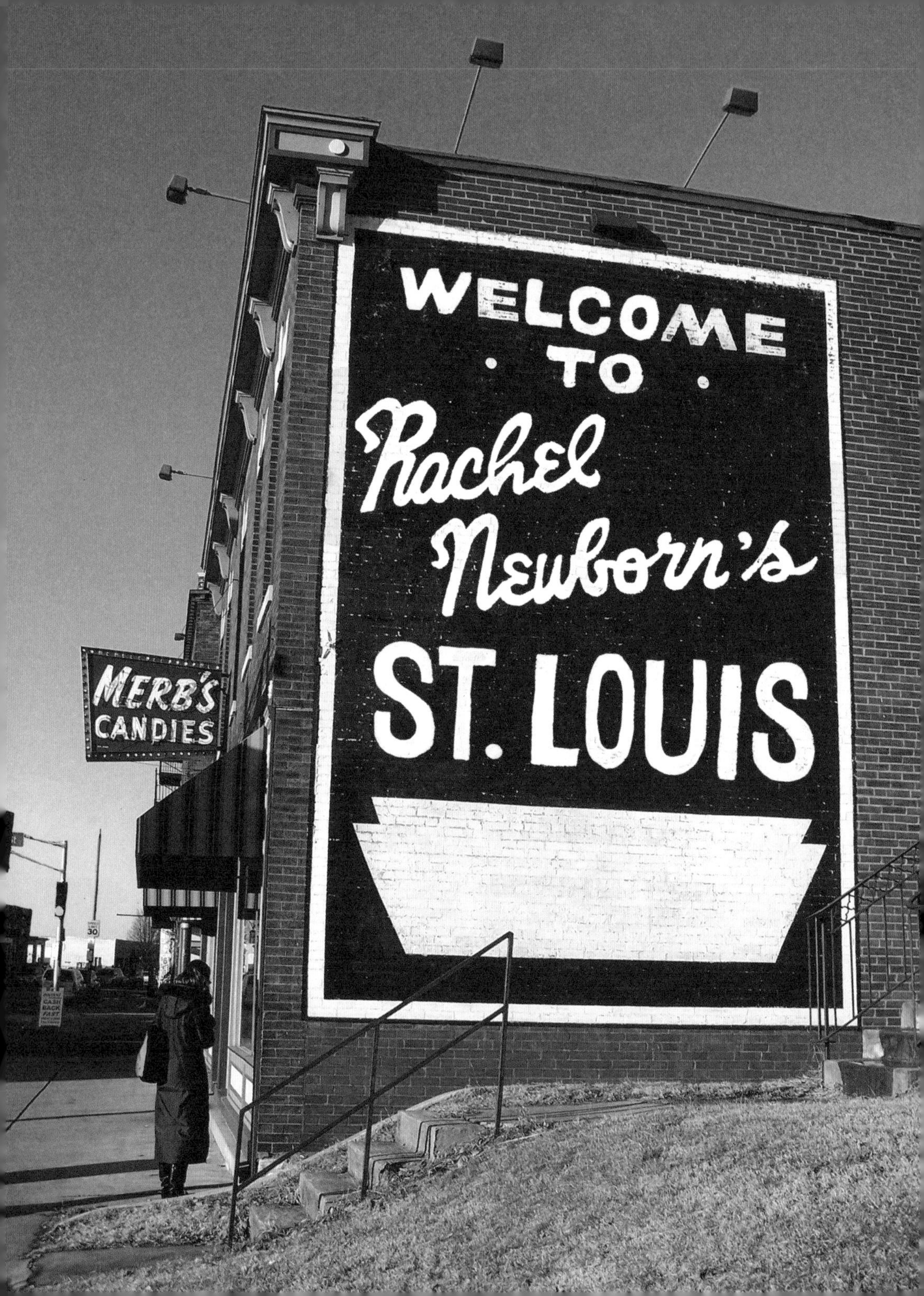
WELCOME
TO
Rachel
Newborn's
ST. LOUIS
MERB'S
CANDIES

ST LOUIS, MISSOURI BY RACHEL NEWBORN

Growing up in Boston, I took public transport for granted. I visited friends, museums, and new neighborhoods without thinking twice, and knew the city's corners and crevices intimately. When I moved to St Louis for college, I was excited to learn the quirks and culture of the city, and assumed I would quickly make it my own. Within a week, I realized this would be more difficult then I expected. Not only was a car essential to get to the most interesting places in the city, but I also had a hard time convincing myself, or my friends, to explore unknown areas in the then most dangerous city in America.

It wasn't until the last half of college that I began to understand the city. Unlike Boston, where every pre-1900 merchant or ship captain's home has been converted into a museum, many St Louis landmarks, such as the historic Lemp Brewery and the Samuel Clemens house, lie in ruin. There's no harborside view and absolutely no tribute to the Revolutionary War. The city's illustrious past as a thriving industrial hub is reduced to the ghosts of old advertisements painted on the sides of buildings and the odd retro candy store. Densely populated neighborhoods and bustling commercial areas now appear desolate or otherwise abandoned.

Of course, this is not always a bad thing. There is a tragic beauty in the brick landscape, which has not gone unnoticed. Artists and entrepreneurs have taken over historic spaces for unexpected venues of art and business. The City Museum, for example, is situated in a turn-of-the-century shoe factory, and it simultaneously honors the building's history, while creating a new space that is pure, unadulterated fun. There is a free-thinking lack of self-consciousness about the city as well. It is home to many independent coffee shops and breweries that roast their own beans and brew their own beer. All public museums and the zoo are free to the public.

St Louis is a city that always believes it could be grander, without realizing that those very cracks that it wants to repair have given a space for pride, tradition, and art to flourish in the unlikely spaces in between.

MOONRISE HOTEL Unfortunately this hotel didn't exist in the days I had cause to visit St Louis as a tourist, but if I ever return with a chunk of change in my pocket, this is where I'm going to stay. Owned by Joe Edwards, local entrepreneur and retro-pop aficionado, it's a real blast with 1950s kitsch signage, a fluorescent staircase, posters of comic book heroes, and plastic ray guns everywhere you look. 6177 Delmar Blvd, St Louis, MO 63112, www.moonrisehotel.com

LEMP MANSION RESTAURANT AND INN In the late 1800s the Lemp family had a monopoly over the beer brewing industry in St Louis, and resided in this impressive mansion. Weirdly, they all met tragic ends – either by suicide or in mysterious circumstances, and today the mansion hosts spooky Halloween events and haunted tours. The rest of the time, it is home to an inn with a beautiful atrium and deck, from which you can see the defunct old brewery. 3322 Demenil Pl, St Louis, MO 63118, www.lempmansion.com

LEHMANN HOUSE This is a very simple, cute, affordable B&B in the beautiful neighborhood of Lafayette Park. It has four rooms decorated with antique furniture and fainting sofas. Although I've never stayed here myself, I've heard that the owner is very accommodating, makes great breakfast and always has a compelling tale to tell. 10 Benton Pl, St Louis, MO 63104, www.lehmannhouse.com

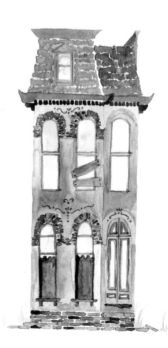

CAFE NATASHA'S KABOB INTERNATIONAL

South Grand is home to many good eats but Kabob International stands out for its great Persian food. It's a quiet restaurant with cobalt blue walls and multicolored lamps. The marinated kabobs are excellent, as is everything else on the menu, including the veggie options. 3200 South Grand Blvd, St Louis, MO 63112, www.cafenatasha.com

AL-TARBOUSH DELI This Middle Eastern counter deli is barely noticeable on a side street off Delmar but they have the best hummus I've ever eaten. Creamy, garlicky perfection. Order it to go, or have it on a juicy, flavorful sandwich. 602 Westgate Ave, St Louis, MO 63130

THE LONDON TEA ROOM Quirky and resolutely British, two young women from the UK run this successful cafe, which has followers so devoted they have the teas shipped across the country. They host knitting afternoons with Knitty Couture, and for the people-watching enthusiast, I've never seen so many hot young dads. 1520 Washington Ave, St Louis, MO 63103, www.londontearoom.com

GREAT PIZZA: DEWEY'S, THE GOOD PIE, PI St Louis is not known for its pizza, certainly not by East Coasters, who feel that the St Louis interpretation of the dish is an abomination (envision a giant matzo cracker with a generous helping of Provolone-flavored American cheese). However, there is a strong following for the few places that haven't missed the mark. Dewey's makes a bready, thicker cut pizza with fresh toppings. The Good Pie does an authentic Napolitano pizza in a brick oven and great daily specials. Pi makes Chicago-style deep-dish pizzas that President Obama liked so much he had them specially delivered to The White House. **DEWEY'S PIZZA:** 559 North And South Rd St Louis, MO 63130, www.deweyspizza.com, **THE GOOD PIE:** 3137 Olive St, St Louis, MO 63103, www.thegoodpie. com, **PI:** 400 North Euclid Ave, St Louis, MO 63108, www.restaurantpi.com

BOOSTER'S CAFE This little cafe is owned and operated by Kevin Winter and Barbara Harrington, and the profits go back to their respective spouses who are promoting AIDS education in Nigeria. Even before I knew about their worthy cause, I loved this place. Their mouth-watering blueberry-pumpkin pancakes hit the spot after a long night out. It's the best place to go if you're craving a slice of home – everything is made with love. 567 Melville Ave, St Louis, MO 63130, www.boosterscafe.com

WORLD'S FAIR DOUGHNUTS This roadside doughnut shop near the botanical gardens is a time capsule of 1960s Americana. It's run by an elderly trio who sport solid beehive hairdos and powder blue eye shadow. The doughnuts are fantastic – crispy on the outside and soft on the inside. 1904 South Vandeventer Ave, St Louis, MO 63110

LORUSSO'S CUCINA This restaurant is a bit more upmarket. It's in the Italian neighbourhood called 'The Hill', and it has a great atmosphere that's both buzzing and romantic. Traditional Italian dishes with fresh robust flavors mean that the place is always packed, so make a reservation. 3121 Watson Rd, St Louis, MO 63139, www.lorussos.com

TASTE BY NICHE Taste is a tiny, intimate restaurant that is perfect for a cozy light dinner and drinks. The staff is very friendly, and the menu features intriguing combinations such as horseradish and dates, or cucumbers, nutmeg, and brine to create flavors that are unexpected but seamlessly combined. 1831 Sidney St, Benton Park, MO 63104, www.nichestlouis.com

BLUEBERRY HILL Frequented by college students and baby boomers alike, Blue Hill, as it's referred to by college folk (not by St Louis natives) is an odd mix. Memorabilia for local sports and music heroes crowd the wooden walls. If you're lucky you might score tickets to see Chuck Berry who, way into his 80's, still places a set every Saturday night. 6504 Delmar Blvd, St Louis, MO 63112, www.blueberryhill.com

BAILEY'S CHOCOLATE BAR Bailey's is just what you'd imagine a swanky dessert restaurant and bar to be. Decorated in red velvet with clusters of tea-lights on the tables, it features a heated, all-weather, wrap around porch with trees growing up through the ceiling. Make a reservation at weekends. 1915 Park Ave, St Louis, MO 63104, www.baileyschocolatebar.com

THE FOUNTAIN A former car showroom turned family-friendly restaurant and ice cream parlor, which is transformed into a stylish bar at night with monthly events like drag and burlesque shows. It's painted with dramatic murals and furnished with early American 20th Century pieces. Their specialties include ice cream cocktails, milkshakes, and baked desserts with homemade hot fudge. They also serve real food, but why wait for dessert? 2027 Locust St, St Louis, MO 63103, www. fountainonlocust.com

VENICE CAFE This bar is like a funhouse tribute to Norman Bates' attic. Bowling memorabilia, stuffed animal heads, broken glass mosaics, and strange portraits crowd the walls, illuminated by colored neon lights. In summer the bar hosts a restaurant on the sculpture patio. 1903 Pestalozzi St, St Louis, MO 63118, www.thevenicecafe.com

FOAM St Louis has many local roasters and breweries, so it's only natural that they'd want to get together. This funky cafe, like many others in the city, serves both coffee and beer. It's an industrial space with bright, retro furniture. Peaceful and chilled out in the mornings for pastry and coffee, and louder and vibrant at night with live bands and a varied beer selection. 3359 South Jefferson Ave, St Louis, MO 63118

THE MAP ROOM A quaint, cozy bar and dessert cafe. Live bands play jazz or swing on the weekends, and couples often get up to dance. The small space gets crowded, but the staff is always ready to help you find a seat at a shared table. 1901 Withnell Ave, St Louis, MO 63118, www.themaproomstl.com

BB'S JAZZ, BLUES, AND SOUPS At night this is a loud, smoky bar. Great if you're in the mood to get lost in the crowd and listen to freeform jazz. During the day they serve Cajun food – po'boys, beans and rice, and gumbo, as well as their signature homemade soups. 700 South Broadway, St Louis, MO 63102, www.bbsjazzbluessoups.com

BLACK BEAR BAKERY Learn about anarchist revolutionaries while sipping a fair trade cup of coffee over vegan buckwheat pancakes. This worker-operated and built cooperative bakery and political arts space has a broad presence in the community, partnering with many local businesses and markets to sell their homemade products. 2639 Cherokee St, St Louis, MO 63118, www.blackbearbakery.org

CROWN CANDY KITCHEN Stranded in a barren area of north St Louis, Crown Candy Kitchen has nonetheless brought in the patrons for almost 100 years, thanks to its handmade chocolates and delicious World's Fair Sundaes. 1401 St Louis Ave, St Louis, MO 63107, www.crowncandykitchen.net

JAY'S INTERNATIONAL MARKET This is a fun market to visit whether you're looking for that special squid ink you've heard so much about, or if you just want to figure out what the heck yogurt soda is. This market sells every type of ingredient you could imagine, and some you'd rather not. 3172 South Grand Blvd, St Louis, MO 63118

SOULARD FARMERS' MARKET/ TOWER GROVE FARMERS' MARKET The Tower Grove Farmers' Market is wonderful outdoor market open in summer/fall. It's located in Tower Grove Park, in the center of a diverse residential neighborhood. Soulard Farmers' Market is the oldest farmers' market west of the Mississippi, and it's huge, with around 200 stands selling everything from locally baked bread to alligator and squirrel meat. **TOWER GROVE:** Northwest Dr and Central Cross Dr, St Louis, MO 63110, www.tgmarket.org, **SOULARD:** 730 Carroll St, St Louis, MO 63104, www.soulardmarket.com

TREASURE AISLES ANTIQUE MALL This is one of my favorite places to hunt for great vintage accessories, furniture or cookware. It is inexpensive, clean and always has new pieces. There are a number of other antique malls nearby, but this is my favorite. 2317 South Big Bend Blvd, St Louis, MO 63143

CULTURE

ST LOUIS ART MUSEUM This museum's ample collection has something for everyone. Its permanent collection is free at all times and the special exhibitions are free every Friday afternoon. Frank Stella and Donald Judd are featured alongside a massive sculpture by Louise Bourgeois. Make sure to check out the sculpture garden, and try to find the dazzling full-scale silver tree amongst the rest of the flora. 1 Fine Arts Dr, St Louis, MO 63110, www.slam.org

THIRD DEGREE GLASS FACTORY Not just a gallery space and a store, the Third Degree Glass Factory has made a name for itself by actively getting the community involved in glass-making. They host parties and demonstrations in their space, and hold night classes in partnership with local universities. Definitely plan to visit during one of their events. 5200 Delmar Blvd, St Louis, MO 63108, www.stlglass.com

MAD ART GALLERY This funky art space operates out of an old police station. There is art displayed in the old prison cells, and they have a rotating gallery show, but they mostly host events including concerts, drag shows, and fundraisers that support charitable causes. 2727 South 12th St, St Louis, MO 63118, www.madart.com

THE MOOLAH THEATER St Louis has a number of movie theaters with a lot of character. The Tivoli (The Loop) is a historic theater built in 1924 that often shows independent and foreign films. Both Webster University and Washington University host film festivals throughout year. The Moolah, however, is my favorite. It's set in an old Shriner's temple that looks like a Las Vegas tribute to the Pharaohs – the brickwork is painted red, gold, and green, and an Egyptian death mask guards the entrance. The theater itself is one large room with comfy couches and end tables. Once a month they host a midnight 'brew&view' night, screening a cult classic like *Rocky Horror* or *The Big Lebowski*. 3821 Lindell Blvd, St Louis, MO 63108, www.stlouiscinemas.com

CITY MUSEUM This is probably the oddest, most disconcerting and simultaneously the most cathartic museum in the US. Appealing to adults and children alike, it features a multicolored slide of paper mache rollers, a gutted airplane suspended from the ceiling, and something that looks like a massive slinky connecting the building to the outdoor sculpture space. There's also a kaleidoscopic tunnel, a carnival funhouse and a pit to roast marshmallows over an open flame. You absolutely must not miss this. 701 North 15th St, St Louis, MO 63103, www.citymuseum.org

FIRECRACKER PRESS One of my favorite places in St Louis, Firecracker is a design studio and printing press that specializes in posters for local cultural venues. From time to time they host events where patrons can watch the letterpress artists in action and even work on the presses themselves. They also have a shop selling posters, cards, and zines. 2838 Cherokee St, St Louis, MO 63118, www. firecrackerpress.com

LAUMEIER SCULPTURE PARK If you have the time to drive a little way outside the city, you must visit this tremendous sculpture park. It's free to enter and amazing to explore. There are hundreds of site-specific pieces ranging from representation pieces to totally abstract work in every conceivable material and media. 12580 Rott Rd, St Louis, MO 63127, www.laumeier.com

THE PULITZER / THE CONTEMPORARY ART MUSEUM This is a two-for-one bargain, not for the price, because both museums are free to enter, but because the two are interconnected. The Pulitzer is worth seeing for Tadao Ando's streamlined, minimalist architecture and Richard Serra's massive steel sculpture, *Joe*, alone. Both museums host intriguing events such as 'Prints Gone Wild', where printmakers from around the Midwest come to sell their work and party. During their Dan Flavin exhibition, the Pulitzer held late openings to properly showcase the light sculptures. 3716 Washington Blvd, St Louis, MO 63108, www.pulitzerarts.org, www.contemporarystl.org

ST LOUIS RIVERFRONT TRAIL / CEMENTLAND This 10-mile walk or bike path starts at the Arch and Laclede's Landing and follows the Mississippi River north. Use public transport to get to the start, and then follow it past the old factories and other abandoned relics of St Louis' industrial past. Bob Cassilly, who developed the City Museum (see Culture) also created an earth sculpture park called Cementland, which you'll pass on the way. Like the City Museum, Cementland is a playspace for kids and adults that's wacky and lots of fun.

WATERFRONT This area is a prime example of the abandonment of revitalization efforts around the once bustling area of the waterfront. It's a nice walk from the arch down along the river, past the Luminaire Casino, under the Eads Bridge and towards the old factories, some of which are now artists' studios, whilst others are left derelict. Eventually the path will connect to the St Louis Riverfront Trail. Be careful to avoid squatters who don't take kindly to people invading their spaces.

THE LOOP

LAFAYETTE PARK Beautiful, elongated brick houses are typical of St Louis, but the decorative front facades of Lafayette Square are unique. It's a great place to walk around, and the community hosts many summer and holiday events, like movies, concerts in the park, open house days, and flea markets. 2101 Park Ave, MO 63104, www.lafayettesquare.org

CAHOKIA MOUNDS This place is just over the border into Illinois, but it's worth the drive. Cahokia is the site of an ancient city inhabited by Mississippian Native Americans from 8th–14th Centuries. Today there is a museum on the site and guided tours, but the best way to explore is to just walk up the man-made, flat-top ceremonial mounds and enjoy the view. 30 Ramey St, Collinsville, IL 62201, http://cahokiamounds.org

MISSOURI BOTANICAL GARDENS This is absolutely one of the best green spaces in St Louis. The Botanical Gardens has lovely grounds, a theater, and a Climatron, that make it worth visiting year round. In the summer, there are free music festivals, art classes, and social events. I once saw a spectacular exhibition of Dale Chihuly's flora-inspired glass sculpture. A few of his pieces are still on display in the collection. 4344 Shaw Blvd, Tower Grove, MO 63110, www.mobot.org

FOREST PARK This park is the largest public space in the area. It's 50 per cent larger than Central Park (take that New York!) and borders the St Louis Art Museum, the St Louis Zoo, and the Missouri History Museum. In the summer, the park is packed with people picnicking or riding bikes. The park hosts lots of events including the fall Balloon Glow, and Shakespeare in the Park. Between Lindell Blvd and Skinker Blvd S

JOSHUA GRAHAM GUENTHER'S

WASHINGTON, DC

WASHINGTON, DISTRICT OF COLUMBIA

BY JOSHUA GRAHAM GUENTHER

Commonly referred to as 'the District' or simply DC, the US capital is unrivalled in its magnificent cocktail of monuments, museums, historic sites, embassies, national organizations, and federal buildings. It's an economic, cultural, and of course, political center for the nation, which means that there's a specific kind of buzz (think community action and political events and rallies) that can be very inspiring. The downside is that it is a major tourist hotspot, attracting about 20 million visitors a year. Try to avoid tourist traps and overpriced restaurants, and focus instead on the fantastic free museums and galleries and the alternative culture, which is bubbling underneath the city's surface.

Washington DC is a very easy city to explore. Its layout is internationally renowned – meticulously planned by Charles L'Enfant, a French 18th Century architect. It's on a grid system, with avenues bisecting city blocks, and plenty of green space. It's divided into four quadrants (Northwest, Northeast, Southeast, and Southwest) that radiate out from the Capitol building. Road names include their location, so it's easy to work out where in the city you are at any given moment. You can get around easily by foot, or use the city's new bike rental system, SmartBike DC. There's also a very efficient metro system, which gets pretty much everywhere in the city. Don't bother renting a car – DC is a major commuter city, and the traffic can get congested with limited and expensive parking.

My favorite time of year is October. It's pleasant during the day and most of the tourist crowds have thinned out. However, the summer can be fun too – with loads of outdoor events and nightlife. Either way, make sure to talk to some locals about underground happenings. You'll find that district dwellers are quite friendly and helpful, and can point you in the direction of the alternative city life that isn't readily apparent to newcomers.

HOTEL PALOMAR A top-end boutique hotel in a great location with a big emphasis on art and design. The rooms are spacious and each one is outfitted with supplies and art games to spark inspiration and creativity. 2121 P St Northwest, Washington, DC 20037, www.hotelpalomar-dc.com

KALORAMA GUEST HOUSE A reasonably priced B&B located in trendy Adam's Morgan, this renovated townhouse offers close proximity to the District's art scene, but is nicely tucked away from crowds. Great if you're looking for an at-home feel. 1854 Mintwood Pl Northwest, Washington, DC 20009, www.kaloramaguesthouse.com

AVERAGE LENGTH OF OVERNIGHT STAY (DAYS)

3.0

116

HOTELS
(27,000 ROOMS)

$
14.5
HOTEL TAX (%)

555

HEIGHT EVERY DISTRICT BUILDING
DOES NOT EXCEED (FEET)

COUCH SURFING I'm a veteran couch surfer. If you haven't heard of couch surfing, it's basically a hospitality exchange network – a community of individuals that host and are hosted by other individuals, providing a personalized – and very economic way of travelling. I highly recommend it, and DC is a good city to experience it in. www.couchsurfing.org

BUS BOYS & POETS A pretty unique institution. It's a restaurant, bookstore, fair-trade market, and "gathering place where people can discuss issues of social justice and peace" (to quote their mission statement). Founded by Anas 'Andy' Shallal in 2005, the name refers to the poet Langston Hughes, who worked as a bus boy. It serves up great vegan and vegetarian dishes, but carnivores are also catered to. 2021 14th St Northwest, Washington, DC 20009, www.busboysandpoets.com

AMMA VEGETARIAN KITCHEN This Indian restaurant is my favorite place for a quick, casual lunch. It's got a friendly home-cooking vibe. 3291 M St Northwest, Washington DC, 20007, www.ammavegkitchen.com

JAVA GREEN CAFE This is a great fair-trade, organic eco-cafe located near Faragut North. I will just tell you up front that they don't offer any meat dishes, but they do serve an awesome vegan breakfast and have gluten-free and raw-food options as well. 1020 19th St Northwest, Washington, DC 20036, www.javagreen.net

MIDCITY CAFFE A quaint little coffeehouse located in the 14th and U Streets corridor above an antiques shop. They serve delicious snacks and absolutely top-notch coffee, plus have Wi-fi access and live poetry and music on Tuesday nights. 1626 14th St Northwest, Washington, DC 20009, www.midcitycaffe.com

EAT

1

AUGUST THROUGH SEPTEMBER

LEAST TOURIST-FILLED MONTHS

INSIDE RESTAURANTS, BARS & PUBLIC BUILDINGS

NO SMOKING

CITY AREA (SQ. MI.)

68.3

STICKY FINGERS This vegan bakery has a great selection of sweets, eats and coffee – a perfect place to satisfy your sweet tooth in a vaguely healthy way. They offer free internet access, serve a great weekend brunch, and have a 'Cupcake Happy Hour' on Wednesdays. 1370 Park Rd Northwest, Washington, DC 20010, www.stickyfingersbakery.com

THE RED DERBY Offering a unique selection of local brews, this well-kept secret (until now at least) is a great neighborhood watering hole, where you can meet like-minded artists. Check out the events page on their website. It's got some great stuff. 3718 14th St Northwest, Washington, DC 20010, www.redderby.com

THE PHARMACY BAR Located off the 18th Street strip of Adam's Morgan, this place will serve you something that you can't really get anywhere else in this area – a relaxed atmosphere. No heaving drunks splashing their rum and coke all down your front, just a mellow vibe and funky decor – medicine cabinets lining the walls and thousands of pills underneath the glass table tops. 2337 18th St Northwest, Washington, DC 20009, www.bardc.com

RANKED U.S. CITY BEST FOR SINGLES

4TH

MINIMUM DRINKING AGE (YEARS)

21

2AM SUN.-THURS.
3AM FRI.-SAT.

LAST CALL FOR ALCOHOL IN BARS

106 ¾

METRO RAIL TRACK (MILES)

THE VELVET LOUNGE A great dive bar with eccentric clientele and liquor bottles galore. The actual bar is on ground-level, but if you head through the front door and directly up the stairs, you'll find a lounge showcasing local bands playing anything from hip-hop to Japanese prog/space rock. 915 U St Northwest, Washington, DC 20001, www.velvetloungedc.com

BLACK CAT An awesome introduction to DC's music scene. This is an opportunity to see local, national and international indie bands up close. Look online to see what's on, and make sure to check out the vintage video game tables inside. 1811 14th St Northwest, Washington, DC 20009, www.blackcatdc.com

MADAME'S ORGAN Another great place to catch some local live music and drinks. Located in Adam's Morgan, Madame's Organ is unmissable – with a giant redheaded lady painted on the side of the building. There's a music venue downstairs and pool tables upstairs – and good bars on both levels. As with most bars in town there's a small entrance fee on weekends. 2461 18th St Northeast, Washington, DC 20018, www.madamsorgan.com

GALAXY HUT This place isn't strictly inside Washington DC, but it's on the Metro, and most definitely worth the haul - there are a few other bars, shops, and restaurants in the neighborhood, if you need added incentive. It's one of my favorite watering holes – a super-relaxed vibe with vintage video game tables and Christmas lights in the windows. You'll feel right at home. 2711 Wilson Blvd, Arlington, VA 22201, www.galaxyhut.com

THE SALOON A brick-walled hangout with a similarly relaxed vibe to Galaxy Hut. It's got a no-standing policy, and its unsung motto is socialization and communication. I like going there to chill out with friends. You don't have to yell to be heard by your buddy sitting across the table. 1207 U St Northwest, Washington, DC 20009

SOLLY'S TAVERN This is another great local gathering spot for events and brews. One of its highlights is Kostume Karaoke – an excuse to revisit your Halloween costume, get lit, and sing your heart out. 1942 11th St Northwest, Washington, DC 20001, www.sollystavern.com

There are plenty of art filled, hipster shops to choose from in the District. However, in terms of general locations, the best places to go shopping are Adam's Morgan and Georgetown in Northwest, as well as Eastern Market in Southeast, listed below.

SMASH! RECORDS Established in 1984, this is the city's premier punk and alternative music and clothing store, stocking a great selection of CDs and vinyl, as well as vintage and indie designer fashions. 2314 18th St Northwest, 2nd Floor, Washington, DC 20009, www.smashrecords.com

CAPITOL HEMP An underground store (literally) entirely dedicated to high-quality products made from industrial hemp. Not everyone's bag, but I like it! 1802 Adams Mill Rd, Washington, DC 20009. www.capitolhemp.com

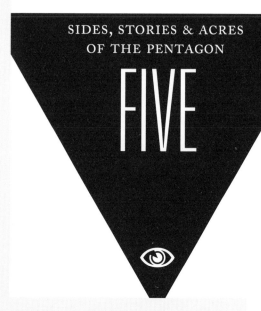

SIDES, STORIES & ACRES
OF THE PENTAGON

FIVE

SHOP

MEEPS VINTAGE FASHIONETTE Great place for finding vintage clothing and costumes for both women and men. They also stock one-off designs by local designers. 2104 18th St Northwest, Washington, DC 20009, www.meepsdc.com

EASTERN MARKET One of my favorite ways to spend a Saturday is at Eastern Market. Vendors sell everything from produce and flowers to clothing and art, and it's got a community atmosphere, which means I'm always bumping into friends. It really is a must experience if you're in town on a weekend. Be sure to check their website for any special events. 225 7th St Southeast, Washington, DC 20003, www.easternmarket.net

POLITICS AND PROSE A little bit out of the way in Chevy Chase, this awesome independent bookstore has great readings by big names, a downstairs cafe, and amazingly friendly and helpful staff – who are not too earnest. It's got a really vibrant buzz about it that is totally DC. 5015 Connecticut Ave Northwest, Washington, DC 20008, www.politics-prose.com

N

2M./9FT.

38:54:18 N

77:00:58 W

ALTITUDE & COORDINATES

HIRSHORN MUSEUM AND SCULPTURE GARDEN
A little bit set back from the Mall, this place is always surprisingly peaceful. It's part of the Smithsonian, and looks like a spaceship – kind of donut shaped with a fountain in the middle. The collection includes some pieces by Warhol, Pollock, Rothko, Lucian Freud, and other heavy hitters, but my favorite parts are the sculpture garden and the seating area at the top, which offers a great view of the Mall. Independence Ave Southwest, Washington, DC 20024 www.hirshhorn.si.edu

TRANSFORMER GALLERY A tiny non-profit gallery with a good program of events as well as some edgy exhibitions by emerging artists. They also hold art auctions if you're into collecting. 1404 P St Northwest, Washington, DC 2005, www.transformergallery.org

HEMPHILL FINE ARTS A classy venue that gets some big names in, as well as younger talent. It's in the now very arty area of 14th Street NW (in Logan Circle), where you'll find other interesting spaces such as G Fine Art, Irvine Contemporary and Curator's Office. 1515 14th St Northwest, Washington, DC 2005, www.hemphillfinearts.com

ADAMSON GALLERIES Another small but elegant gallery in the same building as Hemphill. You'll need to buzz at the door to be let in. Similar to Hemphill, they get some big names in (Chuck Close and Jenny Holzer have featured in the past), and focus primarily on digital prints and photography. 1515 14th St Northwest, Washington, DC 2005, www.adamsongallery.jimdo.com

RANKED U.S. CITY FOR BEST MUSEUMS

NUMBER ONE

CULTURE

255 Washington, DC

CORCORAN GALLERY OF ART This is one of the few galleries in the District that you'll have to pay to enter, so check to see what's on before you go. They've had some amazing photography exhibitions in the past (William Eggleston was particularly inspiring), and their permanent collection features both classical art and more contemporary stuff. 510 17th St Northwest, Washington, DC 20006, www.corcoran.org

ARTOMATIC The best way to see the District's artists is by way of Artomatic – a free, month-long festival held in a rented out office building, attracting over 1,000 visual artists and 600 performance artists. The venue changes from year to year, so be sure to check out their website for dates and locations. www.artomatic.org

SCREEN ON THE GREEN A summertime favorite: free classic movies on a giant screen on the National Mall. Screenings usually take place on Monday nights in the summer, starting around 8:30pm. Some folks claim their spots as early as 5pm, so don't leave it too late. Bring a blanket, food, and beer and enjoy the show. National Mall between 4th and 7th St, Washington DC

DC INDEPENDENT FILM FESTIVAL AND INDEPENDENT MUSIC FESTIVAL Every March, the city comes alive with feature, short, animation, and documentary films, and in tandem, the independent music festival brings acts from all corners of the world. A fun ten days and a great way to see the industries' finest. March 4-14th, www.dciff.org

The Washington Metropolitan area is well known for its cycle trails. Most of them follow simple loops and offer a great alternative to more conventional sightseeing. You can get a free city cycle map from: www.ddot.dc.gov/bike

CHESAPEAKE & OHIO CANAL
The canal is a great historical landmark as well as one of the most accessible locations in the District for walking, running, kayaking, and off-road cycling. The continuous trail starts in Georgetown and ends in Cumberland, Maryland. A great way to access nature and get some exercise. http://bikewashington.org/canal

BIKE

DRUM CIRCLE One of the best unsolicited events that I like to participate in is the historical 'drum-circle' in Meridian Hill Park. On Sunday afternoons, during the warmer months, locals and visitors gather in the park and dance, provide food for the homeless, and drum! The activity has been held since the 1950s and is a really life-enhancing experience. Meridian Hill Park (informally, Malcolm X Park), in Northwest, Washington, DC

CRITICAL MASS If you happen to be a bike messenger or just a cycling enthusiast, make sure to check out this event, which happens on the first Friday of every month, leaving from Dupont Circle at 6pm. It's basically a load of cyclists making themselves seen. As Critical Mass DC puts it, "We're biking to solve our oil crisis and so we can breathe clean air". Make sure to check the website, and contact me if you'd like to ride together! Dupont Circle, Washington, DC 20036, http://cm-dc.mahost.org

#1
RANKED FOR MOST
WALKABLE U.S. CITY

ANNUAL RAINFALL (INCHES)

39.1

COMMON PLUG OUTLET (VOLTS):
60 CYCLES

110-120

$

5.75

SALES TAX (%)

EASTERN
STANDARD
TIME

TIME ZONE

TELEPHONE AREA CODE

202

#

1 MILE
X
400 FEET

NATIONAL MALL DIMENSIONS

M

86

METRO RAIL STATIONS
(41 LOCATED WITHIN THE DISTRICT)

BIOGRAPHIES

LAURA FERACO
Anchorage

I'm a graphic designer by day, closet relief printer, package designer, bookmaker, and paper lush by night. Married to my best friend and biggest critic, Scott S, we share our home with two mischievous cats, Sushi and Bento. I crave beautifully functional things. My goal is to create thought provoking work that makes viewers think about their impact on their neighbors, the planet and themselves.

Characteristics: (the good and the bad) kind, clever, patient, impatient, sarcastic, perfectionist, and stubborn. Secret affinity for: British comedy. Have a maternal instinct for: the protection and conservation of wildlife and our planet. Teased by friends in design school: because I actually like art history. Number of cities lived: 10. Consider myself: a square peg in a round hole. Favorite meal ever: sangria, manchego cheese, baguette and a warm peach - enjoyed while basking in the Mediterranean sun on a tiny beach in Nerja, Spain. Number of nicknames had in my lifetime: 11+. Design motto: white space (although not always followed). Design obsession: typography and architecture. Biggest vice: all things mini. Turn off: inconsiderate people. Most recent realization: a rekindled love of winter.

www.feracodesign.com
www.etsy.com/shop/sushibites

LAURIE FOREHAND
Atlanta

Inspired by the colors, shapes and textures she finds in nature, designer Laurie Forehand's eclectic compositions and modern aesthetic are a mix of the familiar, the unexpected, and the exotic. Her creative use of graphic line art, Art Deco motifs, and hand-drawn sketches have helped define a style all her own; a style that has leant itself well to a variety of mediums.

Her Scandinavian heritage and unique outlook on modern graphic design techniques has been a launching pad for endeavors such as a paper goods line under her design brand, 1201AM. Recently, the brand has extended into the interior product design and textile design market, with licensing deals for area rugs and wall coverings.

www.1201am.com

BRYAN KEPLESKY
Austin

Bryan Keplesky has been designing
professionally since 2002. After cutting his
teeth in Richmond, Virginia, he moved to
Austin in 2004 and has been eating breakfast
tacos ever since. In addition to duties in art
direction, design, and copywriting at indie
ad agency Door Number 3, Bryan co-founded
Austin-centric Misprint Magazine in 2005. He
also takes on a variety of gigs for his friends'
bands, bars, shops, and festivals.

His work has been featured in Communication
Arts, Print, Step Inside Design, Nylon
Magazine, the Chicago International Poster
Biennial, the book you are currently reading,
and, most importantly, the Side Bar.

When not doing any of the above-mentioned
things, Bryan enjoys Kurt Russell movies,
cheap beer and expensive tequila, and
articles about giant squid.

www.roundobject.com
www.misprintmagazine.com
www.dn3austin.com

ELIZABETH GRAEBER
Baltimore

Elizabeth grew up outside of Baltimore and
studied illustration at the Maryland Institute
College of Art where she graduated with a
BFA in 2007. She is now a freelance illustrator
currently living in Washington DC.

She is part of Project Dispatch, an artwork
subscription service, where people receive
original artwork in the mail. She always
carries a sketchbook, drawing every day.
Check out her daily drawing site: http://
illustratedagenda2010.tumblr.com/. You can
also buy her stationery, paintings, drawings
and screenprinted fabrics on Etsy.

www.elizabethgraeber.com
www.projectdispatch.biz

ESTHER UHL
Boston

Esther was born in Southwest Germany, and studied communication design at the University of Applied Sciences in Augsburg. During her studies she spent one year in Valencia, Spain where she focused her interests on animation, film and photography. After graduating, Esther moved to Boston to work for PUMA, creating artwork for the corporate identity and marketing of the international brand. During this time she developed an interest in product design and illustration.

At the moment, Esther is working as an art director at Saint Elmo's in Munich. Her clients include BMW, Lufthansa City Center, Credit Swiss, and SportScheck. She focuses her work on finding innovative design concepts and directing photoshoots. In her personal projects she likes to stay open-minded to all creative mediums, so besides her design and illustration work, she very much enjoys dealing with fashion design, etching, sculpting, and carpentry.

www.estheruhl.com

JAY FLETCHER
Charleston

When I was in the sixth grade I mummified a fish. A trout, to be specific. Our class had spent six months studying the ancient civilizations of Rome, Greece, and Egypt, and the whole thing culminated with each student spending several weeks on a personal project, which would amount to a large portion of their grade. So I mummified a fish. I removed its guts, packed it in salt, waited several weeks, and then wrapped the leathery leftovers in gauze and placed it in a paper mache sarcophagus which I'd painted gold and doodled hieroglyphics all over with a black marker.

I couldn't tell you what I got for a grade, but the project was a huge success (so much so that teachers and their classes visited from other schools just to see it) and something about the story speaks to why I've ended up in the business of creativity. A unique idea had popped into my head, I spent some time making it a reality, and it resonated with people. It's a simple story, but something inside me clicked. On some level, everything I've created since that day has been just another dead fish.

www.jfletcherdesign.com

DANIEL BLACKMAN
Chicago

Daniel Blackman was born and raised in Warren, a small town in the Allegheny National Forest in Pennsylvania, and as a result he is an outdoor lover and finds inspiration in surrounding nature. Since leaving Warren, he has lived a number of places, but now calls Chicago his home.

He has degree in Graphic and Interactive Communication from Ringling College of Art and Design in Sarasota Florida, and since graduating has been freelancing for companies such as Fwis, VSA Partners, Arlo, Tribal DDB, and 160over90. He also enjoys illustration, photography, bookmaking, and collecting. He is currently working on a blog called The Matchbook Registry, showcasing a family collection of matchbook design and typography.

Daniel tries to keep his work simple and fresh, always trying different things. He is inspired by his friends, family, and colleagues. Design for him is a lifelong learning process, whether it be technical, aesthetical or business oriented.

www.dblackman.com
www.thematchbookregistry.com

GWENDA KACZOR
Denver

Gwenda Kaczor is a freelance illustrator and designer based in Denver, Colorado. With a BFA from Art Center College of Design and experience as an illustrator, character designer, and animator, Gwenda has a long list of clients that include Mother Jones, The Wall Street Journal, The New York Times, Utne Reader, American Express, AT&T, and NPR.

Her work has been recognized by American Illustration, Communication Arts, NY Society of Illustrators, HOW, Print, and has been spotlighted at Illustrationmundo.com.

www.gwenda.com

ANGELA DUNCAN
Detroit

Hi! I'm so excited to have been part of this wonderful book, and I'm thrilled that you're reading this right now. It's like we're hanging out, or something. So thanks for that.

We talk with our hands in Michigan, because they make great maps. I grew up near the tip of your pinkie finger, went to college near the middle of your palm, and am writing this further south, sort of by your thumb, in Detroit.

I have a BA in advertising from Michigan State University, and plan to attend a very awesome art school, as soon as I win the lottery. Of course, I'm not blatantly asking for funding... merely hinting at my openness to the idea. Um... I've tried my hand at other careers in photography and advertising copywriting, but my true passion has always been in the physical form: illustration and hand drawn lettering. I've been fortunate enough to turn this passion into a career, simply by doing it a lot and pushing my limits. This is just the beginning, and I'm definitely using every opportunity to make the most of it.

www.theangeladuncan.com

RAMZY MASRI & MORGAN ASHLEY ALLEN
Kansas City

Ramzy Masri (Illustrations and Text)
I like to take bio opportunities to ask myself a more interesting question:
How would describe what you do to a blind child?
I would say:
I'm a feeling-worker. I take feelings. And feel them for a while. And then I look around and collect things that I think give me that feeling. I mix all those things together, in a bunch of different ways until finally, hopefully, I come up with something that gives someone else the same feeling I had.

www.ramzymasri.com

Morgan Ashley Allen (Text)
I believe in the efficient and smart. I look to Eames, Einstein, The Books. I enjoy 3/4 count, alliteration, anecdotes. Kenny Shopsin is my hero, and I try my damndest to live by: "non-participation in anything you believe is evil."

Mention dives, brews, breads or bully breeds, and I'm sure we'll talk for hours if you've got the time.

www.morganashleyallen.com

TAL ROSNER
Los Angeles

Tal is a digital artist and filmmaker. He was born in Jerusalem and raised in the bustling metropolis of Rehovot, Israel. For almost a decade he has been living and working in London.

A lot of his work focuses on collaborating with classical musicians as well as theatre directors and choreographers, translating sounds and rhythms into a personal (and frequently abstract) visual language. He has also worked on a number of short films, and recently a multiple-channel gallery installation called *Family Tree*. Tal's work has been screened in spaces including: the Disney Hall, LA, Forum des Images, Paris, and the Barbican, Royal Festival Hall, and Tate Modern in London. His title sequence for the television drama *Skins* won him a BAFTA award and he is currently working on 2 commissions for the new home of Miami's New World Symphony, designed by Frank Gehry.

Tal loves: German Expressionism, Josef Albers, industrial wastelands, Mad Men, Eugene Ionesco, Basquiat, salted nuts, plaid button shirts, technology, and bread.

www.talrosner.com

ALEX WARBLE
Memphis

Alex Harrison (also known as Alex Warble) is an artist, musician, mural painter, and dreamer living and working in Memphis. He comes from a family of artists and musicians in Fulton Mississippi, and moved to Memphis to study at the Memphis College of Art.

Alex is currently working on a number of projects ranging from CD covers and flyers to a mural project. He takes inspiration from dreams, and his paintings are often obliquely surreal, and yet somehow very humorous. Music is also an important part of Alex's life, and he devotes as much time to his band, the Warble, as he does to his art. His illustrations have featured in various books, magazines and blogs, and his band plays regularly at venues around the city.

www.josephalexharrison.blogspot.com
www.myspace.com/thewarble

MICHELLE WEINBERG
Miami

My aim as an artist and designer is to animate spaces for people to inhabit. Color and pattern build vivid backdrops for human activity – in paintings, rugs, tiles and art for public spaces.

My work freely adapts settings from the built environment around me: fictitious elevations, warped courtyards, pastel warehouse facades, floating perspectives and words inscribed on walls and billboards. In each work, I create a unique space and then leave the door open for the viewer to enter and fill it imaginatively, as a performer injects motivation into a theater set. The bland non-architecture of industrial Miami provides a starting point for me to elaborate on. Filtering urban spaces through an eccentric comic-utopian narrative, I am creating a poetic record of my lived experience.

www.michelleweinberg.com

ANDY BRAWNER AND MIKE KROLL
Milwaukee

Andy Brawner
Rather than write about myself in first or third person, I'll try second person, which I think means using "you" a lot. Andy Brawner, you are a copywriter for Planet Propaganda in Madison, WI, and have lived in Milwaukee, WI, for almost 10 years. You play music under the name Time Since Western. You used to play music with Mike Krol, and you used to work alongside Mike Krol at the aforementioned Planet. Then, one day, Mike Krol left.

http://andybrawnercopywriter.posterous.com

Mike Krol
Mike Krol was born and raised in Milwaukee. Although he loved it in his early years, upon high school graduation, he left to attend the School of Visual Arts in New York City. After 4 years of New York style living and college-style eating, Mike Krol moved back to the Motherland, this time settling down in Madison, where he worked as a designer at Planet Propaganda. Three years of fame, fortune, and ping pong led him to believe he could do this stuff on his own. Currently, Mike Krol works for himself in New Haven Connecticut, where he holds down clients like Nike and MTV. He also works part-time as a designer for the Yale University Art Gallery.

www.mikekrol.com

ADAM TURMAN
Minneapolis

I'm a Minneapolis-based illustrator and screenprinter. I work out of my home studio creating artsy-farty stuff for the best customers and clients in the world. Many of my customers are locally-based, and much of my art includes local subject matter. I'm a homebody. I like to take vacations and trips as long as I know I'm not staying away from Minneapolis too long.

I've been drawing my entire life, got a job right out of school, and realized I wasn't doing enough hand-drawn illustration in my design work. That changed in 2003 when I met DWITT and he introduced me to Steve of Squad 19. I started doing a ton of illustration work for through jobs provided via Squad 19. My style became well-recognized around town. Pro-bono work turned into paying work. Bands, businesses, organizations, and private commissions hire me to produce illustration and prints for their events and projects.

I've heard it said "you can't walk down any street in Minneapolis without seeing something by Adam Turman." I'd like to believe that's true on most days. If you don't find it on the street you can find it on my website.

www.adamturman.com
www.dwitt.com
www.squad19.com

TOM VARISCO
New Orleans

Tom Varisco is sole proprietor and creative director of Tom Varisco Designs, a design / branding studio in New Orleans that has won several awards for a wide variety of clients. In 2007, He was awarded the first "Fellow Award" by the New Orleans chapter of the American Institute of Graphic Arts (AIGA).

Tom's self-published photo book *Spoiled*, about the refrigerators left out after Hurricane Katrina, became a local best seller, and was selected one of the top 50 design books by AIGA in 2006. His second self-published book, *Signs of New Orleans*, is a design and photo book that serves as a brief record of the city's "sign language". *Desire*, his award-winning publication of observations and opinions about New Orleans, features original local artwork and writing, and is in the permanent collections of the New Orleans Public Library and Tulane University Library.

Tom Varisco has taught graphic design to fourth year students in Loyola University's Visual Arts department since 1985. He is a charter member of AIGA New Orleans.

www.tomvariscodesigns.com

CAMILLIA BENBASSAT
New York

Avec is a design studio founded by Camillia BenBassat in 2006 that has worked on the design and implementation of brand identity systems, printed matter, collateral materials, websites and mobile applications. At the end of the day, we take pride in building innovative, valuable, and successful solutions that are always infused with a high quality of design and care.

Our work has been published in several books including *1000 Fonts, The Freelance Design Handbook* and *All Access: The Making of Thirty Extraordinary Graphic Designers*. Avec's awards include Print's Regional Design Annual and Step Design 100. In 2010, Avec's work with greentechmedia.com was honored with a Webby Award, the first time the 'green' category was introduced.

In 2010, Avec launched DesignersAnd.com, an online portal and directory connecting designers with the resources needed to see their ideas realized. The goal is to build a community and forum to support all aspects of the industry, creating a hub where designers can share experiences, find inspiration and communicate with each other.

www.avec.us

KATIE HATZ
Philadelphia

Born and raised in the scenic farmland of Lancaster, Pennsylvania (about 70 miles west of Philly), Katie Hatz earned her MFA in graphic design at Tyler School of Art in 2010. She lives in Philadelphia with her cats, Lady and Indiana Jones, and probably more icky bugs than she cares to think about. Favorite outdoor activities include biking, walking, sitting, standing, eating, and getting lost (although she generally refers to the latter as "going on adventures").

Although she once dreamt of becoming an accountant, Katie is mostly content with her life choices at present. She loves being a designer, as the title justifies the countless hours of unfocused research, book shopping, junk collecting, doodling, pun making, and bullshitting that she'd probably do anyway. Katie's work has been featured in *AIGA 365, American Illustration, Communication Arts, Creative Quarterly, HOW International, The Big Book of Green Design*, and *Logo Lounge*, among others. Her specialties include writing, illustration, and hand lettering.

www.katiehatz.com

JON ASHCROFT
Phoenix

I am a designer and illustrator based in Phoenix Arizona. I live with my beautiful wife Paige, who is a hairstylist, and our dog Sam in a historic neighborhood in central Phoenix. Paige and I are both transplants from Northern New Mexico where we were born and raised and most of our families still reside.

I received a Bachelors of Fine Arts with an emphasis on graphic design and photography from New Mexico State University. During the day I am a graphic designer for Fender Musical Instruments Corporation, where I work with a great little team to create campaigns and collateral for Fender, Gretsch, Jackson, and other musical instrument manufacturers. I am also heavily involved at Praxis Church where I serve on a creative team producing artwork, videos, and informational materials.

I am very active in the Phoenix design community, often exhibiting my personal illustration pieces and working with fellow creatives on social outreach projects. I'm a music junkie, design connoisseur, and lover of simple pleasures.

www.jonashcroft.com

BRIAR LEVIT
Portland

Briar is West Coast girl, through-and-through. Raised in the California Bay Area, she studied graphic design in London, but returned to the 'left coast' of the US. This time, she set up in Portland, Oregon, and it's here that she plans on laying down roots for her career, friends, and family.

Briar teaches design at Portland State University and does freelance work, primarily for nonprofits and sustainable businesses, under the name BriarMade.

www.briarmade.com

ADAM LUCAS
Providence

I attended Kenyon College in Gambier, OH (a bustling metropolis that somehow escaped being one of the featured cities in this book), where I studied English and Art and played lacrosse.

I am currently pursuing an MFA in Graphic Design at the Rhode Island School of Design. I would like to give a shout-out to my family's dog, Tootsie Bear. She is a sweet old girl.

www.adamlucas.org

CAMERON EWING
San Francisco

Cameron Ewing is a brand and innovation designer. He works with ambitious clients to challenge convention and deliver imaginative visual communication. The work he does stretches across multiple mediums, including traditional print, brand and identity, digital and motion graphics.

Cameron received his MFA in Graphic Design from California Institute of the Arts, a Post-Baccalaureate degree in Design at the Minneapolis College of Art & Design, and his BA in Politics, alongside a minor in Spanish Literature from Princeton University. Cameron stays active in the world of academia by leading a variety of typography, branding, and other similar design workshops.

Cameron has been the recipient of several design awards including ID Magazine's Design Review Award as the Addy Awards Best In Show Category for his thesis work completed at CalArts. Additionally, Cameron has worked at top design firms in Los Angeles, New York, London and most recently San Francisco, where he continues to pursue his career as a Senior Designer at Apple and his work as a practicing artist.

www.cameronewing.com

BJÖRN SONESON
Seattle

Born on the East Coast and raised in Midwest, Björn Soneson is a multi-disciplinary designer now working, living, and soaking up life with his wonderful girlfriend, Lia, in Seattle. While design is his one passion, travel is his other. His curiosity has led him around the world from visiting his roots in Sweden, to perusing fish markets in Japan, to summiting peaks in Switzerland, to running with the bulls in Pamplona, to working in London, to exploring the Cascades near his home in Seattle.

Feel free to get in contact if you'd like to know more about him, his work, his city, or if you'd like to donate to his growing moist towelette collection. Also, check out Björn and Lia on couchsurfing.com if you'd like to meet up while in Seattle.

www.bjornsoneson.com

RACHEL NEWBORN
St Louis

Rachel Newborn grew up north of Boston and finished her undergraduate education at Washington University in St Louis. She returned to Boston to pursue a career as a graphic designer in trade publishing.

Rachel is a huge lover of music, photography, pop culture, and crafts of all kinds. She also loves to spend time traveling and learning about other parts of the United States in her spare time. She hopes this book will help her make traveling more fulfilling.

http://newbornrachel.blogspot.com

JOSHUA GRAHAM GUENTHER
Washington DC

Joshua Graham Guenther works in
Washington, DC making posters, books,
magazines, newspapers, clothing, photos,
and illustrations. Doodling away night and
day, he creates new typefaces and sundry
graphics that inevitably evolve into his new
work, exercising the great belief that the
generating of piles is the sincerest form of
creative process.

Please feel free to contact him with
questions, or for whatever your design, type,
art direction, or art needs may be.

www.cargocollective.com/guenther

ACKNOWLEDGEMENTS

Thanks firstly to all the contributors, who put
in so much time and effort, and who produced
such fantastic work.

Joana Niemeyer at Studio-April is the
originator of the Graphic Guide concept, and
together with Lisa Sjukur, was responsible
for its overall layout. Thanks, as always, for
being simultaneously so imaginative and
professional.

Thanks also to Andrius Juknys and Mark
Garland at Thames and Hudson distribution,
and Todd Bradway at D.A.P.

Catherine Hodkinson and Maggie Cheung
at SNP-Toppan.

Tom Nurse for assistance with design, and
Diana Hanaor for help with proofing.

Thanks also to Nommi Elsley for not coming
early, and to Edie for being so patient.